Wish Me Luck

Born in 1945, Roger Fowler grew up in and around Stourbridge in the West Midlands. He studied automobile engineering before going into the motor trade and eventually switched to the building industry, working for a volume house builder.

Recently retired from jointly running a commercial property business, his interests are motor sport, tennis, skiing, and sailing –which has included three transatlantic passages. Having recently completed the restoration of a classic racing car he now competes in historic motor sport events.

After being based in Worcester for a number of years, he moved to an attractive village on the edge of the Cotswolds where he enjoys walking and the countryside.

Although this is his first book, he has written several articles for motoring and sailing magazines.

Wish Me Luck

A Journey around the World

Roger Fowler

Wish Me Luck
Roger Fowler

Published by Aspect Design 2019
Malvern, Worcestershire, United Kingdom.

Designed, printed and bound by Aspect Design
89 Newtown Road, Malvern, Worcs. WR14 1PD
United Kingdom
Tel: 01684 561567
E-mail: allan@aspect-design.net
Website: www.aspect-design.net

ISBN 978-1-909219-60-1

This book is dedicated to my late parents,
Brook and Peggy Fowler,
and to all those who helped me on my way.

To Peter
With all good wishes.
Roger

Contents

Preface

A number of people thought this book would never get finished – including me! The idea of writing an account of my journey was first suggested by friends just after I returned home, but events moved on and the thought passed, as thoughts do. In any case there is no way that I could have done it in longhand, or by using a typewriter. Modern laptops make corrections, additions, and alterations, so much easier. The task was also made easier by the fact that I had kept a diary the whole time, together with most of the correspondence I had sent to my parents, and received from various quarters. In addition were all the photographs I had taken; but choosing which to use from the hundreds available was quite a dilemma. Anyway here it is at last – forty-six years later.

I would like to take this opportunity to thank my proof readers, Judith Armstrong, Becky Vale, Mike Walker, and my partner Sue Duffy for all her help and encouragement with finishing the project.

Chapter One
An Idea Develops

It's a curious fact of life that sometimes a seemingly insignificant event, or chance remark, can subconsciously trigger an idea in one's mind. In my case it was the latter, when I sat as a spectator at the Shelsley Walsh speed hill climb in Worcestershire. It was a gloriously hot summer day in July 1970, and the view from the enclosure out across the Teme Valley with its patchwork of fields and woods, never fails to impress. Add fast cars to the scene and you have a sight to gladden the heart of any enthusiast.

Behind me sat two older gentlemen, and absent-mindedly I caught snatches of their conversation. At one point one of them started a sentence with the words 'When I was in Hong Kong . . .' I don't remember the rest of what he said, but that particular phrase stuck in my mind. How wonderful I thought, to have experienced such an exotic place, and to have seen something of the wider world.

I was twenty-four at the time and life was not really going the way I wanted. A long held ambition to make the grade in motor racing had fizzled out a couple of years earlier, when the expense of it all had overtaken me, and I had to sell the Lotus that I'd been racing. Since then I had been earning a rather precarious living in the used car business, which although having its amusing moments, did not hold out great hopes for the long-term future.

Over the next few weeks the idea of travelling overseas began to dominate my thoughts. The question was where to go? Australia seemed to be the destination of many Brits: a friend of mine was somewhere in Queensland working on a sugar cane plantation. It was still the day of the £10 'Pom', and therefore no work permit or visa would be required. So I paid a visit to the Australian Consulate in Birmingham where they gave me a lot of information – and what's more they seemed quite keen to have me!

Continuing to mull over the idea, by the time I set off for home from a holiday in France that September, I had made the decision not to return to my old life. Australia seemed a good choice, but rather than just stepping on to a ship or plane I wanted to combine the journey with an adventure. Studying the travel sections of the papers I decided to place an advertisement in the *Sunday Times* to see what came up. And so a couple of weeks later my advert appeared, reading 'Young man wishes to travel. Anything legal considered'.

There were only two replies, the most promising of which came from two electrical engineers from Buckinghamshire, who were planning to drive overland to Australia in a Land Rover. They were looking for a third person to join them and contribute towards expenses. We decided to meet in Banbury to discuss the idea further, and see if we all gelled. Geoff Smith and Bob Rossiter were slightly older than me and seemed nice guys, but I was very surprised to see that Geoff, who owned the vehicle, was a paraplegic. He assured me that despite his condition he was quite capable of managing, and explained that the long wheelbase diesel Land Rover was fitted with hand controls. In the back there were fold-down beds to sleep three, and a small gas cooker. I suppose it was a measure of my determination (or desperation!) to proceed with the idea that I was not put off by Geoff's situation.

Their plan was to drive across Europe via Greece to Istanbul, before continuing across Turkey, Persia, Afghanistan, and Pakistan, to Madras on the east coast of India. From there they planned to take a British India Line ship to Penang, Malaysia, and drive down to Singapore, from where they could get another ship to Darwin, and then probably make for Sydney. Depending on how things went, the general idea was to get jobs and see what Oz had to offer, with thoughts of later perhaps touring some of Australia too.

For a couple of weeks I chewed over their proposition, and in the absence of anything better emerging I telephoned my acceptance. So we arranged to meet again to discuss finance, timetables, and general arrangements in more detail. By now it was late October and it was proposed to make a start the following month, which didn't leave me a lot of time. Among other things I had to be inoculated against diseases like cholera, smallpox, yellow fever, typhoid, etc. until I felt like a pin cushion. Also there was the business to wind up, the hardest part of which was to sell off my stock of about half a dozen cars. But being based at my parents' home I had no lease commitments to fulfil. I managed to sell all but one car in the next few weeks, and this was passed on to a fellow trader to dispose of for me.

My father kindly presented me with a second hand 35mm Agfa 'Solinette' camera, which although old-fashioned with its fold down front, was quite compact. It had an excellent lens, and once I got the hang of using all the settings it really took some great photos. I still have it to this day. Throughout my journey I took colour slide photographs for convenience, and tried to use Kodak film if possible which I found gave the best results. Usually I posted the pre-paid film to Kodak in England for development, and they then forwarded it on to my parents' address. In this way my progress could be followed.

A stroke of luck was an introduction through a friend to David Collins, one of two army officers who had done the journey on motorcycles, although their trip had been from east to west. He was full of information about such things as the condition of the roads on our intended route, medical requirements, insurance, and currency. For instance he strongly advised us to take the bulk of our money in cash, and only keep travellers cheques as a safe reserve. The reason was that all countries from Greece onwards had a thriving black market which was generally situated in the bazaar area of big towns, and at which you could expect up to twice the rate of exchange for sterling or US dollars than that offered by the banks. Of course you needed to know the rate before doing business, and to check the notes carefully. I found later that it helped to have a mate keeping watch too. David also advised that useful forms of currency were watches, electrical appliances such as shavers, film etc. and that we could make a lot of money in India where foreign goods were almost completely prohibited. It was best to avoid all officials who he said were most pedantic and appallingly difficult to deal with. Apparently bribery was often necessary. He warned that in Eastern Turkey there were many stories of travellers being murdered by the locals, and that some perhaps were true. They had been stoned on one occasion in the area, and took the precaution of stopping at dusk every evening and camping well off the road, if possible amongst trees.

Further advice included keeping clear of local women throughout the journey, and being especially careful about taking photographs. 'Enormous offence could be caused by snapping without permission'. And far better to carry too many vehicle spares than too few, as one had to pay fabulous prices for genuine factory parts. In the letter David wrote to me, his advice on eating at the local cafés makes interesting reading after some forty-seven years. 'Enter politely, and demand to see the kitchen.' 'Inspect the pots and select your meal.' 'Fix the price before you eat.' 'Eat!' 'They will respect your guile, and all along the route it's a battle not to be parted from your money.' Forewarned is forearmed. Amazingly, if we got tired of local food, roast beef and Yorkshire pudding were available at one hotel in Kabul, Afghanistan! More worryingly he had heard that the Greek-Turkish border had recently been closed, but we would have to hope for the best.

My last weekend at home was taken up with packing, taking phone calls from well wishers, and being interviewed by the local *Express & Star* newspaper who had somehow heard of my plans. They sent a photographer round and my sister and I posed on the driveway with a map of the world. The story appeared a couple of days later under the heading 'Going out of business'. I'm sure the neighbours were delighted.

Suddenly the departure date of Monday November 23rd had arrived. I managed to cram the last few things into the one large suitcase which we were each allowed, before going into Stourbridge to get 500 pounds in cash and travellers' cheques. In addition I bought a sleeping bag from the Army and Navy stores, had a haircut, and made arrangements for the car. My mother gave me the address of some relatives in Adelaide – just in case I got that far and they were still there. The family had originally emigrated in the 1800s, and she had last heard from their descendants about twenty years previously.

After a quick lunch, my parents ran me down to meet Geoff in Banbury, and as we left home the reality hit me of leaving all my friends and family, and I felt rather choked. My father was full of admiration for Geoff undertaking such a journey with his handicap. We said a last goodbye and they wished me luck before Geoff and I set off for his mother's home near Aylesbury.

Mrs Smith was a kindly grey haired lady who made me most welcome, and did not appear overly concerned by the challenging and possibly dangerous journey that her son intended to make. At least if she was, she hid her feelings very well.

Bob was working almost to the last minute at the nearby Stoke Mandeville Hospital, (where he and Geoff had met) and so the following morning Geoff and I drove into London and left our three passports at the Persian Embassy to get the visa stamps. We picked them up at 3.30pm after some haggling, and rushed them round to the Afghan Embassy just before they closed. Back we went the next day and rather to our surprise all was in order. As India and Pakistan were Commonwealth countries no documents were needed; unlike today.

A Tesco supermarket was the next port of call, where we stocked up with food, most of which was in cans for obvious reasons; plus a supply of long-life milk and bottled drinking water. And last but not least on the list were a dozen loo rolls. We hoped to buy fresh vegetables en route, and for washing, shaving, and cooking we would carry a large jerry can of water.

The next three days were mainly taken up with maintenance jobs on the Land Rover, such as bleeding the brakes, changing the oil, and fitting air horns. We seemed to have an extraordinary amount of equipment with all our luggage, food, vehicle spares and tools, but after re-packing several times we eventually got it all in. The roof rack was a big help, and that was where Geoff's wheelchair finally ended up.

Of major concern was that Bob was having trouble getting his money together, and things were taking him longer to sort out than expected.

We had set Monday November 30th as our start date, but were apprehensive when Bob failed to appear as planned at Geoff's home on the Sunday. The next morning was spent on the last few jobs, but there was still no word from him. He was not on the phone, and this being long before the days of mobiles, Geoff and I set off to his digs in Buckingham, where there was no sign of him. We both thought he had changed his mind, but much to our relief we finally caught up with him back in Aylesbury. He explained that there had been a last minute problem with finances and settling his affairs, and so after loading all his gear we rushed off to catch the 11.30 pm Dover ferry to Zeebrugge in Belgium.

I for one was hugely relieved and happy that we were on our way at last. The great adventure was about to begin!

Chapter Two
On the Road

We docked at Zeebrugge at 4.00 am on December 1st in pouring rain, and drove over the nearby border into Holland to re-fuel as it was cheaper there. Our route took us through Ghent and on to bypass Brussels, where we took the wrong road towards Antwerp for a while before joining the autoroute to Liege. Indeed our first day was not without incident as it was near there that we had a puncture, and then a bit further on a leaking radiator hose. It was not much fun carrying out roadside repairs in very wet weather, and I felt knackered by the time we pulled into a clearing in the Ardennes forest to spend our first night. My sleeping bag proved to be pretty useless and I was frozen by the next morning when we drove on into Bastogne, the scene of a famous Second World War battle. Geoff had a friend there and we stopped to breakfast with him. Everything was pulled out of the vehicle again and after re-packing it all and carrying out a few checks, we pushed on in the late afternoon through Luxembourg to reach Trier in Germany. Stopping for the night in a well appointed Youth Hostel we found the only problem was getting old Geoff up and down some steep stairs in his wheelchair.

The weather was still awful but we drove all day on the excellent autobahns and at least the scenery was attractive, especially along the Rhine. Munich, the city of colourful clocks, music boxes and Oktoberfest was the next destination, and as we couldn't get into the hostel we found a comfortable pension nearby. The distance now covered since leaving home was about eight hundred miles.

After getting the puncture repaired we went sightseeing, and decided to visit the infamous Dachau concentration camp which lies just outside the city. They have a museum there showing some of the awful experiments carried out on the inmates, and seeing the place first-hand after various television documentaries and newsreel coverage over the years, brought the true horror of it all to life. I found it interesting but very morbid.

Much more agreeable was the excellent Deutsches Museum,

and for me the technical section with the famous pre-war Mercedes and Auto-Union racing cars was the highlight. They were so advanced and ahead of their time, and I found it particularly fascinating to see them 'in the metal'. Unfortunately it required a lot more time than we had available to see it all. With David Collins' advice in mind I also bought a gold ring from a jeweller, as future collateral.

Our route took us on into Austria and we reached Mozart's Salzburg, dominated by the Hohensalzburg castle, that evening. Next morning we left the hostel early and went up to Berchtesgaden just back over the German border. Our intention was to reach the Eagle's Nest, Hitler's famous mountain retreat, but it was closed during the winter. However it was possible to look around the old SS barracks about halfway up the mountain, and even from there the view down the valley was awe inspiring. It was easy to imagine the Fuhrer up in his 'eyrie' gazing out of the huge picture window at the surrounding mountains.

Graz was our next stop where Geoff had another contact, but as we couldn't locate him, we found a room for the night just outside the city. My diary stated that 'things were going satisfactorily and we all seemed to be getting on well'.

Western Europe was expensive so we kept moving at a fairly fast pace. The rain had ceased and although cold, thus far there had been no snow. Most people associate a certain tune with a particular time or event in their lives. We had a good supply of cassette tapes in the vehicle, and whenever I hear Long John Baldry singing 'Mexico', it reminds me of that ride across Europe in late 1970.

For convenience sake I had now started to grow a beard. The general opinion seemed to be quite favourable and I kept it for many years, finally shaving it off in 1988.

On December 6th we crossed the Yugoslav (now Slovenian) border at Maribor, from where I sent off a couple of postcards home. We were all slightly apprehensive about travelling into a

Lunch break on the Yugoslav coast

On the Cator Pass looking towards Macedonia

Communist country, as these were still the days of the Cold War. The change from wealthy Western Europe was very noticeable, and as we made our way through attractive countryside towards Ljubljana, now the capital city, we pulled onto the side of the road for a sandwich. There were some women toiling away in nearby fields, and using mostly sign language, they asked us how it was that we could be driving in leisurely fashion through their country while they had to work? We explained that we were from a capitalist, not a communist country and were on holiday, which may not have gone down very well . . . Nevertheless, so far the people seemed friendly although there were large numbers of troops everywhere.

From Ljubljana there was a terrific descent lasting about an hour and a half down the mountains to Rijeka, and we saw some serious accidents with badly crashed cars on the way. It was an attractive port on the northern coast and we stopped in the Land Rover for the night just outside town, and cooked up a meal of omelettes.

Next morning we continued down the very desolate coast road which followed almost every inlet and creek, but it had the great advantage of being virtually brand new, with a lovely smooth surface. Traffic was sparse so that most of the time we had it to ourselves. There were islands lying offshore all the way, which made for some spectacular views, and at a town called Zadar, which is now a beach resort, we stopped and bought some bread for lunch. Driving was taken in turns with the usual stint being about two hours each, and Geoff proved most adept with the hand controls.

Stopping just outside Split for the night we came upon a shack standing seemingly in the middle of nowhere, which served as a local bar. Our mistake was to sample far too much of the local 'plonk' in our enthusiasm to fraternise with the other customers, and that night I was violently sick.

Feeling the worse for wear we set off next day towards

Dubrovnik, following the road past some very scenic lakes and rivers. On arrival we were fined twenty dinars on the spot by a truculent policeman for going up a one-way street the wrong way, and had no doubt that the money went straight into his pocket.

Nevertheless it was a spectacular medieval port with its turrets and fortifications, and the 'placa' or main promenade featured many attractive three and four story terraced buildings and impressive domed church towers. Furthermore the sun shone from a clear blue sky, which made us all feel better. We booked into the Hotel Petka (yes it's still there), and after doing some washing went to sleep for the afternoon. Just before turning in for an early night we heard on my radio that there was a power cut at home, and wondered how everyone was managing.

Bob was not very popular next morning when he took us on the wrong road for three quarters of an hour, but at least we were still blessed with fine weather. Continuing down the scenic coast to a town called Virpazar, where the route turns inland, we took a small ferry across the still waters of Lake Scutari. A wall of rock faced us and it was hard to believe that any road could exist up this, but a tortuous winding ascent of the almost vertical mountainside began. After an hour and a half of hairpin bends and with a sheer drop on one side, we finally reached the top and heaved big sighs of relief. The town below could still be seen and the view was breathtaking, although to my great regret it was just too dark for photography. Pressing on along a narrow twisty road which crossed a plateau, we had to reverse several times on sharp bends to let large trucks pass, before reaching Titograd, (now Podgorica). We settled down for another freezing night a few miles beyond the city in more mountainous scenery, where the road ran along the side of a huge gorge above the River Moraca.

Next morning we had our first taste of rough going as we ascended the Cator Pass which took us most of the day, and brought us to a height of 6,600 feet, giving some fantastic views.

It was mostly second gear work and we stopped periodically to look back down the track as it followed the contours of the mountain sides, before eventually reaching the summit in quite deep snow.

From there we could look towards Greece, but first came the descent into Macedonia where the Turkish influence from the days of the old Ottoman Empire was still strong. It felt quite different from anything previously encountered. I didn't like the people, who seemed very unfriendly, or the place, which was extremely primitive. It was my first taste of the third world and I suppose I was out of my comfort zone: But this was what I had left home to see and with hindsight I should have been more relaxed about it.

The usual means of transport was the ox cart, and it was risky driving at night as they carried no lights. Despite having a few near misses we eventually found the scruffy Youth Hostel in Skopje, the town that was eighty per cent destroyed in the 1963 earthquake. The bed sheets were filthy as was the rest of the place, and the pillow was like a bag of cement, but surprisingly I spent a reasonable night. The place didn't look any better in daylight, with rubble everywhere, and the people mostly seemed to live in tin shacks.

Turbans and old fashioned baggy Turkish trousers were the fashion for men, reminding us of Ali Baba and the forty thieves. A sense of unease fostered by the general atmosphere increased my feelings of apprehension about reaching Turkey itself.

I was glad to leave early next morning, and good progress was made on the crude road which followed the River Vardar to the Greek border near Gevgelija. (Don't ask me how that's pronounced.) The Greek customs officer told us he wanted everything out of the vehicle, but changed his mind when he saw the shambles inside! Our next stop was Thessaloniki, but the Youth Hostel there was shut. So at this point we decided to detour south from our route and visit Athens.

Throughout Greece there were little shrines at intervals along the road in which a lighted candle was placed at night, and most Greek trucks were festooned with different coloured lights after dark. The drivers had photographs of their wives and children hanging in their cabs, but these seemed to have little effect as they still drove like lunatics. A great number of army vehicles and personnel were evident together with signs proclaiming '21 April 1967' the date when the king was dethroned and the army took over government. The whole country gave the impression of being on standby, although people were always friendly and helpful. Surprisingly most public buildings still had large portraits of the king and queen hanging from their exteriors.

After nearly running out of fuel, we dropped in to a little roadside café near Larisa in the evening and started on the local wine again. But I had learned my lesson this time and didn't over indulge, although I spent another freezing uncomfortable night and decided that I'd have to do something about my sleeping bag.

However the sun was shining next morning and we reached Athens at midday, although Geoff insisted on driving in the heavy traffic which Bob and I did find rather unnerving. Having checked in at the hostel we toured the flea market and then went for a meal, before watching *Coronation Street* on TV with Greek subtitles! A lazy day was spent in tourist mode and we visited the Acropolis, which together with the amphitheatre impressed us very much. Fortunately this was still possible in 1970, because in later years access to the site was barred. As the superb weather continued there were glorious views over the city, and we lounged around in the sun before returning to the hostel for supper. That evening we had a long chat with some fellow travellers and an obliging Australian gave us some first-hand information on his homeland.

It had been our intention to visit the museum next day, but as it was closed we set off at mid morning and decided to take the old road back towards Thessaloniki, instead of the toll road on which we had travelled down. This nearly proved our undoing as, approaching a town called Lamia at dusk on a downhill stretch of mountain road; we came upon some black ice half way round a bend. The Land Rover spun right round and nearly went backwards over the unguarded cliff edge. I was driving at the time and having locked over the steering we stopped with the rear of the vehicle almost against the rock face, but away from an almost sheer drop. We all sat in a cold sweat for a minute imagining what could have been our fate. After recovering we drove on carefully to the hostel north of Larisa and encountered more black ice in the Vale of Tembi, seeing a bad accident in which a car had gone under a lorry. Once again the hostel was shut, so another night was spent in the Land Rover, but we had covered three hundred miles that day so were quite happy with our progress – especially in view of our narrow escape.

The road followed the Aegean coast, but although overcast the weather was very mild, and stopping for lunch by the flat calm water's edge, we cooked up a meal from some of our tins. Continuing through Xanthi the country was rather featureless up to the border near Ipsala which we reached at 9.30 pm.

The Greek customs post was a scene of amusing chaos. One of the officers was sitting in pyjamas playing cards, and when Bob offered his passport he showed no interest but just told him to pick one! The Turks were equally unconcerned, and just stamped everything they could lay their hands on. They then found that they had stamped the wrong forms and after screwing them up, waved us through. So we were into Turkey and our first night was spent in the Land Rover at a garage just down the road from the border post.

We woke up to grey skies and pouring rain which didn't improve our mood after another cold night, so without wasting time we got going and reached the Yucel Tourist Hostel in the Sultanhamet district of Istanbul by early afternoon. Although the exterior looked rather dingy it was quite comfortably furnished and the manager, a short smartly dressed man spoke good English, having been a submariner in the Turkish navy. He told us that he had spent time at Barrow-in-Furness on occasions while his vessel was re-fitted.

Being a confirmed petrol head I noticed that there were lots of old American cars from the Forties and Fifties about the place, rather as in Cuba today. The whole city seemed pretty chaotic to me although Geoff was quite enamoured of it. Over the next few days my impression was reinforced by the sight of whistling policemen directing the idiotic drivers, who usually stood around scratching their heads in amazement at the scene of every accident.

We had now completed the European section of the journey and felt satisfied with our progress, but with the weather so bad there were no celebrations, and we settled down in the hostel for an early (and warmer) night.

Chapter Three
Disaster!

The city stands at the junction of Europe and Asia, and was a focal point for travellers going either east or west. Over the centuries it has had three names. First it was known as Byzantium, then Constantinople after the Roman Emperor Constantine, and now as Istanbul. We had decided to have a break here for a few days before heading out into the wilds of eastern Turkey, and quickly found that the main hangout was a restaurant going by the unlikely name of the Pudding Shop.

It was a buzzing hive of busy waiters and noisy conversation in the smoky atmosphere from the assortment of back packers and travellers, which included quite a sprinkling of the hippie fraternity. On one wall was a large notice board with adverts from people looking for lifts, and also for equipment for sale, and from this we bought a couple of sleeping bags. We took most of our meals there, and heard various stories of people being swindled in one form or another. The place had an 'edge' to it which I felt was reflected in the city as a whole.

The following day confirmed this view when we walked around the famous indoor bazaar. I had never seen such a lot of rogues and con men, with even the children continually pestering us to buy something. Waiters with small trays of tea weaved their way through the crowds, and dodgy looking money changers touted for business. All kinds of goods were for sale. Rugs hung from the ceiling, brass samovars and hookah pipes were plentiful, but my overriding impression was that it was nearly all cheap rubbish.

Then in the evening someone threw a brick through one

The Pudding Shop, Istanbul

View up the Bosporus

Arriving in Tenerife

of the Land Rover's windows while it was parked outside the hostel, and we had to move it to a garage for the night. Although nothing seemed to be missing we were assured that this was a common occurrence.

With hindsight I was very foolish next day to try and change some money with a black market street dealer. The man was incredibly quick and even with Bob looking on he managed to steal 140 dollars in traveller's cheques while negotiations were in progress. This was a real bind and meant that I had to go to the American Express office to arrange reimbursement, which involved having my photograph taken and filling in several forms. It was a big relief to get the money back next day and having learned a valuable lesson, I always wore a money belt from then on. What with this, and having to rush round unsuccessfully trying to get the broken window replaced, we had hardly seen anything of the wider city. Geoff didn't seem particularly bothered by events, but by that evening Bob and I felt pretty depressed, and altogether fed up with Istanbul.

Over the next few days we did manage to do some sightseeing, and because Geoff was not feeling well we decided to remain in the city over Christmas to allow him a good rest. He spent several days in bed with what appeared to be flu-like symptoms, although we didn't imagine it was anything serious and thought he would soon recover. Meanwhile Bob and I had the Land Rover window repaired and visited various tourist attractions.

The Topkapi Palace Museum was the official residence of the Ottoman Sultans for four hundred years until 1856, and contains the most holy relics of the Muslim world. Amongst these are the cloak and sword of the Prophet Muhammad, and artefacts of the various Sultans. One evening we also went to a service at the famous Blue Mosque, which with its domes and tall minarets is a city landmark and somewhere that all tourists visit. The massive 17th century structure is famous for its richly decorated walls and ceilings, covered with decorative tiles in subtle tones of green and blue. While there I had a long conversation with an old Turkish gentleman who spoke good English and who was interested in our story. It was a novelty leaving our shoes outside beforehand and with our experiences to date it was something of a surprise to find them still there afterwards! Another attraction was the large Turkish Military Museum, and having a fascination for the First World War, I found the Gallipoli memorabilia particularly interesting.

Our room at the hostel was shared with various nationalities, and amongst these were three Americans, an Australian who had been mugged by black marketers, and two English lads who were travelling east in a 1947 Austin 10, which I thought exceedingly brave. By now a week had passed and the manager started asking when we would be leaving. I had the impression that they were as fed up with us as we were with them and I was itching to get moving again, but Geoff was still not feeling too good.

On Christmas Eve therefore we decided to take him for a check up to the American hospital, the only Western hospital in the city, before setting off again. There was some concern about the possibly excessive expense of this, but he seemed confident that his insurance policy would be adequate. Much to our surprise they told us that he must remain under observation for a few days, and this news did nothing to improve our gloomy feelings. We arranged to call back and see him next day and make sure he had everything he needed.

It was my first Christmas in a non Christian country, and the only sign I had seen of anything festive was a foreign car with a Christmas tree tied on the roof. I guessed that it must be some lucky diplomat on the way home that evening, and felt very envious. We went out later to try and find a bit of life but there was nothing happening and we returned to the hostel, where we did at least have a laugh with Chuck, Jan, and Glenn, the Americans in our room. On the radio, Christmas Carols were playing and I really felt quite homesick for the first time, wishing I was back in my local with friends.

Next morning it was hard to believe that it was Christmas Day, but because the weather was fine and quite warm Bob, Jan, and I took a bus ride for a few miles along the Bosporus to a little fishing village called Dolmabache, near the Black Sea. It was really pleasant to get out of Istanbul, and some of the villages on the water's edge with their colourful boats tied up reminded me of Greece. Here and there lay old city walls and the remains of the odd palace from days gone by. We had a relaxed lunch at a small waterside bar populated by cats who lounged on heaps of fishing nets. Raising a glass to our respective families, it was easy to picture them tucking into a traditional Christmas meal at home. Afterwards we took the ferry back, and from the water, which was full of jelly fish, one could see the haze of filth above the city. As Jan had to catch his train to Sofia, we rushed back to the hostel and were accosted by the usual money changers on the way.

In the evening we drove to the hospital to see Geoff who was rather noncommittal, but did say they had given him oxygen and a glucose drip. Bob thought the situation was more serious than we had imagined, and that we could be stuck in Istanbul for weeks rather than days. And a Happy Christmas to you I thought.

Our worst fears were confirmed when we returned to the hospital next day. Geoff looked in a terrible state, with oxygen pipes up his nose and a glucose drip in his arm, and in fact had nearly died that afternoon. The authorities told us that he would not be able to carry on with the journey, and must fly home when fit enough, which could be several weeks. We were told that he had pneumonia which was compounded by the fact that he only had one lung. Apparently this was due to his having been in a bad car crash some years earlier, and I realised that this must be the cause of his paraplegia. He had never mentioned the reason previously and I hadn't wanted to ask.

It was hard to immediately take in all the consequences of

this shock news, and our long term plans were now thrown into jeopardy. Bob and I thought that we might be able to carry on, but as the Land Rover belonged to Geoff, it was a very awkward situation. For one thing because of our planned extensive stay in Australia we each had too much luggage to become back-packers; and we couldn't just abandon it all. Also, having only recently left home, I couldn't contemplate returning so soon to face all my friends, and going back to my old life.

Over the course of the next few days we considered all our options while continuing to visit Geoff who was gradually improving. At one point he said that we could take the Land Rover and continue – before later changing his mind.

We spent an evening looking at all the maps but couldn't decide what to do. It was then that Bob announced that he had a pal in Jamaica who he used to work with at Stoke Mandeville, and had an open invitation to visit him. He said that he had his address and could write and let him know that we were planning to come over. What did I think of this suggestion? My original reason for leaving home had been to travel and see the world, and in many ways I was not too bothered where I went. The West Indies sounded as good as anywhere, especially in winter, and as it was a Commonwealth country we shouldn't have any problems on arrival. After sleeping on the idea overnight I accepted his proposal.

Immediately we both felt much better! Now we had a plan and the next step was to inform the British authorities about Geoff, and to try and work out how we were going to get from Istanbul to Jamaica.

It took us two hours to find the British Consulate that morning, and then a further two hours waiting before we could see the Consul and tell him the full story. He was sympathetic in a very businesslike way, but his brisk manner gave us the strong impression that diplomats don't like having their schedules disturbed by unforeseen events. However he made a note of all

Geoff's details and promised that someone would visit him and keep an eye on his situation.

Later that day we called on several travel agents, and were told that the most likely place to catch a ship across the Atlantic was from Lisbon in Portugal. We had thoughts of driving there, but when we saw Geoff later that day and brought him up to date he didn't seem keen on the idea of lending us the Land Rover. In retrospect this was hardly surprising.

Working our passages to Jamaica as merchant seamen was also contemplated, and so we visited several shipping offices, but as neither of us had the necessary paperwork this plan soon came to nothing. The idea of flying there was never considered, as apart from the cost it would have defeated our original object of seeing as many countries as possible, and combining the journey with an element of adventure.

Returning to the hostel, we found that another brick had been thrown through a window of the Land Rover, and Bob went absolutely mad. Neither of us could wait to get out of bloody Istanbul! Later when we saw Geoff he told us that borrowing the Land Rover was definitely out of the question as he had decided to drive home in it when fit enough. He seemed very offhand and was no doubt most disappointed about the cancellation of the trip. But then that applied to all of us.

Next morning therefore we began to work out our best way of getting to Lisbon. It appeared that there was a Turkish ship, the *Karadeniz*, which sailed via Izmir, Athens, and Naples, to Marseilles in southern France. From there we would have to travel by train across France and Spain to Portugal. The big problem was that she sailed at 8pm the next day which was New Years Eve, leaving very little time to sort out all our affairs. But beggars can't be choosers and after a quick discussion we booked the cheapest tickets available for 38 US dollars.

The remainder of that day and the next were one mad rush during which we had the Land Rover window repaired again, got all Geoff's affairs straight, collected our tickets, and divided up the food, some of which we sold to the hostel staff. To save money we had been having meals up in our room which caused some amusement to the other inmates but didn't impress the manager.

I sent a letter off home explaining what had happened and outlining our future plans, which I imagine must have given my parents quite a shock. It wasn't the last they would have however.

On the last evening we went to see Geoff to bring him up to date with all the arrangements and wish him well. Not surprisingly he was sorry to see us go, and each of us felt sad to see the expedition breaking up. We had started out with such high hopes and now the future looked pretty uncertain, but all we could do was trust that things would work out for each of us one way or another.

The hectic pace continued on our final day in Istanbul and the first job was to collect our boat tickets. We had arranged to leave the Land Rover at the British Consulate where it would be safe from further damage, pending Geoff's discharge from hospital. So we duly drove over there and it was locked up securely in their compound. After this we returned to the hostel to pack up all our gear, which was quite a task. Eventually we crammed everything into the available space and much to management's relief settled our bill, before rushing in a sweat down to the docks.

We were pleasantly surprised at our first sight of the *Karadeniz*, as she lay alongside the wharf with her white paintwork gleaming in the late afternoon sun. She was a modern German built ship of nine thousand tons, and having produced our passports and tickets five times in as many seconds to a variety of officials we were allowed on board. Our sleeping quarters with iron bunks were down in the hold, and I was worried about the security of our luggage because we were sharing the space with a couple of shifty looking strangers.

However the problem was soon solved as we met up with a couple of English lads, Dave and Lyndon, from Solihull who had travelled from India in a V.W. Caravanette. They kindly let us put the bulk of our luggage in their vehicle which was locked up on deck for the duration of the voyage.

But Istanbul wasn't going to relinquish its grip on us too easily, as our departure was delayed firstly by a dock strike, and then by an injured seaman, and it wasn't until 11.00pm that we finally slipped our mooring lines. After sixteen days I was just so glad to see the back of the place and particularly the Yucel Tourist Hostel.

Dave and Lyndon were fast workers and soon befriended one of the Turkish crew. His name was Nihat and he was the ship's radio operator, and consequently spoke good English. He treated us to some local wine and got us into the First Class lounge where there was a band providing entertainment for the New Year celebrations. With a great feeling of relief Bob and I raised our glasses to each other and sincerely hoped that 1971 would bring us better fortune with our new adventure. This called for another toast which then led to another, and the Old Year slipped smoothly into the new one!

Some last memories of Istanbul include: the wailing loudspeaker from the Mosque over the road which woke me up every morning; the multitude of porters bent almost double by the huge loads on their backs; the waiters with their little trays of tea or coffee; the eternal money changers; the whistling policemen on point duty, with their white helmets and gloves, directing the manic horn blowing drivers; and finally the Pudding Shop which a few years later I found mentioned in the book *Midnight Express*.

Chapter Four
A New Beginning

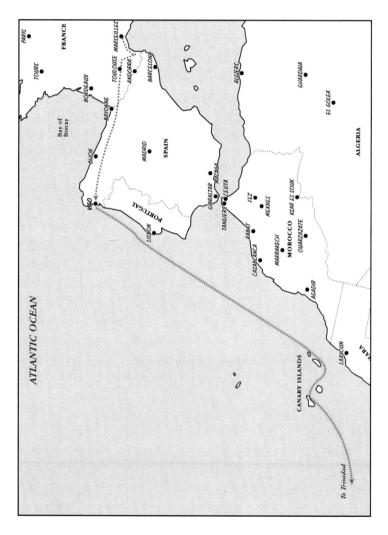

I woke up to the most incredibly rough sea which did my hangover no good at all. The *Karadeniz* was ploughing her way across the Sea of Marmara, and her bow which would normally be about fifty feet above the water was disappearing completely beneath it. Our portholes were also submerged and were battened over by a seaman, and I guessed the wind strength to be about force 9. Happy New Year!

Fortunately I managed not to be sick as some of the others were, and as we passed through the Dardanelles and out into the Aegean later in the day the wind and sea moderated. We played cards and looked around the ship before arriving at Izmir on the southern coast of Turkey at about five thirty in the afternoon.

Several of us shared a taxi into the town, which appeared very clean, and a big improvement on Istanbul; but that was not difficult as far as I was concerned. Stocking up with bread and a few other staples, as our tickets limited us to only one meal a day, I also treated myself to a new pair of boots.

Our next port of call was Athens which was reached the following morning, and Dave, Lyndon, Bob and I, took the tube into the city centre. I tried unsuccessfully to get a student card in Omonia Square, as I had been told that they enabled one to get reduced rail and bus fares.

Dave and Lyndon wanted to see the Acropolis so we took a walk up there. It seemed odd being back again so soon, and I thought of all that had happened since our last visit a few short weeks ago. Against all expectations here we were going in exactly the opposite direction.

Back on board Nihat, the friendly Turk surprised us by providing a good meal which we ate in his radio cabin, before putting on an old Nigel Patrick crime film in the evening.

Crossing the Ionian Sea the next day was fairly rough and as I wasn't feeling too clever I returned to bed until early afternoon. The rest of the day was spent playing pontoon before going on deck that evening to watch as we passed through the Straights of Messina, the narrow passage between Sicily and the 'toe' of Italy.

The smell of Naples preceded our first sighting of the city next morning, and we docked in pouring rain. Because of the weather our intended visit to Pompeii was abandoned, so Bob and I checked out a few shipping offices for possible transatlantic sailings. We had no success with this so joined the others for a very good lunch of spaghetti bolognese, with a bottle of red wine that cost fourteen hundred lire for the two of us. Excellent value for what amounted to one pound. With Naples looking very dreary and being at a loose end, we spent the rest of the afternoon in a couple of seedy cafés before meeting up with Nihat. He obviously knew the city from previous visits and took us to a disco where he proceeded to buy us quite a few drinks. What, if anything, he expected in return none of us was sure, but fortunately there appeared to be no ulterior motive. We just made it back to the ship in time and I was pleased to buy an English paper on the way.

The final day of the voyage passed quietly with a calm sea, and steady progress was made towards Marseilles. We played cards and read in the lounge where there were a number of Americans, some of them discussing politics in loud voices, before Nihat put on another of his epic film productions in the evening. This time it was a black and white 1947 John Wayne Western. It was punctuated by frequent loss of sound and vision, which all added to the entertainment. But Wayne was outdone when a fight broke out between two of the waiters that was much more exciting!

January 6th Marseilles, France. It's 7.00 am and I'm woken up by someone shouting for us to come up and show our passports to the authorities. A frantic packing session ensued with Bob protesting loudly, and my case had been shipped ashore in Lyndon's van, so I had to go and retrieve it. While I finished packing, the customs officer made Bob empty all his bags again; which didn't go down at all well with Mr Rossiter!

Saying a hurried farewell to Nihat we rushed ashore, where

Dave and Lyndon kindly took us and our baggage up to the Youth Hostel, for which we were very grateful as it was some way from the city centre. We all had lunch at a dockside café before wishing each other good luck, and I remember feeling rather envious as they set off for Paris. They had successfully completed their trip and were now heading home, whereas our expedition had come to a sad end.

That afternoon was spent doing the rounds of shipping and travel agents again, and contrary to the advice in Istanbul, none of them had any information on suitable ships sailing from Lisbon. The only boat crossing the Atlantic that we discovered left from Cannes, although not until February 4th and even so not bound for Jamaica. We couldn't wait that long and feeling tired and rather fed up we trudged back to the hostel, which was in an old château.

Much to my surprise there was snow on the ground early next morning, as I hadn't realised that it spread this far south in France.

We must have called on every shipping agent in the city before eventually finding one possibility; a Spanish ship called the *Begona*, leaving from Vigo in Northern Spain, and going via the Canaries and Venezuela, to Kingston, Jamaica. It made a marvellous change to have a positive answer to our enquiries, instead of the usual Gallic shrug and a reply of 'Non'. To celebrate, we bought tickets for the film *Lawrence of Arabia* at a cinema on La Canabiere, the City's wide main thoroughfare. Even though it was in French with no subtitles we didn't mind, as we knew the basic story. In fact I was pleasantly surprised that my schoolboy French seemed to be holding up fairly well. We retired to bed feeling pretty whacked as we must have walked I don't know how many miles, and to cap it all I had a stinking cold.

Having had a lie-in next morning and thought over our options, we decided to make our way to Vigo and wait there for the *Begona* which sailed on the twenty-ninth. Much as we liked Marseilles with its wide streets, and large impressive cathedrals, we found everything very expensive and it would cost far too much to stay for long. So tickets were purchased at one hundred and fifty six francs, or just less than 30 dollars, for a train which left at quarter past midnight. The route was via Narbonne and Toulouse to Pau, where we would change.

Back at the hostel we packed our kit, and the old fellow in charge helpfully arranged a taxi to the station for us. We caught the train all right but didn't realise that we had to change at Narbonne, and carried on south to Perpignan before realising our mistake. So it was out with all our gear and on to another train back to Narbonne. What a sweat!

But the weather was perfect as we travelled across France, the sun shining from a clear blue sky and sparkling on the snow-capped peaks of the distant Pyrenees.

Arriving in Pau I recognised parts of this lovely old city from a visit I had made five years earlier, for the annual motor race. Some of the public roads are closed for this event, which creates a true street circuit in the old European tradition. I would have liked a wander round but regrettably there wasn't time, as the onward train was due.

Much to our relief this one took us straight through to Vigo, as it was a tiring business hauling our luggage in and out of carriages. 'Rather a problem' as Bob kept saying. Managing to get a compartment to ourselves we later pulled down the blinds and lay along the seats in our sleeping bags. Somewhat annoyingly we were awoken at two am by a man and a boy coming in, so had to make room for them. But the view out of the window was some compensation, as we sped along over flat snow-covered countryside illuminated by a brilliant full moon, which gave way to another clear day.

Both our fellow travellers were engrossed in reading strip cartoon comics until our arrival at the Spanish border, where we had to grab everything again and move up the train as our coach was being detached.

Finally we reached Vigo just after midday, and an enterprising porter led us across the road from the station to a suitable looking hostel where we took a room. No doubt he was amply rewarded by the proprietor, but past caring that we might have found somewhere cheaper, our top priority was to have a bath, as we both felt pretty filthy.

Later in the afternoon, after having a meal from our dwindling supplies and feeling better, we went for a look around, but forgetting it was Sunday found most places were closed. Vigo, in the Galicia region of North West Spain, was a sizeable city of about two hundred thousand inhabitants, with some wide avenues and fine old buildings. It had a large modern port, and two islands form a natural breakwater protecting the Bay of Vigo from the violence of the Atlantic. We noted that there was a passenger liner about to leave for Buenos Aires, and having studied some sailing timetables, it seemed that the place held out a good possibility of finding a suitable transatlantic ship. I was even more cheered when I managed to pick up Alan Freeman and *Pick of the Pops* on my radio that evening.

However the next two and a half weeks were a mixture of boredom and frustration. On Monday we went for a tour of the shipping offices but they all agreed that the *Begona* on January 29th was our only hope. A very helpful little clerk at one office suggested catching a boat to Las Palmas in the Canary Islands and waiting there, but we thought it would mean extra expense without any real advantage. It was decided to cut costs by finding cheaper accommodation but when we told the hostel we were moving, the price per night magically came down from 200 to 160 pesetas! So we stayed put.

While Thomas Cook's office made enquiries for us on sailings from Lisbon, we passed the time exploring the city which was very clean and had an extraordinary variety of shops. One could buy anything from a mini tractor to a bar of soap, and I remember thinking that it compared favourably with my previous memories of Spain in the sixties, and certainly with Istanbul. Unfortunately the weather was shocking a lot of the time, with frequent rain storms and hailstones like golf balls. Trying to dry our clothes wasn't easy and the entire hostel was damp, which didn't help poor old Bob who suffered from asthma. The man in the next room had a terrible cough and sounded as though he was at death's door. His snoring also carried through the wall and kept us awake at night, which all added to the fun. However we did find a very good library with books in English, and so passed time there reading and drying out.

We also visited the amiable British Consul who didn't seem to have much to do either. Obligingly he phoned the main office in Madrid for us to enquire about the situation in Jamaica regarding work permits etc, and the reply was quite encouraging. He didn't mind us coming in to read his stock of English magazines, and told us about an old retired Postmaster who lived in the city, promising to put him in touch with us.

Sure enough a couple of days later we were woken by the Landlord bashing on the door. Apparently the Postmaster was downstairs asking for us, so we hurriedly dressed and rushed down to meet him. His name was Mr McCormack, and he was a small man, of Irish origin in his late sixties, who wore a black beret in the Basque fashion. He was a most pleasant old boy and having been born in Argentina, spoke fluent Spanish. He was very well travelled and had worked in Africa and Gibraltar amongst other places. After we had recounted our story to date he very kindly bought us lunch at his hotel, and we chatted nearly all afternoon about a great variety of subjects, such as politics, travel, and religion. We were most grateful for his company, as we were both suffering from being cooped up together so much in our damp and claustrophobic room.

First thing next morning there was more bashing on the door, and the old boy was downstairs again where he relayed some bad news. It transpired that the *Begona* was up the coast in dry dock having its propeller repaired. On enquiring at the shipping office they told us that she would not be sailing until March. Great! Why they didn't know this earlier was a mystery to us. It was suggested that we take a smaller boat down to Tenerife in the Canaries, and wait for the *Montserrat* her sister ship, which was due to sail from there to Kingston on February 14th. Mr McCormack was a great help in translating all this information and the three of us adjourned to a nearby café to talk things through. Despite earlier concerns about the cost of going to Las Palmas, it appeared that it really would be no more expensive to wait in Tenerife which should at least be warmer; because all we seemed to do every day was dodge in and out of doorways trying to avoid the rain. The decision was made easier when Cooks finally informed us that there were no ships sailing from Lisbon to Jamaica after all.

Our minds were made up next day when the foul weather reached new heights, with terrific winds which whipped the tops off street lamps, took tiles off roofs, and broke glass doors and windows. There were absolute rivers of water running off the gutters and down the streets in the steeper parts of town, all of which brought to mind the old line about the 'rain in Spain'. Although I never imagined that it got this bad and we certainly weren't 'in the plain'. At one point the landlord's wife came into our room and was most upset to find that the lights AND radiator were on, so we went over to Mr McCormack's hotel in the evening where at least it was warm, and we could listen to the news on his radio.

Boredom was becoming a serious issue, and it was with high hopes that we set off early down to the docks a couple of days later only to find that there was no sign of the boat to Tenerife which was called *Domine*. Nevertheless at the office they insisted that she was expected at any time so we reserved our places, before spending another wet day wandering around town, reading in the library, and washing clothes. The only relief was viewing the

TV at Mr McCormack's in the evening, and having a glass of wine in a bar on the way home.

Sure enough the *Domine* did arrive next day but stayed anchored out in the bay apparently because of the high winds and trouble with the rudder! All very reassuring, but we were informed that she would definitely sail the following day. In one respect the delay was lucky as I found at the post office a letter from home in reply to one of mine, which had been there for a week. There was no real news but my parents wanted to post it before a threatened strike, and it did contain a couple of addresses in Jamaica that might be useful. I wrote to them again with a news update and for various reasons this was the last they were to hear from me for nearly three months.

On Wednesday January 27th we were off again at last. We bought our third class tickets that morning for 1,256 pesetas each, and then went back to the Hostel Panton for the final time to pack our bags and settle up. What a relief! A taxi took us down to the docks where we were met by Mr McCormack who had come to see us off, and who had very kindly bought us a couple of bottles of wine for the voyage. He had been good company and a great help to us, and we promised to drop him a line when we reached Tenerife. Thanking him and saying our goodbyes just before sailing at 6.30pm, we watched from the aft deck as Vigo gradually disappeared under dismal dark skies. The solitary figure in the black beret stood waving in the distance before turning to walk away. I hoped we had proved an interesting diversion for the short time that we spent in his company.

Chapter Five
Goodbye Europe

The steward called us in promptly for a four course supper consisting of soup, fish and lettuce, beef with mashed potato, and finally fruit. Considering that the total fare for the voyage was about seven pounds and five shillings this represented fantastic value. After this feast I went for a look around the ship which was a small coastal steamer taking cargo and a few passengers between the Spanish mainland and the Canary Islands. She had been built in 1935 and naturally looked rather dated but everything was spotlessly clean, including the engine room, where a man with half his right hand missing lurched around with an oil can. The ornate wooden staircases featured brass finials, which together with all the copper work were kept highly polished. Our cabin, which we shared with four other third class passengers, was directly above the propeller, and our bunks had small curtains around them which swung out at alarming angles as the boat began rolling. Things started banging about up above, and obviously expecting the worst, the crew began lashing everything down.

Bright sunlight streaming through the porthole woke me, and considering the movement of the ship I had slept reasonably well. Fortunately I usually get my sea legs fairly quickly, but Bob had a lie-in till midday before being woken by the noise of the crew chipping away at the odd rust spots around the ship. They painted over them with red lead, and a boy had the job of washing away any rust stains.

Our meals were taken in a separate saloon above our cabin and the food was surprisingly good throughout the voyage. As quite heavy seas were washing over the rail the steward did well to carry trays of food from the galley to the dining saloon. He had to time his run along the deck to coincide with the retreat of the water, dashing out from one door and in through another without getting soaked. There were twelve passengers in total, all Spanish, so there wasn't much communication but I passed the time reading and taking a few photos, happy in the knowledge that we were at least moving in the right direction. Towards evening on the second day the sea really got up, which made supper like the scene in the Charlie Chaplin film where plates and cutlery kept sliding everywhere. The confusion increased half way through the meal when all the lights went out!

Our first stop was the island of Lanzarote and I woke up just as we docked next morning. We watched the crew unloading cargo for a while before walking three miles into the main town of Arrecife. It was overlooked by volcanic mountains which were active until the previous century, and there wasn't much there except for one big new hotel. It was quite evident where huge lava flows had poured into the sea and the main attraction was some hot springs, although we weren't able to sample them. Everything was covered in fine black dust which blew about in the strong wind, and it didn't strike me at the time as being a future holiday destination, which was apparently the long-term plan. I've never been tempted to go back there although it seems quite popular these days. We were late for supper after walking back to the ship, although I'm glad to say that we were not responsible for the delayed departure for Las Palmas at 9.30 pm.

We duly arrived first thing next morning, and the docks were large and very busy, with everything from a herd of goats to a new Rolls Royce being unloaded. The weather had finally improved and most of the day was spent looking around the town which had some pleasant parks. At one of these there was a seven month old lioness for sale at the bargain price of 3,500 pesetas! The beaches were crowded and there were some very affluent looking characters wandering about enjoying the winter sun. I had a look inside the rather posh yacht club as I was having thoughts of trying to get a crewing position on anything bound for the Caribbean. But nobody spoke English so we resorted to looking at the ships that were in port, most of which were going to South Africa.

Back at the *Domine* later on, an interesting spectacle occurred when a chap rode up on a motor scooter loaded with boxes of cigarettes. The crew had some sort of smuggling scam going on which the Captain obviously suspected, as he was pacing up and down the quayside gnashing his teeth. The rider hid behind a trolley load of wood and when the Captain's back was turned he would dash out and throw some of the boxes on to the ship. Eventually one crew man was caught in the act and received a terrific rocket in front of everybody! Whether the matter ended there we never found out. All I know is that when I retired to bed that night my feet were so sore they felt as if they were going to drop off.

Beautiful warm sunshine greeted us when we arrived in Tenerife at noon next day. What a change from Vigo! A four-masted sail training ship was tied up at the quayside as we entered harbour, and with the mountains as a back drop she made a lovely sight. We said farewell to the *Domine* and hauled our luggage ashore and into the island's capital, Santa Cruz, and then the heat became less welcome. It took us some time to find a hostel, and when we eventually did we collapsed onto our beds exhausted, and I decided I would have to ditch some of my kit. Our hostel was on Calle Castillo, one of the town's main shopping streets, and after recovering I had a walk around and was favourably impressed. Being smaller and much less commercial than Las Palmas it was more like the picturesque little haven I had envisaged. The more I saw of the place the more I liked it. Everything was beautifully laid out with gorgeous parks

Carnival in Santa Cruz

and squares displaying colourful plant and flower arrangements.
The yacht club was very much in keeping with all this and had a
swimming pool and tennis courts. I sat on a terrace there in the
evening sun drinking orange juice and felt like a million dollars!

Two more weeks passed during which we had unfulfilled
hopes of finding a ship leaving before the *Montserrat* on February
14th. Quite some time was spent tramping round various travel
and shipping agents, until we got sick of the sight of them. The
possibility of going on to Cape Town was also investigated,
but that turned out to be a non starter because unless one was
emigrating, a return fare was required, plus enough money to
cover one's stay etc. I even went on board a transatlantic Russian
cruise liner which had a large number of British passengers and
spoke to the purser, who assured me they were full. Perhaps they
were but anyway you can't argue with a Russian.

The harbour for fishing boats was a mile or so out of town,
and we learned that any yachts making the Atlantic crossing
berthed there. Bob felt that we should be trying to hitch a ride
on one, but it occurred to me that I was doing all the leg work

needed to check this out. I spoke to two Swedes with a ketch going to Antigua, and also an Australian couple who promised to make enquiries for us. Our hopes were raised of getting a free trip across the 'Pond', avoiding having to pay an expensive fare. Disappointingly nothing came of it as the majority of yachts making the passage had apparently left about a month previously. Eventually I reached the conclusion that it would be better to just enjoy our time on the island.

Besides sightseeing we spent time having long debates on subjects such as politics, and history, writing letters, or just reading in our room. I shall always remember it was here that we heard the shock news that Rolls Royce had gone bust, and could only imagine the reaction at home. I managed to sell a sleeping bag to an American at the hostel, but couldn't find a customer for a pair of London fireman's boots bought at the Army and Navy stores.

After a last unsuccessful visit to the yacht harbour that possibility was finally exhausted, and we reluctantly splashed out 95 pounds for the *Montserrat* ticket on the day before departure. It was a lot of money and meant that I would have to find work quickly on reaching Jamaica. Bob wrote to his friend to advise him of our arrival date and we also sent a card to Mr McCormack before packing our gear. Our last night was spent watching a superb carnival from our balcony. It lasted for about three hours and involved hundreds of people and dozens of very colourful and elaborate floats. Afterwards everyone seemed to go wild and people danced in the streets whilst various musical groups played in the crowded bars until the early hours. I was delighted that we happened to catch this festival before we left.

And so it came about that we finally boarded the good ship *Montserrat* to take us across the Atlantic. She was built in 1945 and was a converted wartime Liberty ship but, showing no signs of her former life, looked very smart and well equipped. Our route to Kingston was to be via Trinidad, Venezuela, and Curacao in the Dutch Antilles. Unlike us, most of the passengers had boarded at the start of the voyage in Southampton, and were West Indians returning home to Jamaica, some for a holiday but the majority permanently. I noted in my diary that Enoch Powell would be pleased at this turn of events! Some of them were quite rowdy and early in the voyage one was gaoled for being drunk and disorderly. A large number of noisy children ran around adding to the air of chaos, which was heightened by the fact that the crew spoke very little English. No doubt they would have made an absorbing study for a psychologist.

My sunbathing on our first day at sea was interrupted by lifeboat drill which was attended by everyone except Bob, who had not heard the call. For some reason we were separated at dinner, and I had to share a table with a girl who had two gurgling babies that screamed almost continuously and threw their food and cutlery around. In charge of all this mayhem was the splendidly named Captain Don Adolfo F. Lopez Merino – although we never discovered what the 'F' stood for.

I started to have more doubts as to whether I was doing the right thing, as the ticket had taken most of my remaining money. But having asked a couple of helpful Jamaicans about jobs in their homeland, I was reassured when they told me that I would have no trouble getting work of some sort. This sounded promising and I had thoughts of perhaps getting a hotel job.

On the second evening I was sitting in the Atlantic bar having a Coke when the door opened and into my life walked a genial American called Frank Hartley IV. There was hardly anyone else about and he asked what I was drinking, in that easy-going way that most Americans have. I thanked him and asked for another Coke, but he immediately retorted that I should have a proper drink! So as they (surprisingly) had Watney's Pale Ale on draft, I ordered a pint. He was of medium height but well built with a swarthy complexion. We introduced ourselves and he told me that his name derived from the fact that he was the fourth generation of his family to be called 'Frank'. He had graduated from Yale University and spoke fluent Spanish but was quite an Anglophile and a big admirer of Winston Churchill. Frank could give a more than passable imitation of our great wartime leader's voice, whilst quoting freely from some of his famous speeches. He had been holidaying in Spain for a month, and having also joined the ship in Tenerife was intending to fly back from Jamaica to his home near Boston. Whilst on holiday he had met the daughter of a retired Scottish couple, had proposed to her in the space of about two weeks, and been accepted! It was planned that he and his fiancé would be reunited in America when all the paperwork had been completed.

Frank was most interested in my story and we found that we had a similar sense of humour and enjoyed each other's company. He smoked a corn cob pipe – a habit which I thought appealing and later took up for a few years myself – and he certainly liked a drink! I was introduced to Martini Rosso, his current favourite tipple. We spent a lot of time in the swimming pool and also at the bar which helped take my mind off, but didn't improve my financial situation. I saw less of Bob, not because we had fallen out, but really as a result of having been cooped up together for so long. All topics of conversation had been exhausted and I think we both needed some space.

Entertainment was provided by a variety of films, dancing, clay pigeon shooting, games, and fancy dress competitions. One of these was won by a girl doing a brilliant impersonation of Charlie Chaplin complete with a twirling cane. Entertainment of a different kind continued at meal times as many of the passengers voiced their opinion of the rather indifferent food. A big row developed at breakfast one morning between two West Indians and the head waiter. They sat banging their cutlery on their plates and tempers started to run very high until the purser was called to cool things down. I witnessed a comical scene one evening when a small Manuel-like waiter with a large bowl of baked beans went up to a huge Jamaican. He nudged the man on the elbow and said 'Hey you wanna beans?' Barely pausing in his conversation, the Jamaican replied, 'Nah man, you eat 'em'! Frank was highly amused when I relayed this story.

The heat intensified as we sailed south through the area known as the doldrums, where the sea was flat calm and there was hardly a breath of wind. Our cabin was like a greenhouse but it was wonderful to sit outside at night watching a film. We did not see much of Captain Don Adolfo, but he would usually appear on the bridge at mid morning in his immaculate white tropical uniform. I saw my first flying fish and was impressed by the distance they could travel. Other sights were a huge manta ray which floated lazily away as we passed, and a hammerhead shark that swam up for a closer look at us before deciding to leave us alone.

The passengers continued to provide unwitting entertainment. An English fellow got very drunk one afternoon and after somehow losing all his clothes jumped completely naked into the swimming pool. He was fished out by the crew and led away calling for another bottle of Champagne and two trained nurses! I do admire a man with stamina.

A farewell party was arranged on the last evening before we reached Trinidad, beginning with operatic recitals in Spanish by members of the theatre group. We were then treated to a Spanish comedian whose jokes were completely unintelligible to us English speakers. Having sat through these two acts the West Indian contingent became decidedly restless with shouts of 'Fetch de Captain,' and calls for Calypso music instead. I found their behaviour increasingly amusing. The suave Captain Don Adolfo did appear later to preside over the silly dancing competitions which were much more enthusiastically received.

On Sunday February 21st after seven days at sea, we sighted a smudge of land on the horizon, which by degrees materialized into a tropical island. As we approached Trinidad it looked wonderful, with waving palm trees and inviting white beaches, and was just how I had imagined a typical Caribbean island. Port of Spain sounded so romantic and we were escorted into harbour by two speed boats before docking at midday in very humid conditions. Some of the passengers disembarked here and Frank and I went into town, but we were soon brought down to earth. The place exuded poverty and was terribly overgrown and run-down with the most ramshackle wooden buildings, nearly all with rusty corrugated iron roofs. This was definitely a shock and we were both tremendously disappointed. After having a meal at a ropey Chinese restaurant we had a lengthy confrontation with the manager. It seemed that he would accept almost any currency except pesetas, which was all we had, and so eventually he had no option but to take them. Unfortunately we had no chance to see more of the island which might well have given us a better impression.

Departure was punctual next morning at 11.00 am. Captain Don Adolfo didn't hang about and our next stop was La Guairá, the port for Caracas in Venezuela. The sun was now really strong and it was essential to cover up. It was fascinating to see our first dolphins and they travelled with us for some distance, playing around the ship, leaping out of the water, and no doubt calling to each other in their distinctive squeaking language. They reappeared, sometimes swimming five or six abreast right under the bow, to escort us into the harbour which lay alongside the busy airstrip, with its runway built out into the sea.

Once ashore we were mobbed by taxi drivers but somehow managed to escape to the bus station, and travelled into Caracas via a modern four lane highway which at one point tunnelled through a mountain. The journey took fifty minutes and cost 1.5 bolivars; another new currency to juggle with. It was here that I adopted Frank's practice of saving a low denomination bank note as a souvenir of every country I visited. Many years later I had them all framed and they make an attractive display.

The approach to the city was dominated by multicoloured

slum houses called favelas, perching precariously on the surrounding hillsides. However, oil wealth had given birth to modern Caracas which had wide boulevards with many high rise buildings comprising apartments, offices, and shopping centres. Frank took my photo in front of the beautiful white Parliament buildings which were formed around an attractive courtyard with palm trees and ornate fountains. The heavily armed police were much in evidence, festooned with ammunition belts, and toting a variety of weapons from pistols to sub-machine guns. Hopefully they were keeping an eye on some of the more unsavoury looking characters who hung around the place. Unfortunately we were unable to take the cable car up to the top of the mountain overlooking the city, but as we arrived back at the ship we were interested to see a Venezuelan submarine surface and enter the harbour. There was just time for a quick drink (Frank's idea) on board a very luxurious Italian liner before we sailed promptly at 8.00 pm for Willemstad on the Dutch island of Curacao.

Rather surprisingly I was on deck at 6.30 am next morning, to find the ship just moving up to her berth in part of a wide inland waterway. We entered this after passing a floating pontoon bridge across the mouth, which had swung open to let us through. The island is governed by the Dutch and the town of Willemstad looked really attractive, the older buildings in a variety of pastel colours typically with gabled red tiled roofs. Once again Frank and I went ashore and the contrast with Port of Spain could not have been greater. It was clean, obviously well run and had many modern buildings. The downside was that everything was a lot more expensive, the inevitable beers costing a bomb, but we had a decent meal at a little bar where they spoke English, Spanish, and Dutch. Similarly three different currencies were in use: Dutch guilders, American dollars, and the Venezuelan bolivar, which made for some confusion, but it was all very relaxed with no problems. On our return aboard I visited the ship's barber who only seemed to know one length – exceedingly short! But I hoped this would help make a good impression when we reached Jamaica. We were off again at 4.00 pm sliding down channel past the attractive waterfront and out into the open sea, accompanied by the now ever present dolphins.

With the voyage almost over, it was most exciting to realise that after all our tribulations we had crossed the Atlantic, and our objective, set in Istanbul, was in sight. The Jamaican passengers were restless at the thought of reaching home, and amongst the crew there was a distinctly 'end of term' feeling. Surprisingly they moved Bob and me into a bigger cabin, so I did some washing and started packing. Frank, who had invited me to visit him if I ever reached the States, bought a bottle of champagne that evening and the three of us drank to a successful voyage.

Chapter Six
Jamaica

At last the *Montserrat* edged into her berth at Kingston on a hot Friday afternoon – but then our troubles started. Nobody was allowed to leave the customs area unless they had an onward ticket by sea or air off the island. Even the returning Jamaicans got a cool reception from the immigration authorities, and one of those who told me I would have no problems on arrival apologetically explained that things had changed since he left. After a hurried farewell, Frank rushed off to buy his air ticket home, and Bob quickly decided to do the same. For £4-5-0 shillings (£4-25p) I bought the cheapest ticket available which was deck class on a banana boat to the nearest island of St. Kitts. But the biggest blow was that they would only stamp my passport for a ten-day stay, which put me in a critical position as I was down to my last £25. Dependent on finding a job, I was just about at my wits' end as to what to do next. This was a dire and completely unexpected turn of events.

It appeared that the easiest way to reach Bob's friend Joe Lawson, who owned an inn on the north coast, was by train but we had some time to wait. Leaving Bob at the station I decided to visit the nearby British Seaman's Club with the vague hope that I might be able to pick up information on some sort of work. I met a sympathetic fellow there who was not a seaman, but having told me that jobs on the island were pretty impossible, he directed me to a Mrs Penkethman at the British Embassy. She was more than helpful but also explained that things were very difficult. However she made enquiries and confirmed that Joe was definitely at the address we had, and that by pulling a few

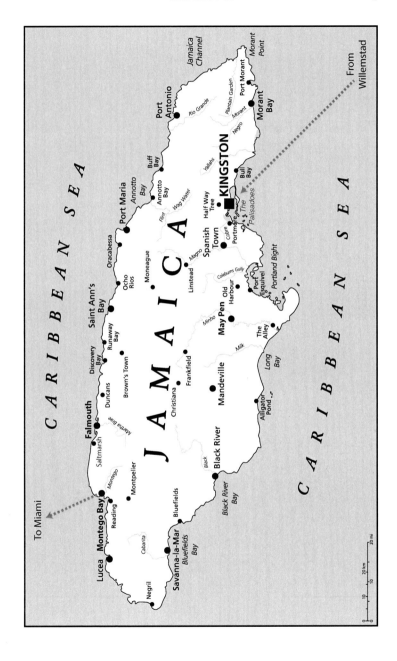

Leaving Willemstad

Eric's garden, Kingston

(*Left to right*) Carol, Bud, Eric, Madeline

strings she might be able to get me an American visa, should I need one. In addition she offered to make further job enquiries on my behalf on Monday, for which I was tremendously grateful, and this helped cheer me up somewhat.

Having bought his air ticket back to the UK, Bob was given a month's stay and thought that owing to the work situation, he would probably make a holiday of his visit and then fly home. I decided to accompany him up to Joe's until after the weekend anyway, and so we caught the train from Kingston in the South East of the island, to Montego Bay which is on the northwest coast – a distance of about a hundred and twenty miles. It was an odd journey on the single narrow gauge railway line through sugar cane fields and around mountains, and we passed through remote little places with familiar names such as Ipswich and Cambridge. They seemed very primitive with dwellings similar to the ones we had seen in Port of Spain, and there was nothing but jungle to look at for much of the time. Then a preacher appeared and after handing out hymn sheets he made us all sing. I needed this like a hole in the head, and when the inevitable collection came round I'm now rather ashamed to admit that in my black mood I made no contribution.

After six hours we arrived in darkness at Montego Bay to find that there were no buses, and reluctantly had to take an expensive taxi ride some fifteen miles out to Joe's at a place called Salt Marsh. Much to our relief we were expected, and after a warm welcome and a meal of chicken salad we flopped exhaustedly on to our beds to end what was undoubtedly the most demoralizing day of my life. I was so shattered I fell asleep in no time.

Joe Lawson was a rotund Jamaican in his mid fifties with a lethargic gait and a kindly manner and he spoke a widely used patois version of English, which often abbreviated a normal sentence. It took a little getting used to but nothing seemed too much trouble and he readily accepted me as a friend of Bob. The Lobster Inn was a fairly isolated roadside restaurant some miles from the town of Falmouth on the north coast of the island, and Joe's nephew Barry, a lad of about seventeen, helped with the cooking and general running of the place. To the rear of the building was a marsh which gave the district its name, so that although the sea came in quite close, it was difficult to reach and very shallow. Our room overlooked this and I was bitten like hell at night by various insects that had no problem gaining access.

I had intended going into Montego Bay next morning to check out the situation, but having no car, Joe had arranged for a friend of his, a Mr Stainrod the local fire chief, to take us on an entertaining tour of the surrounding area. This was incredibly beautiful with an abundance of palm trees and exotic plants, and surprisingly many of the roads, especially higher up in the hills, were reminiscent of a country lane in Devon or Cornwall.

We visited a sugar mill and were introduced to over proof white rum which comes straight from raw sugar cane and is absolute 'rocket fuel'; however, the old gate keeper in whose office we had this initiation could knock it back in one go! A delightful river called the Martha Brae on which you could hire a raft and be punted downstream for about three miles was a less volatile attraction, and where each bend presented a new vista of jungle creepers and exotic blooms. Apparently it was close to there that the Spanish first settled on the island.

After showing us his fire station at nearby Falmouth, which had the quiet air of a market town, with its brightly painted houses and white picket fences, we visited an attractive restaurant – with a difference. Here they kept a live alligator and we were glad to see that it was securely tethered and not listed on the menu!

The fireman then decided that he wanted some bananas, so we visited his uncle who lived in a primitive wooden shack on a remote coconut plantation on the edge of what is called 'Cockpit Country'. This is a near-impenetrable rainforest where escaped slaves known as Maroons once hid out. Some say they their descendants still do. The old peasant took a machete and went off into the jungle, returning with some big bunches of bananas, after which we drank coconut juice mixed with more rum. When the juice has been drunk the coconut is broken open and the jelly is scooped out with a sliver of shell. I really struggled with this although apparently it's an acquired taste. Not by me though, I'm afraid.

However, after our reception in Kingston we were most grateful for this friendly and unusual insight into Jamaica, which was unlikely to be experienced by the average tourist. It certainly helped take my mind off my job worries for a while.

Sunday was spent relaxing and I caught a bus into Montego Bay first thing on Monday morning to try my luck with a job. Mo Bay (as it was known by the locals) was an exotic resort with some tasteful buildings and a large number of well heeled American visitors. After trying a couple of hotels the situation appeared quite hopeless without the work permit required by a foreigner, which was apparently almost unobtainable. I felt that I might as well forget the idea and was back to wondering what on earth to do next. Someone suggested trying the Cayman Islands but I thought the situation would probably be much the same there. Things were fearfully expensive and there was a definite attitude of 'let's fleece the tourist'. Although unexceptional Doctor's Cave beach was the prime spot for sun bathing, volleyball games, and general relaxation, and I sat there awhile taking in the scene. What impressed me most was the wonderful turquoise colour of the sea, which was unlike anything I had seen previously.

Next morning I went into Mo Bay again with Barry and Bob, who seemed a lot brighter since our arrival, and I phoned Mrs Penkethman at the Embassy. She had no more news of a job, so I arranged to 'phone again and we returned with some supplies to the Lobster Inn, where things were quiet and business seemed none too brisk. The *Star* newspaper was full of reports of the latest gun battle in Kingston between local gangsters and the

police. From all accounts it resembled Dodge City, with at least
one shooting or armed robbery every day, and Joe told me that I
would get killed if I went to work there. He was quite serious too
and seemed genuinely concerned.

At the suggestion of his brother Vince, who kindly drove me
up there, I enquired about work at a large hotel nearby called the
Rose Hall Holiday Inn. This was situated on the site of a historic
sugar plantation and was originally the owner's palatial mansion,
but had now become the area's premier hotel. Depressingly, it
proved to be another dead end. Vince also made enquiries at
Montego Bay airport where he worked, and I got quite excited
when he returned to say that I should go down there the following
day. By now we were halfway through the week so time was
running out.

Jamaica Air Taxi was a small company operating a shuttle
service around the island with Cessna and Piper light aircraft,
and was owned by a sizeable and rather ungainly American called
Rudy Mantell. He had a tendency common to many Americans,
as I was to discover, of wearing white socks with black shoes
and dark trousers, but was an accomplished pilot with his own
stunt plane. Although there wasn't any chance of work with the
company, one of their employees, a friendly young chap called
Jimmy Hilton, suggested I try an aircraft maintenance outfit in
Kingston. He offered to speak to them and try to organise a free
flight down there for me, which would be a great help in terms
of time and money. So, arranging to be back early the following
morning, I returned to Joe's full of hope. But my luck was out
as there were no planes flying, and to cap it all the weather
turned really nasty with a heavy rainstorm later. I phoned Mrs
Penkethman again who said they might have something for me,
but sounding slightly annoyed, she stated that I should have been
at the immigration department that day instead of the following
Monday. I had now been in Jamaica for a week so it was vital that
I return to Kingston after the weekend to try and extend my visa.

I was back at the airport again on the Saturday morning but there was no news of Monday's flight schedules. Jimmy kindly offered to let me stay at his house on the Sunday night so that I could be at the railway station first thing on Monday, and I trudged wearily most of the way back to Joe's. It was a long way and I was getting very fed up with trying to hitch lifts, but one ride did produce an introduction to a most affable young American called Tom Thompson, who gave me his address and a welcome offer of accommodation when I was in Kingston.

Joe had taken a fancy to my watch so I sold it, and also gave him the gold ring bought in Munich as a 'thank you' for my lodging. By now Bob had become rather morose and I was keen to move out. The following day I went spear fishing with Barry in the stretch of sheltered but rather muddy water behind the inn. I managed the raft while Barry got a couple of snapper, and it was an interesting diversion from job seeking. Later on I hitched back to Mo Bay and met up with Jimmy for a drink, before he ran me back to his pleasant bungalow for the night.

I caught the early Monday morning train which eventually reached Kingston at 3.00 pm instead of 11.20 am as scheduled, after a terrible journey which included swapping trains part way. Added to this there were four more fanatical bible-thumping preachers to contend with, who I reckoned would put most people off religion for life. Nervously entering the immigration department, I managed to get my visa extended until March 25th, which was a big help as it gave me another seventeen days stay. However Mrs Penkethman at the Embassy was none too pleased with me and again said I should have come down the previous week to investigate a possible job offer. This opportunity had apparently now lapsed and my next call was to the aircraft company that Jimmy had mentioned. A taxi took me out along the Palisadoes isthmus on the far side of the harbour, to the airport where they were located.

The Palisadoes Maintenance Company was run by two

Canadians and I met Eric Saide one of the directors, and explained my background and current situation. He was pleasant enough and after I had filled out a CV said that there could be an opening for me with the company, in view of my previous motor engineering experience. They could only offer an initial salary of 25 pounds per week which wasn't great, but I was delighted with this opportunity and he promised to investigate the possibility of a work permit. Eric advised that I would do a lot better in the USA or Canada, and I resolved to try and move on there with my remaining funds if nothing came of the job. It was left that I would check back with him at the end of the week.

I stayed the night with Tom Thompson and his wife Nina at their modern flat in central Kingston, and they kindly let me doss down in their living room. Both were from New Orleans and I got to know them well and very much enjoyed their company. Tom worked for an American education firm and regularly travelled up to Montego Bay on business. They had a lively four year old son called Matthew, and I can still hear Tom with his Southern drawl saying 'Maathew, will you quit fart'n around'!

Jimmy Hilton had told me previously that there was a chance of a free flight back to Mo Bay with Jamaica Air Taxi, and as Tom had some free time he offered to run me to the airport. He was very surprised when I marched up the control tower to enquire about JAT flights. The fellow there was very inquisitive and asked a number of searching questions as to where I had come from etc. I had to waffle a bit of a story but cadged a flight with JAT to Port Antonio, a quaint backwater of tin roofed dwellings and dilapidated clapboard mansions on the northeast coast. Its tranquillity obviously attracted Marilyn Monroe who honeymooned there in 1957.

The third largest Caribbean island, Jamaica is about a hundred and forty miles long by fifty miles at its widest point. The Blue Mountains run across the island from east to west with the summit, Blue Mountain Peak, near the eastern end, standing at a height of 7,400 feet. We passed over this in what was only my second flight in a light plane, and it was an exciting experience with terrific air pockets making the small Cessna rise and fall as though in a lift. The pilot could not take me any further as there were paying passengers to collect, so I had to hitchhike and walk in blazing heat along the north coast back to Salt Marsh; a distance of about a hundred miles.

Once again there were familiar names as the island is divided into three counties: Cornwall, Middlesex, and Surrey, which are split into various parishes. It was impossible not to be impressed by the sheer scenic beauty, as the irregularly surfaced road followed the coastline and wound through attractive resorts with intriguing names like Ocho Rios, and Runaway Bay, (so named after the escape of a slave in colonial times). These places were smaller and less Americanised than Montego Bay. Near Oracabessa I passed the entrance to Ian Fleming's house *Goldeneye*, where all the James Bond books were written, and eventually returned exhausted to Joe's about 8.00 pm. All things considered it had been a successful trip, and from arriving knowing no-one to cadging a free plane ride in such a short time I felt was pretty good progress.

Back at the Lobster Inn there was some commotion when the barmaid who was found to be on probation was caught stealing, and was summarily dismissed. She had bought a watch from me so I was very relieved to get the money from her before she departed.

The next few days were spent helping Barry spear fish by paddling the bamboo raft, and in between visits to Mo Bay I wrote to Frank asking him for an invitation letter to visit the States in case nothing came of the job. I visited the Yacht Club out of interest and had a chat with Mr Round the secretary. There was a lovely English boat leaving the following week for New York, and he told me they needed crew. Courtesy of Vince I also applied for a job with a large Ford garage, who promised to let me know by post, so I had a few irons in the fire and felt more hopeful.

And then came the news I had been waiting for. At the end of the week I phoned Eric Saide who told me I could start work anyway until my permit came through. What a break! I was delighted and contacted Tom who was in Mo Bay, to arrange a lift with him down to Kingston.

So on that Saturday afternoon after saying cheerio to everyone at the Lobster Inn and promising to keep in touch, we set off in Tom's VW Beetle with an ice box full of the local Red Stripe beer, (no drink/drive worries in those days!) and travelled back along the north shore stopping on the way for what was my first proper swim in the Caribbean. It was wonderfully clear warm water and felt marvellous, except that Tom lost his car keys in it and I had to hot wire the ignition to get us going again. But all was well and after enjoying the spectacular scenery in comfort this time, we reached Kingston, and the four of us went to an Italian restaurant that evening. A day at the beach followed, with some of Tom's work colleagues, before we returned to a good supper cooked by Nina and a lively game of Monopoly. They really were a marvellous couple and I was tremendously grateful for their hospitality.

Feeling a little nervous at the thought of actually starting work after my four month 'holiday', I caught the bus out to the airport and checked in at Palisadoes Maintenance Co. Bud Wood was Eric's compatriot and co-director, and in contrast to Eric an altogether more taciturn character. Although he was pleasant enough, I soon realised that he didn't suffer fools gladly. Both were in their mid forties and with Jamaican backers had only recently started the business. Eric's wife Carol, who was expecting their first child, did the books. She was about my age and originally from British Guiana where they had met. It was arranged that they would put me up for the time being at their bungalow in the Barbican area of Kingston. This was set in a good sized garden with mango trees and a lovely view of the Blue Mountains. I had a comfortable room with shower and the situation suited me a treat, especially as it was near to the Thompsons'. It was to be the first of many long days and after a slow start we finally knocked off that night at 10.15 pm.

Besides Eric and Bud the workforce consisted of three Jamaican lads who were trainees, plus Lloyd the jovial chief mechanic, who until fairly recently had worked in the airport canteen. He rolled up every day in the most clapped out old Morris Oxford called 'Betsy', loaded down with his workmates, and one morning it got stuck in a huge pothole and we all had to lift it out. The others were Robbie, Perkins, and Prince, who were decent guys in their early twenties and there was an enjoyable working atmosphere. Everyone in Jamaica seemed to be addressed as 'man' even if they were a woman or a baby, and the usual exclamation if anything went wrong or was unexpected was 'Laaaard Gaaard' (Lord God)! The aircraft were known by their registration initials: i.e. CG was Charlie Golf, EZ Echo Zulu etc. My first week was spent on a variety of jobs on planes and also on maintaining Eric's battered Ford Escort, and we finished late every night.

Arriving home on the second evening we found that the house had been ransacked. Nothing much seemed to have been taken, although I lost a few items plus my small radio. It could have been worse, but as it was the second burglary in a month Carol was very fed up. A man from the CID arrived at breakfast time and took a few details, and three more were waiting when we returned that evening.

My work permit was applied for but very disappointingly Eric did not feel that there was much chance of success. It was worth a try though and I had to hope for the best. The week ended with another long day but I had the use of Eric's car, and was glad to meet up with Tom and Nina who were giving a dinner for a colleague of Tom's who was returning to the States. That

Palisadoes Maintenance Company

Jamaica days. Working on the DC3 near May Pen.

weekend I met Bud's wife Madeline when I was invited to stay a couple of nights at their spacious house, which was perched on a hillside to the east of the city with a gorgeous view of the sea. She was friendly enough but gave the impression of being rather a hard case like Bud. Surprisingly she preferred the far north of Canada where they had previously lived, to the balmy Caribbean climate, and stated that if anything happened between them she would return there like a shot! In fact both Eric and Bud agreed that the frozen north was the place to make money. They were probably right but I wondered if I could stand the cold, which was well illustrated on a couple of occasions when Eric showed us his cine films of Canada, together with those of his time in Guyana.

In contrast I walked down to the sea that Sunday afternoon for another swim before returning to join all four for an enjoyable meal. Bud produced a variety of drinks which loosened him up but he was back to normal when he drove us in to work that Monday. However rather than the mad thrash first thing at the Saides' with Eric chivvying Carol on, we rolled in comfortably at 9.30 am.

Work continued on different aircraft, together with ongoing maintenance of Eric's Ford Escort. A Curtiss C46 cargo plane came in one evening with a defective engine, and I was detailed to help Eric and Robbie strip it down, which was especially interesting. The C46 was a large twin radial engine plane originally used during WW II as a military transport, and although production ceased at the end of the war, many were still in service. The job took three days and we finished at 8.00 pm on a Friday evening, after which we took the crew for a meal to a restaurant at Spanish Court, an attractive mall in New Kingston. During the course of the conversation they told me that I could earn fantastic money as a waiter in New York. So I was certainly getting plenty of advice!

With baited breath I returned one morning to the immigration department and much to my surprise they agreed to extend my stay for another month. Hearing that the postal strike in the UK was over I resolved to write home but was so shattered after work most evenings that I found it an effort. However to my parents' relief we did re-establish contact and it was good to get their news again – as well as that of friends. The police had apprehended our burglar and so I made a visit to Constance Spring police station to make a statement and identify my shirt, penknife, and belt. Meanwhile I helped Lloyd with spray painting a Piper Cherokee and an engine change on a Cessna, which was all good experience.

Despite the heavy workload I managed to stay in contact with Tom and Nina and would nip in at odd times whenever I could. Tom would produce sherry and cigars which he bought as rejects from the factory, and although previously a non-smoker I became quite partial to them. Invariably a mad game of scrabble would ensue with all sorts of very unlikely words coming up and much light-hearted arguing over their legitimacy! Unheard of English slang was unacceptable to them as were some of their Americanisms to me. I was also introduced to the local marijuana or 'ganja' as it was known. Despite trying it on a number of occasions I felt no effect whatsoever and wondered what all the fuss was about. It was to be the following year after quite a bit more experimentation before I found out!

Another new experience was a visit one evening to a drive-in movie when they took me to see *Ryan's Daughter* starring Trevor Howard and John Mills. The novelty of watching a film in the open air was a wonderful experience but I remember being more impressed with the cinema than the movie.

A couple of weeks after my move to Kingston, Tom had called at the Lobster Inn on his way past and told me that Joe was quite concerned as to my whereabouts. Worrying news was that Bob was apparently in Falmouth hospital with some bug, and I decided that I would have to get up there at the first opportunity.

But there was no immediate chance as the long hours continued, and one evening Robbie got really upset at having to work late and lapsed into one of his unintelligible tirades. These used to crack me up and the only word I could make out was 'Raas', a common local swear word which appeared at frequent intervals in his performance. One lunch time he took me to his home in down-town Kingston and introduced me to his family. Normally it would have been very dangerous for a white man to venture into the area on his own, and I did get some menacing looks from loitering Rastafarians. But Robbie's folks were lovely people and made me most welcome. I was amused that the wooden houses often had half numbers; such as 47 ½ George Street.

It was during my third week that Bud told me that the authorities knew I was working there and that he had been given a quiet word of warning about the situation. It seemed that a work permit was out of the question and I would not be able to continue for much longer, which was a big blow. Apparently if I'd had just a year's experience with aircraft, even without any qualifications, a permit might have been possible. So as not to be seen working on planes too much I concentrated on Eric's car, together with running errands for Carol and Bud. I was reacquainted with Jimmy Hilton when he came to Kingston to take an aircraft related exam. We nipped up to my usual lunch time haunt at the flying club for a sandwich, and it was good to catch up on each other's news.

At last I had two days off and I sat with my diary early one Friday on Eric's terrace, gazing at another perfect Jamaican morning. There was not a cloud in the sky and with the Blue Mountains shimmering in a distant haze it all seemed too fantastic for words. Later on Tom called and we set off for Mo Bay with the car loaded as usual with cigars and an ice box full of Red Stripe beers. It was a magical drive over the mountains, with breathtaking waterfalls and bridges over foaming torrents, then along the north shore with Tom playing his kazoo and me singing an accompaniment, interrupted by our fits of laughter. They were good times which I shall always remember.

He dropped me at Joe's which was just the same and everyone seemed quite pleased to see me. Bob had returned from hospital the previous day after having had a blood transfusion, which didn't sound at all good, and it had gradually become more obvious over the months that he wasn't particularly well. But he seemed to be recovering satisfactorily and having mellowed somewhat, was rather more affable. Tom picked me up later and we returned to Mo Bay, stopping on the way at various hostelries. At one of these we collected a large Jamaican girl who took us to a dance. Things got interesting when she started asking if we had any money and while I was bopping away Tom gleefully did a runner, leaving me stranded with her – the bastard! I eventually managed to escape and made my way to his guest house, where I collapsed into the back of the VW to spend an uncomfortable night.

On my second free day I awoke feeling decidedly groggy but an early swim improved things and it really felt marvellous to laze on the beach all morning. I called again on Mr Round at the yacht club but there were no suitable boats leaving, although he promised to get in touch if anything did come up. We had another wonderful run back, punctuated by numerous stops for rum and coke and a swim at an idyllic little beach. I never ceased to be amazed at the beauty of the scenery and knew that I'd miss it tremendously if I had to leave. On our return Nina cooked us a chicken supper, after which we had another hilarious game of Monopoly that went on late and left me completely knackered – and broke!

So ended my short rest and it was back to work on Sunday morning, painting the interior of the new offices, which kept me out of sight of any casual observers. This was interspersed over the next few days with running numerous errands and a visit to the American Consulate to obtain a visa. Armed with Frank's letter inviting me for a visit I gave a full account to the official of my travels so far, and explained that my goal was still to reach Australia. He asked a lot of questions but accepted my story and stamped my passport there and then! Somebody waiting in the queue expressed some surprise at this and the ease with which I had completed the process. As I told him though, it was all true.

The new offices were starting to look very smart and we even managed to knock off work at a reasonable time for a couple of evenings, one of which was spent with an English family called Shelton who were friends of the Saides', and who had a split-level type house with a pool. Mr Shelton was building a small stunt bi-plane called a Pitts Special in his living room, but was going to have to partly dismantle it again on completion to get it out of the house.

Tom had found some scruffy tennis courts nearby and having wangled another Friday off, we had our long overdue match. As expected this developed into the usual boisterous affair although he beat me comfortably. But with the mountains as a backdrop the setting was exceptional, and I have never again played amid such splendid scenery. Then it was off to Gunboat Beach out by the airport for the afternoon, which was enlivened for all the wrong reasons when some poor local fellow drowned. There was a cursory enquiry by the authorities but no trace was found and nobody seemed particularly concerned, which struck me as typical of the general attitude.

At the end of the Palisadoes causeway lay the remains of Port Royal, the original capital of Jamaica, and once known as 'The Wickedest City on Earth'. It had a turbulent history of fires and flooding and had been a haven for privateers and pirates such as Sir Henry Morgan, who preyed upon and plundered Spanish treasure ships. Twice devastated by earthquakes in 1692 and again in 1907, it was gradually being rebuilt, and after the beach we went to look at the restoration works. Much remained to be

done but a number of original cannon and other artefacts had
been recovered from the sea, and it was an interesting reminder
of the country's early history.

Another barmy game of Scrabble finished off the day, but I
was starting to feel like some night life after so many evenings in,
although at least I wasn't spending much money.

After several weeks of nonstop sunshine it is surprising how
welcome a cloudy day becomes, especially when you are working
in the heat. That weekend was the Easter holiday but typically
the weather gods overdid things, and there were tremendous
deluges of rain. Together with the Woods and Saides I set off to
a house they rented at Ocho Rios on the north coast. Over the
mountains the rain poured down in torrents and we couldn't
reach the place because of a flooded river, so disappointingly we
returned home where the Shelton clan joined us for a barbecue
that evening. Things improved the next day and while everyone
sat around reading I borrowed the car and drove up into the hills
behind the house to take some photos. The views across Kingston
were magnificent, as were the houses in the appropriately named
area of Beverly Hills, but because of the high crime rate each
had its quota of Doberman and Alsatian guard dogs. More
tennis followed with Tom and a friend of his, and the evening
degenerated into further mad card and Scrabble tournaments!

Work continued with a vengeance and I spent most of the
time completing my painting and cleaning the place up in
readiness for a forthcoming board meeting. Just as I was getting
concerned as to how to proceed on the next stage of my journey,
we had news that a plane had force-landed at a disused wartime
airfield some fifty miles west of Kingston.

The following evening, having just been released from jail,
the pilot turned up. He was an American called Robert (Bob)
Holden, and was under suspicion of smuggling marijuana because
the airstrip he had come down at was out in the bush, ten miles
from the nearest town of May Pen. I was asked to go with him

back to the plane, so after calling at Eric's to pick up my kit we left immediately in his hire car. The plan was to carry out temporary repairs before flying it back to Kingston, and when we eventually arrived at 10.30 pm the DC3 was under police guard. Bob and his co-pilot who remained in custody, had been questioned as to why they had been trying to land on such an isolated strip, and his explanation to me was that they had been forced down by the previous Sunday's bad weather. He certainly didn't appear the sort of fellow to be involved in anything illegal.

Introduced in 1936, the Douglas DC3 was a very advanced passenger and transport plane for the time, and it became the allies' workhorse during WW11. The interior of this one had been converted for executive use and was quite luxurious, so I settled down on a couch for the night and slept in style. The airstrip was an old American base called Vernam Field, and although the concrete runway was over a mile long and in quite good condition, there were no facilities and we had to wash at a nearby farm.

Eric and another mechanic from Kingston arrived early next day and we started making repairs to the leading edge of the starboard wing. The plane had come in at night too high and too fast and gone off the end of the runway into some trees, but fortunately the damage wasn't too bad. It meant removing the de-icing strip from the leading wing edge and riveting sheets of aluminium over the damaged areas; which was hot work out in the open. After the other two left I was happy to carry on until sunset, whereupon Bob and I had our supper by torchlight before settling down to our second night on board.

With a good night's sleep I continued again at 7.30 am and Eric turned up later, this time with Robbie. It was another burning hot day and without a hat Eric suffered from sunstroke and didn't feel too good. Fortunately though, we finished the job by midday and so drove into May Pen to get some lunch and phone Kingston. It was decided that I stay with Bob at the plane, and after going for a good wash at the farm I spent a quiet afternoon reading and trying to keep cool. Further welcome news had come from home as Eric had brought out a letter, and I was pleased to hear that all was well. Later a curious little group of locals huddled in the shade under the wing, and were very keen to look inside the 'iron bird' as one fellow called it! We were offered 'ganja' but as Bob had generously offered me a free lift on his return to the States I really hoped he wouldn't be tempted to do anything foolish. Darkness eventually descended, and after a third night aboard I was looking forward to getting back now that the work was completed.

Bob went into town next morning to check the situation and then returned to collect his kit before leaving for Kingston. He couldn't say when the pilots would arrive to collect the plane and as the noise of his car died away I felt quite marooned. With no one about it was an eerie feeling sitting in the shade of the wing watching the heat waves rise off the deserted runway.

The silence was interrupted later by a crop duster plane which, after circling around, landed and taxied up to enquire 'the form'. The pilot was a craggy looking English fellow and after my brief explanation he shot off again to continue his work.

Happily that afternoon Bud Wood and the DC3's other pilot Steve Cavender, were ferried over in a couple of our customers' aircraft to collect me and fly the plane out. After a check around they climbed aboard, and with a roar and a great sheet of flame from the exhausts of its two big radial engines it hurtled down the runway and into the air. I had an enjoyable flight back in a Piper Cherokee and obtained some good aerial photos of Kingston. It had been an interesting episode and just the sort of unusual experience I was hoping for when I left home.

A picture of the DC3 and an account of its forced landing appeared in the paper; alongside a report of a gun battle in Kingston at Easter between police and gang members when four people were shot dead . . .

I was due a day off that Sunday but Eric and Carol went in for their Board meeting, and on returning Eric told me that I would have to finish after Tuesday – which amounted to giving me my marching orders. Understandably I suppose he didn't want me hanging around indefinitely, and now that I had to go I was keen to move on. Equally disappointingly the DC3 was going to be grounded for a month and there would be no chance of a free ride to the States.

So I began preparations for departure and the first thing I needed was yet another extension from the immigration department, which I duly obtained. It was an awful business retrieving my stolen items from the incredibly obstinate local police, even though I explained that I was leaving Jamaica imminently. I collected a letter at the post office from my mother, written two months earlier, and three more arrived just in time before I left. One of these contained an article she had read on how you could get around America delivering cars which vehicle rental companies needed to relocate. It was to be tremendously useful in the coming weeks.

After some thought and advice I decided to leave from Montego Bay, as besides needing to say cheerio to Bob and Joe, I could check on any yachts departing from there, or failing that, get a flight to Miami. My last day in Kingston was spent running a few errands for Eric and gathering my things together. Later Tom and I had another game of tennis followed by a terrific birthday supper for Colin, a colleague of his. A number of friends came over and a fair amount of celebrating took place, which all made for a good last night. I was back late and ended up playing cards with Eric – not too successfully I might add.

It had been arranged with JAT that they would give me a lift up next evening, so after a final tennis match I said a rather sad farewell to Tom, Nina, and Matthew. They had been fantastic company and had really enhanced my stay in Kingston. We swapped addresses because as Tom said 'We wanna see yuh agin

yuh hear?' I certainly expected
to renew our friendship and
we corresponded for some time
afterwards, but sadly eventually
lost contact. Meeting wonderful
people is a great part of the
whole travelling experience; the
downside being that so often
your paths never cross again.

Tom, Nina, and Matthew

    As I did my packing the
old butterflies returned at the
thought of beginning another
stage of the journey – but this
time on my own. Robbie collected me from Eric's and ran me
to the airport where I said goodbye to all the lads. They were
genuinely sorry to see me go, with Lloyd commenting that I was
only trying to earn a living. I wished Eric and Carol luck with
the baby and thanked them for everything, including a letter
of recommendation and the name of a contact in Canada. Even
though things hadn't worked out I hoped I had repaid their
hospitality and helped in a small way with the development of
their business. Through them I had been able to see a good part
of Jamaica, and I was certainly grateful for the improvement in
my finances.

    I flew up to Montego Bay with Rudy Mantell and one of his
pilots in a Cessna and Jimmy Hilton kindly offered his spare
room until I departed, so we had a night on the town with Will
Drew who ran The Ledge guest house. Jim seemed to be having
constant woman problems: they either didn't show up or if they
did they were a disappointment. Coupled with sometimes having
to work late this often left him in a pretty foul mood. One
lady that he had lined up from New York cancelled at the last
minute, and furthermore the reverse charge phone call cost him
25 dollars! But a visit to the Toby Inn cheered him up, as a few

drinks generally did, and he introduced me to some of Montego Bay's more popular bars and night spots.

It took a week and several visits to the yacht club before I finally gave up all thoughts of sailing to America. I went aboard a boat that was supposed to be going to Miami and spoke to the broker who had flown down to inspect it, but there were problems to sort out and in the end it came to nothing. Another yacht was going to San Diego through the Panama Canal, and although that could have been an enjoyable two month voyage it was well out of my way and would have cost me 100 dollars, so after some consideration I ruled out the idea. Eventually it boiled down to buying a plane ticket to Miami for 65 dollars, and after making that decision and sending a card to Frank I relaxed and settled for a day at Doctors Cave beach.

At the airport I met Bob who had also extended his stay, but was coming to the end of his holiday and was planning to fly home. After buying my ticket we returned to the Lobster Inn where I was very pleased to retrieve letters from my father and Frank. Bob's attitude had completely changed and he had become most affable now that I was leaving. We had been through a lot together and, but for him, I would not have seen Jamaica, so I was glad that we parted on good terms. Looking back I really don't know what I'd have done had he decided to just fly home from Istanbul . . .

Nothing had changed at the Inn and after spending a quiet day I said a final farewell to everybody and made my way back to Jim's. I was certainly doing a lot of walking and my feet were killing me. As I noted in my diary I must have walked more miles since Istanbul than in the whole of my life to date.

In readiness for my departure I spent next morning at the house doing some washing and trimming my beard, before going to Doctors Cave beach for a last swim in the Caribbean. Would I ever do so again I wondered? After supper with Jimmy at the Pelican Inn we had an uneventful cruise around town; and so ended my last day in Jamaica.

Despite an awful start it had been a wonderful experience and I list some of the things that stayed in my memory such as: the monotonous Reggae beat blaring out from shops and bars and seemingly whirling round constantly in the people's heads; Red Stripe beer and the *Daily Gleaner* newspaper; the little carts with steering wheels that people used to push their goods about on; goats everywhere (goat meat was a staple food); the journey to work every morning along the Palisadoes road with Kingston Harbour like a mill pond, and Eric as impatient as ever with the car and Carol. Then there were the multi-coloured irregular buses all with individual names such as Field Marshal; people chewing sugar cane; and of course the palm, banana, and mango trees; with the latters' fruit being especially prized. Shanty villages were in abundance with nearly all the houses having corrugated iron roofs, and at the other end of the scale were some of the most beautiful and luxurious mansions imaginable.

Some things were so familiar that it was like seeing England in a tropical setting; examples being official uniforms, parish boundaries, road signs, driving on the left, L plates on cars, red painted letter boxes, and very often being politely addressed as 'Sir'. On the minus side the bureaucracy and petty officialdom could be infuriating; as when I tried to retrieve my stolen goods from the police.

I would always remember the hills in front of Eric's house with their views over Kingston, and the lush green scenery of the island, and wondered if I would ever return.

Chapter Seven
On to the USA

Friday April 30th, 1971, and it was departure day for the big bad USA! Jim took me down to the airport and we dropped my bags off at Caribair's desk, where thankfully I had no excess luggage problems. Only a few questions about a return ticket which I evaded, because by now I really felt that I couldn't care less about rules and regulations. If I was refused entry, well so be it. Then after a quick farewell drink with Jim I thanked him for all his help and hospitality and hurried on board. Disappointingly I had an aisle seat (where I couldn't see anything) next to an unusually reserved American couple. We touched down on American soil with a terrible one wheel landing, and as I left the plane the humid heat hit me so immediately that I thought it was coming from an engine! It was oppressively hot as I made my way nervously towards the Immigration Department, but fortunately once inside air conditioning took over.

Facing me were about a dozen booths and I scanned the different officers until I saw a white haired older man who I thought might give me an easier time. I joined his queue and sure enough when he heard my English accent he became positively chatty. He said he'd been to England with the US Navy and I gave him a potted version of my plans, whereupon he stamped my passport for a six month stay and waved me through. Six whole months! After all the hassle in Jamaica I was over the moon and when I'd collected my bags and cleared customs I immediately headed for the nearest bar, dubiously titled Sir Robert's Pub, to celebrate with an unheard of beer called a Budweiser.

Now that I had successfully entered America my plan was

to travel up to see Frank via New York, taking in as much as I could on the way, before going on to Canada. Using the recommendation letter and contact name given me by Eric I had thoughts of continuing to work on aircraft.

Everything seemed fantastically expensive and after changing all my money I had 180 dollars (about 75 pounds). I decided to try and see something of the Indianapolis 500 mile race, one of the major events of the American sporting calendar due to take place at the end of May. With this in mind I approached some car hire firms, and Avis looked the best bet as they wanted cars delivered there. I couldn't afford to stay too long in Miami and arranged to be at their office next morning.

The next step was to find somewhere for the night so after leaving my large case in a lock-up I caught a downtown bus with a very helpful driver who had emigrated from Folkestone in 1958. He dropped me off at a small hotel called the Pittsburgh where I put up for 5 dollars a night. My feet were killing me but after a wash I couldn't resist going for a walk round.

I still had to pinch myself to believe that I was in the States, but everything was just as shown on TV at home. There were large blocks of high rise buildings with open air bars, palm trees, and of course huge cars, but a surprise was that the district was largely Spanish speaking. I went to bed tired but extremely happy with the way things had gone.

A box of cheese biscuits bought the previous evening sufficed for breakfast, and I then took a bus ride across Miami, with its numerous attractive waterways to the Avis office. Known as the 'Venice of America' the city consisted of many huge hotels and very plush holiday bungalows with boats moored at the end of their gardens. Meanwhile a large Goodyear airship droned overhead giving tourists a birds-eye view of it all. I thought things were going too well and so it proved, as when I arrived the last car had gone. They put me on the phone to a delivery agency where a coarse sounding character told me they would only pay

20 dollars towards petrol for the journey. In no position to argue I went back across town to his office where I gave him all my details, plus the required four passport photos taken en route.

The car, which turned out to be a Dodge Dart, a mid-size saloon, had to be collected from the private address of an elderly couple. They were very timid and only with some reluctance let me into the house when I asked for a glass of water. However the tank was full and I was soon on my way, although it was rather nerve-racking navigating through the city's tangled traffic in a left hand drive car. It was a relief to collect my case from the airport and after getting a map I drove north on Route 27, until stopping for a snack at a truck driver's pull-in invitingly named Lew's Pure Oil Truck Stop.

The country was very flat and marshy and it rained hard at one stage, but I kept going past lots of caravan parks and boat dealers before pulling off the road into an orange grove to spend a rather uncomfortable night in the car. Due to the humidity it took me some time to get to sleep.

Setting off again at 7.30 am I stopped for a coffee in the sleepy town of Sebring. Being a petrol-head I made a small detour to see its race circuit, which looked rather scruffy. The course is marked out with oil drums around a small airfield and is most famously used for the annual twelve hour sports car race, which first took place in 1953.

Having checked the map I saw that I had only covered about a hundred and seventy miles out of a total distance to Indianapolis of twelve hundred, and realised that my fuel allowance wouldn't go very far and I had better press on. I weakened the carburettor mixture to improve things and petrol at least was cheap at $4-10 cents a tank full.

The scenery remained rather monotonous for a while before gradually giving way to large wooded areas, and I passed lots of camp sites and motels before stopping for petrol just before reaching Highway 75 at Leesburg, north west of Orlando. It was easy driving and I cruised all day at 60-70 mph apart from stopping for lunch and a snooze after my second fill up, but was then concerned to see that no oil was showing on the dipstick. I felt rather miffed at having to spend some of my dwindling dollars on topping it up.

By 8.00 pm that evening I had reached the outskirts of Atlanta, Georgia, and the setting sun had painted the clouds a lovely purple colour. It seemed an attractive area which a drive around confirmed; the streets, homes, and gardens all being very neat and tidy. I stopped in the centre of town to stretch my legs, but then had difficulty finding my way back on to Highway 75 north again. Eventually I made it and followed a yellow Triumph TR3 sports car in pouring rain for several miles. 'Rainy Night in Georgia' would have been most appropriate, but instead the radio was playing 'Our Day Will Come' by Ruby and the Romantics, which always reminds me of that bit of the journey.

Although it was noticeably colder I slept much better on my second night in the car, but remember thinking that it must be the only vehicle in America without a heater.

My route cut across the western edge of the heavily wooded Appalachian Mountains, the Continent's oldest mountain range, and just south of Chattanooga I crossed the State boundary into North Carolina. Very soon this had changed again to become Tennessee, and continuing in a north westerly direction I passed through Nashville, famed for its Country and Western music.

I was making good time so decided to leave Route 65, the Interstate Highway, and take the more scenic road for most of the way to Louisville. This was wonderful driving through the beautiful Kentucky landscape, with its long rolling hills, panoramic views, and wide rivers. The neatness of the countryside, dotted with wooden homesteads was impressive, and eventually I came upon Abraham Lincoln's birthplace, a small town called Hodgenville, before entering Louisville itself.

Here there were many picturesque streets with enchanting

Georgian style houses, which could have come from a film set. I
filled up with petrol for what I hoped was the last time, as by now
I had used up my 20 dollar fuel allowance, and I was concerned
that the car was using a lot of oil.

Having crossed the majestic Ohio River I had now entered
Indiana, and after some food and a wash I stopped behind a café
for my third night about ten miles north of the State line. I was
disturbed around midnight by a large dog and then its master,
the café owner, who told me to get the car nearer the road or
otherwise he said 'the cops will move you on'.

Even allowing for my being acclimatized to the tropics I could
not believe how cold it was; far more so than I had anticipated for
May. I awoke chilled to the bone and got on the road at 6.00 am,
driving due north on the main highway, before breakfasting at
another truck stop.

By 9.30 am and sooner than expected I had reached
Indianapolis. In order to stay for the race it was my intention to
get a temporary job, but feeling unsure where to start looking I
first decided to have a clean up in a garage 'rest room'. A hotel
seemed a likely possibility and I drove downtown and found the
Hilton, where I waited unsuccessfully for about two hours to
see the personnel officer. Finally giving up I went across to the
YMCA to drop my bags before driving out to the track, where I
registered without too much optimism for any casual work.

After some difficulty finding the delivery address, another
private house, and spending $2.25 cents getting it washed I
delivered the car but didn't get the expected tip, although
they did run me back to the YMCA. Having been told that
everything was madly expensive at race time I reconsidered
my plan to stay, as it would also mean finding more permanent
accommodation. I didn't really care for the city much anyway as
it was quite industrial and I found most people very brash and
not particularly helpful. Nevertheless on the bus out to the track
next day a woman offered me free citizenship of Indianapolis if

I filled out a form and sent it off to her! It sounds ungrateful but I didn't like to say that I wasn't too enamoured of the place so wouldn't be taking up her offer.

After being woken up at 6.00 am by a noisy newspaper seller on the corner, I spent all next day watching the novice drivers doing their 'rookie tests'. This involved them doing a certain number of laps at a designated speed, and then repeating these at gradually increasing speeds as instructed by the officials. Several drivers were engaged in this exercise including David Hobbs, an Englishman who had driven for a team I had worked for a few years previously. I later regretted that I hadn't picked an opportune moment to re-acquaint myself with him, as it occurred to me that he might have been able to fix me a temporary job.

It was a pity that practice was stopped early when rain set in, as unlike us Europeans the Americans don't race when it's wet. But it did give me a chance to spend time in the extensive museum which told the history of the race going back before the First World War, and I recorded my stay by signing the large visitor's book.

Walking around town that evening I witnessed a fire at the Columbia Club in the main square which gave a good demonstration of the US fire and ambulance services in action, the latter fortunately not needed. Having first sent some postcards home, a combination of the gloomy weather and my dwindling finances made me decide to investigate moving on to New York the next day.

The bloody newspaper seller was in action again at 6.00 am so I was up and out early, and later managed to get another car delivery courtesy of a company called Auto Driveaway. This was a Plymouth Station Wagon owned by Sergeant First Class Charles T. Schneider (I don't know why but his name has stuck in my memory) which had to be delivered to the Military Ocean Terminal at Bayonne, New Jersey. From there it was to be shipped to Hawaii where he was being posted. Lucky man! The arrangement was ideal as it was

David Hobbs, Penske Lola, Indianapolis

Sloane House YMCA, New York

very near to New York, but took up most of the morning as I had to go for a strict medical check up. Apparently I should have done this before making the last trip, and had a shock when told that the fine for ignoring the rule was 1000 dollars! Eventually all was sorted out and after collecting my bags I went back to the track for the afternoon.

As it was sunny there were a lot more cars going round and the American Mark Donohue set a new lap record of 177.9 mph. It was an interesting and colourful scene with the officials in smart jackets and big baseball caps presiding over the famous Gasoline Alley. This is where the teams are housed and their garages were very plush with most having portable TVs and air conditioning. The McLaren team even had the floor tiled in their colours of orange and blue, which you could have eaten your dinner off. There was no sweating to move the cars around either as they were pushed about by mini tractors. All very efficient!

It had been an interesting interlude but I was under way again at 5.30 pm on US 70 east, stopping four hours later just short of Richmond for the night. The Plymouth was much more comfortable for sleeping as with the rear seat folded down I could lie full length in the back.

Awoke at 6.00 am very cold again and after a wash in another garage rest room I continued eastwards towards Dayton, and crossed the State line into Ohio. Near to Pittsburgh I came upon a small place called Ligonier. This was the site of a famous British fortification from the French and Indian War of 1758–66. The wooden fort had been fully reconstructed and restored with a museum, and it was nice to see the Union flag flying proudly above it. I took an hour or so to rest and wander round the site taking photos, and found it reminiscent of many an old Western film.

Like the fort most American houses I passed were of all wooden construction and although the roads were good I found the signs very confusing. Annoyingly I went miles out of my way at one stage en route to Harrisburg.

Staying off the main turnpike as much as possible was not only cheaper, but much more enjoyable driving on relatively deserted roads, before the night's stop just outside Allentown. This had taken me through another time zone and I had gained an hour and almost crossed Pennsylvania to spend what would be my final night in the car. True to form I was again woken in the early hours by someone unknown who disconcertingly asked if I was O.K.; I was fine until he disturbed me.

After some thought I decided to make the delivery the next day, a Saturday, rather than keep the car over the weekend – and so headed straight for the city passing through some pretty grim areas on the way. In common with most American cities the streets are laid out on a grid system which, once you get used to it, makes finding your way about quite straightforward. I took the Lincoln Tunnel under the Hudson River for midtown New York City which sits on Long Island, and having found the YMCA on 34th Street and 9th Avenue surprisingly easily, I managed to check in and drop off my bags without attracting a parking ticket.

There was torrential rain for most of the day which didn't help, but I eventually reached the Military Ocean Terminal at Bayonne which was back into New Jersey overlooking Upper New York Bay. After checking everything out, the fellow there drove me to a bus stop and in isolation I sheltered in a doorway from the weather. Luckily I didn't have long to wait, and in half an hour was back in the city again. It was exciting to arrive in New York with its mighty skyscrapers and I estimated the cost of getting from Indianapolis at about 13 dollars, which was gratifying as the car ran well and used no oil.

After a quick snack I went to see the film *Patton* with George C. Scott at a cinema just off Times Square, but thought it rather disappointing. I was to be even more disappointed later when I studied my fellow inmates at the YMCA. I had never seen such a collection of 'dossers' and 'drop outs' in all my life, and anything less like young Christian men would be hard to imagine. Where they got the money for the room rent I couldn't think, but at least I slept well after two nights in the car.

It seemed that the most economical way to see something of the city was to take a bus tour for $7-50 cents, and I strolled down Broadway to the depot. It was exhilarating to be on the street where all the principal theatres were situated and where some of the greatest shows became world famous.

The tour guide was quite a dandy and happily reeled off his six Christian names when introducing himself. We took in most of the main landmarks such as 5th Avenue with its famous shops: Saks, Bloomingdales, and Macy's: the Rockefeller Centre, Wall Street the financial hub, Central Park, and after visiting China Town we viewed the Statue of Liberty at a distance across the river. But surprisingly he also took great delight in pointing out all the prisons, mental homes, alcoholics in the Bowery, and filth in Haarlem, so we certainly had a balanced view of everything! The Stars and Stripes hung in abundance from many buildings, and an unusual feature of the city was the plumes of steam coming from gratings in the streets. We were told that this was because rather than heat their own water all the big hotels and office blocks found it cheaper to have it heated at a central plant, and then piped to them underground at high pressure.

The first task next morning was to collect my 50 dollars deposit from the Auto Driveaway office, and this was followed by a sightseeing-cum-job search expedition. I took the lift to the 102nd floor observatory of the Empire State Building which was then the world's tallest building at 1,472 feet, and luckily it was a fine day with visibility for fifteen miles. This offered a wonderful view of the city and beyond, with pedestrians being almost invisible and the ubiquitous yellow cabs smaller than children's toys. It was also possible to see, rising skywards in the distance, the ill-fated twin towers then under construction. Who could have foreseen the manner of their downfall thirty years later?

I made a fruitless visit to the Canadian Embassy to enquire about a work permit but was told by an official that there were no short cuts, and I would have to go through all the usual channels, which would take about five months. In fact he said that it would be advisable to make the application from the UK. This was a huge blow and I returned to the hostel feeling totally despondent. Sitting in my room later I was at a very low ebb and back to wondering what to do next. Again it seemed that a return home was the most likely outcome and the end of my journey was at hand.

But that evening in the common room there was a discussion on employment opportunities which gave rise to a few useful pointers. Afterwards I got into conversation with two other guys named Dick and Art who differed greatly from the majority of residents, and we all agreed to check out the situation the following day. Dick was a couple of years younger than me while Art was in his early thirties and hoped to get a book published from a manuscript he had written. It was good to have some company again and we all went over the road to a diner called The Flame Steak, where steak and chips with a Coke were to be had for the bargain price of 1 dollar.

A Social Security card was a vital requirement for any kind of work and they suggested we call at the Labour office next morning where they could wangle one for me. This they duly did by using Art's details and my name on the application card, which, to hide my English accent, Dick presented for processing. Easy! We then visited a very helpful employment agency recommended by the YMCA, who told us to call back next day.

A visit to the Australian Embassy confirmed that I could go straight in, so I decided to forget the Canadian idea and try to earn enough in America to take me the rest of the way there. I was further heartened by some gorgeous weather and a letter from home that was waiting at the huge Central Post Office. What a difference a day makes!

At 7.45 am next morning Art and I were waiting at the employment agency where we sat until 9.30 am with no success. So I continued visiting other agencies while Art set off with his manuscript to call on publishers. During lunch time I went into the central library but after half an hour everyone was hustled out by the police because of a bomb scare; which happily proved to be a false alarm. Later I put in a call to Frank and left a message letting him know where I was.

We made contact again at 7.00am next morning when I was awoken by his familiar voice on the phone wanting to know when I was coming up to Maine? It was great to catch up on each other's news and I agreed to check on travel arrangements later on.

Vigo type rain storms hindered job hunting but Art and I nipped out at one point and went round Macy's on 5th Avenue which is reputedly the largest department store in the world. Just about anything was available: the latest in fashionable clothing and shoes, wedding gifts, jewellery and watches, his and hers bathrooms, bedding and household goods etc, which could all be shipped world-wide.

Life moved at a fast pace in NYC and everyone seemed to be in a hurry. One afternoon on my way back from an employment agency down near Brooklyn Bridge, a car screeched up to the kerb, several men with drawn pistols jumped out, and two fellows walking twenty yards ahead of me were pushed against the wall with their hands raised and frisked for weapons. They were then handcuffed and bundled into the car, which rushed away at great speed. All in the space of about forty seconds!

After a couple of false starts the end of the week brought very good news with the possibility of a live-in hotel job, which sounded fairly definite. And then like buses, another option came along through Dick, with the offer of a job in a nursing home. This was not really my cup of tea but I decided to consider things over the next few days while visiting Frank.

So, packing all my kit but leaving my case at the hostel, I walked to the Greyhound bus depot accompanied by Art. The journey took all day in lovely sunshine but we stayed on the main highway, so didn't pass through many of the attractive looking little villages of upstate New York. A rest stop in Boston, Massachusetts, allowed a brief walk around and eventually we crossed into New Hampshire, and arrived in Portsmouth where I was met by Frank and his handsome Alsatian dog, Boy.

It was great to see him again looking just the same as ever and we drove out of town over the Piscataqua River (an original Indian name) into his home state of Maine. First stop was a tea shop by the pier in the lovely New England fishing village of Kittery. All the houses were of wooden clapboard construction, mostly painted white, but with the odd red one amongst them making a most attractive contrast. It was near here that the Kennedy family had a holiday home.

Frank's farmhouse was approached along an unmade drive and stood on high ground in a large tract of land with a panoramic view overlooking a creek. It was basically 150 years old – a single storey white painted clapboard building with a cedar shingle roof, and had been in the family for several generations. Frank had inherited it some years previously when his father died.

The main part of the house was let to some sailors from the naval base at Portsmouth, while Frank occupied one end of the building. He lived in a somewhat chaotic bachelor style amongst souvenirs of his many travels, and a variety of photos and pictures covered the walls. It was very homely though and just how I felt I would like my own place to be. It intrigued me that he drove a smart Mercedes saloon and dashed off around the world at the drop of a hat, yet his cooking facilities were quite basic and all washing up was done in the bathroom basin! He had a married brother, John, who lived in Cambridge Massachusetts near Boston and whom I was soon to meet. But relations with his mother who owned an art gallery nearby were apparently somewhat difficult, and they met only occasionally. To my appreciative surprise he was also something of a car collector, for his barn contained a 1953 Jaguar XK 120 coupe, a rare 1948 MG Y type tourer, and his first car – a very sound and attractive 1929 Ford Model 'A' cabriolet.

That evening we were invited to a party being given by the sailors and we went along for a while before returning to open the bottle of Martini I had brought. I find it difficult to believe now that I drank so much of the stuff.

Despite poor weather on Sunday we took a trip up the creek in his motor boat and viewed the many expensive looking yachts in the harbour. Some were original Maine designs built of wood with lovely traditional lines, which would no doubt require painstaking upkeep. Attention to their teak decks and varnished coach roofs and taffrails was a labour of love. Several tall concrete submarine towers still existed; the explanation being that these were used to try and spot marauding German submarines during the Second World War. As I was beginning to realise, no journey with FH IV was complete without a restorative, and we were suitably fortified by frequent nips of rum which he kept on board.

After a leisurely start next morning Frank made some enquiries for me about a genuine Social Security card, as he didn't think my current arrangement very satisfactory. He rang the local office in Portsmouth and asked how one obtained a Social Security card for an Englishman. 'Oh just bring him down here and we will issue one' they replied! Off we drove into town and to my surprise they did just that; so now I was entirely legal, which certainly felt more reassuring.

A visit to a historic house was next. 'Historic' in America is of course a relative term and at that time the country had still to celebrate its bi-centennial, as independence from Britain became a reality in 1776. Anything over a hundred years old was viewed as historic, and many such houses took their names from former residents and were preserved with their personal effects on display.

R.F. and Boy

Lesley, Irene, Boy, and Frank

As the weather was fine we went out in the boat again and called on the retired headmistress of Frank's old school. Her name was Gertrude and she was a jolly lady in her mid sixties with a twinkle in her eye, who plied us with rum and coke. It was during this session that the idea was suggested of my giving a talk next day to the school children, about England and my travels to date. Under some pressure I agreed, and we both returned to the boat feeling rather the worse for wear. Later, reality set in as the thought of what lay ahead dawned on me.

Surprisingly next morning I didn't feel too nervous at the prospect of facing two hundred American school children. I made some notes before Frank took me on a tour of the school which catered for children between the ages of six to twelve years old, and I met the headmaster prior to getting under way at 1.00 pm. After a brief introduction by him I described my journey so far and my original reasons for leaving home, and then gave them my impressions of the USA and my future plans to get to Australia. This all seemed to be well received and we then moved on to a question and answer session. These ranged from the lack of National Service in the UK (conscription was in force as the Vietnam War was still raging), to why our police did not carry guns, and one child wanted to know if Houdini ever escaped from Scotland Yard! My English accent intrigued them, and I later overheard one girl say to another: 'They talk sharp don't they'?

The children were very polite and at the end I received a big round of applause and Frank and Gertrude were most enthusiastic about the whole event. I was very pleased and relieved too, for after my initial doubts I had really enjoyed the experience.

Frank had a part-time job as a supply teacher, but he had also recently invested money in a joint property venture with a friend of his in Cambridge, near Boston. This apparently was a large block of flats which his business partner Don Byron managed. He explained that Don also had several other properties and employed students to carry out redecoration and general maintenance work, and that there might be an opening for me with him. After he telephoned Don on my behalf I was offered a week's trial starting the following Monday. This was great news and solved my previous job dilemma; in addition I was assured quite rightly that Cambridge was a much nicer environment than New York City.

Having enjoyed my week in Kittery I said cheerio to Frank before he left for work on the Friday morning, and took a taxi to Portsmouth where I boarded the midday Greyhound back to The Big Apple. Art was still at the 'Y' but was due to leave on Monday for an out of town hotel job, which was lucky as he was down to his last few dollars. Dick was also now working at a hotel where we met that evening, before all dining out on another 1 dollar meal at the Flame Steak. 'The best value in town'!

After a 60 cent breakfast next morning Art helped carry my bags to the bus terminal. We shook hands and I wished him luck before boarding the 11.00 am for Boston and another new start. I hope things worked out for him as he was a good bloke and very welcome company. Perhaps he made a fortune from his book – it would be nice to think so.

Chapter Eight
The Byron's of Cambridge

My large suitcase was nearly pulling my arms out, (three cheers for modern wheeled cases!) and in desperation I booked into a hotel. Separated from Boston by the Charles River, Cambridge is an attractive dormitory town and home to world renowned Harvard University. I decided to make a start looking for accommodation there straight away, and having bought the local paper I went over to see a room advertised for rent in a boarding house.

It was situated in a pleasant tree lined road called Ellsworth Avenue, near to Harvard Square as Frank had advised, and comprised a bedsit with a communal kitchen which was quite suitable. Returning to the hotel I explained the situation and they kindly let me check out again without charge, and so back I went with all my gear. Having bought some food supplies, I felt tired but satisfied that evening with the way that events had unfolded. Several times during the day I had wondered how an old school friend's wedding had gone. I imagined my chums having a fairly wild time and missed their company.

Sunday dawned gloriously sunny and after a late breakfast I set out to explore Cambridge. The hub of the town was Harvard Square on which are located the attractive ivy covered buildings and gate of the University. In the centre is the subway station known as the 'T' which runs into Boston, and there were many restaurants, galleries, clubs, bookshops, theatres, bars and even a pseudo half-timbered English pub selling Watney's Red Barrel at 70 cents for half a pint! It was just as Frank had described, a fascinating scene which I felt would be most enjoyable for my envisaged two month stay. Most of the afternoon was spent lying by the Charles River watching speed boats dashing up and down, and generally soaking up the atmosphere. Returning to my room I wondered what the following day would bring.

Promptly at 9.00 am on Monday morning I reported for work at Don Byron's office, which was within easy walking distance of my digs. He was a youthful looking 44 year old man of medium height and slim build with a welcoming smile, and he described his background while waiting for his foreman to arrive. Originally he had hoped to make a living as a writer and had bought his first property, which he converted into flats, to provide a steady income. He would write during the morning and work on the building in the afternoon. Eventually though he had given up writing to concentrate full time on property development, and appeared to be making quite a success of it. Don now owned a number of apartment buildings in and around Cambridge and his latest venture was the one involving Frank. After an initial trial I was promised 120 dollars per week which was good money and would allow me to save for the onward journey.

Don's only permanent employee turned out to be a chubby fellow with a crew-cut called George St. Pierre, who had worked for him for several years. Of French Canadian origin he could turn his hand to almost anything, and most notably, never got annoyed or swore, however awkward the job in hand. After a couple of days I had no doubt that we would get on fine as he was very easy-going with an infectious chuckle.

Our first job was repairing a chimney on the roof of an older building containing several flats, one of which was let to a doctor. The conversion had been done very cleverly giving it great character, and it appealed to me immensely as an ideal bachelor pad. The financial aspect aside, learning about building maintenance was to stand me in good stead in future years, and the difference between American and English terms was an education in itself. For instance what we call plasterboard is known there as 'sheet rock', Rawlplugs are 'anchors', and

Polyfilla goes by the delightful name of 'spackle'. For the rest of the week we carried out small external repairs on several different properties, in continuing sunny weather.

Another acquaintance at this time was a real odd-ball called Bill Hammill. Bill occupied a basement flat in one of Don's buildings and cycled around doing odd cleaning jobs for him. He spoke in a slow nasal drawl, and, conscious of being almost bald grew his hair at the back so long that he could sweep it forward over the top of his head, and then back again in a quiff which was held in place on his forehead with Sellotape! This was supposed to make him more attractive to women, or 'broads' as he called them. We nicknamed him the phantom cyclist, and tales of his latest amorous encounters and observations on the opposite sex had George in stitches of laughter.

With the exception of a friendly fellow named Dan who lived downstairs, I didn't see anything of my fellow tenants. He was kind enough to let me watch the 'Indy 500' on his TV, and having visited the track I was especially interested to see the actual race which was unfortunately fraught with spectacular crashes. I didn't go out much, and after buying supplies at the local supermarket and cooking my evening meal I usually went to bed and read. Just as I was thinking of looking for somewhere with a bit more life, Don Byron came up with a most surprising proposal at the end of the week. 'Would I like to live rent free at his ex wife's house as she was going on holiday and didn't want to leave their teenage son Alan on his own?' This would certainly boost my finances and it was agreed that we would have a meeting in the next couple of weeks. So my job situation looked more secure.

That first weekend was Memorial Day Holiday, a federal holiday to remember those who died serving in the armed forces, and predictably the weather turned dull. But after working all Saturday, Dan kindly lent me his bike and I rode off to further investigate my surroundings.

The Blue Parrot, The Idler, and the Ha'penny Pub were an interesting selection of bars and coffee houses recommended by Frank, and all situated around Harvard Square. The legal drinking age in Massachusetts was twenty-one but it was common for those younger to use false identity cards. The advice in the Boston–Cambridge student guide book was 'if you are going to use one, at least make sure it's realistic'! This booklet was a mine of information on eating, drinking, transport, dating bars, clubs, cinemas, newspapers, radio stations, television channels, museums, etc. – and still makes fascinating reading.

Students from around the world congregated in these various establishments and music from an impromptu street band could often be heard drifting through the air. Bob Dylan's anti-Vietnam war protest songs would remind one of the burning issue of the day, and Carol King's classic new album *Tapestry* was also a huge favourite. A rock festival was held every Sunday in the park and at the first one I attended everyone had brought their pets. These ranged from a St Bernard dog through a variety of birds to a tame stoat on a lead.

Just off Harvard Square lay the Brattle Street Theatre, a basement cinema specialising in black and white classics, and I treated myself to the 1932 gangster film *Public Enemy* starring James Cagney. Great stuff! Whenever they showed a Humphrey Bogart movie tickets were half price, and the audience would often applaud and shout comments at the screen, which all added to the entertainment.

A particularly noticeable sound was that of the almost permanently wailing sirens of police cars and ambulances, which were much louder than those at home. Cycle theft was a big issue too, as I was to discover later when my borrowed bike was pinched. Everywhere the Stars and Stripes were displayed: on public buildings, cars, houses, police and other officials' uniforms. It was as though the population needed a constant reaffirmation of their nationality and self-belief. 'America – Love it or leave it' was a common slogan.

During the week I called in on Frank's brother John and his attractive wife Sue who lived nearby. John resembled Frank but was much less extrovert; a quieter chap altogether, who didn't seem to have a job of any kind at that time.

There was also an invitation to meet Don's ex wife Mary at her home to discuss my proposed move there. Mary was slightly older than Don and had apparently taken some persuading that marriage was a good idea. She spoke with a pronounced Southern accent, a result she explained, of being brought up by a Negro nanny from Louisiana, and was followed everywhere by her doleful Basset Hound Honey. A pleasant arty type she had a rather vague manner and described at length all the problems they had been having with Alan, who had been smoking 'pot'. Her mother had a house in New Hampshire and Mary planned to spend more time there over the summer, but was concerned about leaving her son alone. Cue yours truly. Alan, the cause of all the concern, was sixteen with shoulder length hair in the fashion of the time, and seemed an introspective lad who, when at home, was usually ensconced in his room. His older sister Valerie was away at school. So it was arranged that I would move in the following week.

I was also introduced to Don's second wife Ruth. She was a bespectacled studious looking English girl from Wimbledon, and about twelve years younger than Don. Their first child was due imminently and they lived just around the corner from Mary; unusually the relationship between them all was very amicable, with frequent social visits to each other's houses.

After three weeks a postcard arrived from Frank inviting me up for the weekend, and on the Friday evening I took the Trailways bus to Portsmouth. This was a big improvement over the Greyhound service with a hostess, free coffee and cake, books, and playing cards. It felt good to be leaving town for a change of scene.

We were to attend a local wedding the following day, and

disconcertingly Frank admitted to having cold feet over his own impending nuptials to Irene, who was arriving at the end of the month. I hoped this was just nerves and at the reception, at which he looked very dapper in a white linen suit, he was his usual boisterous self, dancing very professionally and generally fooling around with old friends and acquaintances. We met John, Sue, and his mother but it was noticeable that he hardly spoke to her all day. Some guests returned to the farm later and we joined up with the sailors who were having their usual Saturday night party.

After a dull start, Sunday brightened up, which was lucky as Frank had arranged a boat trip with the daughters of a local doctor who lived across the harbour. Elise Strauss and her younger sister Jess, whose mother was French, had put together a picnic, and before stopping along the shore for lunch we went for a look over the old coastguard's house on a small island in the bay. We were invited back to supper and I was rather concerned when Dr Strauss started questioning me closely about my job. He had apparently tried unsuccessfully to obtain a work permit for his French nephew, and was surprised that I had succeeded. But the moment passed and we had a pleasant evening before Frank ran me back to the bus. It had been a most enjoyable break.

Finally at the end of the week Mary came round in her old Plymouth station wagon to collect my kit, and I moved into her home at 239 Mount Auburn Street. Mary's driving style was something of a novelty. As the seatbelt fixing had broken, she would hold on tightly to the belt with her left hand whilst steering with her right; this being possible as the car was an automatic. Meanwhile the passenger had the interesting experience of seeing the road going along beneath his feet through a hole in the floor!

The house was a typically white painted wooden structure with a balcony running across it at first floor level, supported by two columns either side of the front door. It was partly screened by trees from the road, on the other side of which ran the Charles River. My comfortable ground floor bedroom overlooked this and had been occupied some years previously by Frank when teaching at Harvard. So here I was, following in his footsteps. A large dining kitchen lay to the rear and at the very back were Alan's quarters. Upstairs was a rather bohemian sitting area together with Mary and her daughter's rooms. A driveway at the side led to a gate through to the back garden in which sat another smaller house in the same style, No. 237, let to three girls. I was having supper one evening when one of them looked in and introduced herself as Carole. She was a freelance researcher at Massachusetts Institute of Technology; the famous M.I.T. It was a pleasant surprise to have some female company and she filled in more background detail on the Byrons and Cambridge life in general.

Gradually I came to know her fellow tenants who were called Amy and Lesley. Amy, the most serious of the three was studying law, and was attractive in a scholarly way but quite highly strung; whereas Carole and Lesley, whom I would later meet on her return from holiday, were much more relaxed and light hearted.

Mary continued to come and go at will and I subsequently met her daughter Valerie, a shy willowy girl of about seventeen with the same rather vague manner as her mother.

Meanwhile summer got into its stride and the Cambridge air became very oppressive, making manual work quite tiring, but I was delighted when Don offered me the use of his small Honda motorcycle, and I obtained my learner's permit. We took it to a large car park for some practice and I began using it for work and leisure which gave me a great feeling of independence. Things were going well apart from a rather quiet social life. I missed my friends and dashing around the area to parties and favourite pubs in our sports cars, together with our frequent trips to London.

However things livened up when Mary gave the first of her celebrated Friday evening drinks parties. The girls and I were invited, also Don and Ruth, together with an extraordinary assortment of characters ranging from artists and university

personnel, to the odd taxi driver. It was here that I met Mary's
English cousin The Hon. Jimmy Sandilands. Jimmy was the
quintessentially eccentric professor type. With unkempt hair,
baggy suit, shoes with broken laces, and a tie that was gravitating
towards his left ear. But he was a charming fellow who taught at
Harvard, and later I believe inherited the family title, to become
Lord Torphichen. By an extraordinary coincidence it transpired
that I had been at preparatory school in Birmingham with his
son. As they say, it's a small world.

One Sunday I was invited on a day trip by a chap called Stan,
one of Don's temporary workers, to a place called Truro on the
Cape Cod peninsular and once again it was lovely to exchange the
humidity of town for a coastal breeze. We had a most enjoyable
run down and saw a replica of the *Mayflower* at Plymouth Rock
before going swimming on the Cape. Although, much to my
surprise the sea was freezing, especially after the Caribbean, so
we didn't linger in the water.

At the end of June another postcard arrived from Frank,
inviting me to dinner one Friday evening at friends of his at
Kittery Point. Here I was to meet Irene who had arrived from
Spain. She was slim, slightly taller than Frank, and as soon
became apparent, quite conventional. She was horrified to hear
during the meal that Frank had smoked 'grass' a few times in
his college days, and after an enjoyable start to the evening the
atmosphere became quite tense. Like me, before leaving home
she had never experienced the stuff, and I suppose it was a shock
to find that her future husband had indulged, even if it had been
in his youth.

Frank appeared next morning with a glass of orange juice
and we had a long chat. The previous evening appeared to have
rekindled his doubts about marriage and he asked for my views
on the situation. This was not easy and all I could suggest was
that perhaps they should give themselves more time.

Anyway it had been arranged that we would pick up Elise

Strauss, and so after a snack lunch at her house we drove up the coast to Kennebunkport and visited Mrs Hartley's art gallery. This was in a beautiful position right on the water's edge and Frank introduced Irene to his mother, who I thought seemed very pleasant. On this occasion he was much more civil to her than he had been at the wedding and fortunately the visit passed off most amicably. We stopped for tea at a delightful little restaurant on the way home, which completed a pleasant day out.

Sunday was Independence Day and Frank had organised a party at the farm which took place out in the front garden in lovely sunny weather. We made a punch in a large silver bowl and provided a good selection of food, and the sailors and a number of friends arrived. As the only Limey present I came in for a certain amount of ribbing, but it was all good natured and the day ended with a spectacular firework display across the creek.

The holiday was extended with an invitation to sail on the Strauss' yacht next day, which I found to be great fun – the first time I had sailed for years, and I resolved to take it up again. It is a perfect boating area with a fascinating variety of small islands, bays and creeks to probe. If you could run a tape measure along the entire Maine coast line it would total three and a half thousand miles. A barbecue supper and a nightcap with Frank and Irene rounded off a wonderful day.

Life continued with a mixture of work, cinema going, further investigation of the area, and keeping an eye on Alan who, with his pals, was likely to turn the house upside down if given half a chance. Reassuringly Don asked me to stay on for at least another six months, to which I agreed – authorities permitting. He also became a father for the third time when Ruth gave birth to a healthy baby boy named Douglas, who would grow up to become a US Air Force pilot.

I greatly enjoyed cycling around the Beacon Hill and Back Bay areas of Boston. Back Bay was built a hundred years previously on reclaimed land facing the Charles River, and contains Newbury Street, which is the high fashion centre of the city and also a lively social scene. Attractive bow-fronted red brick buildings housed expensive boutiques, gift shops, and art galleries, interspersed with numerous outdoor restaurants and coffee shops.

Traditionally Beacon Hill is where Boston's wealthiest families live, or at least have their addresses. Teddy Kennedy had a house there and Mt. Vernon Street has been the home of at least fifty of the most influential families to shape the country's history. The lovely Georgian houses set in small shaded squares or on steep narrow streets, many not wide enough for a car, with quaint gas lamps lend the locality an air of charming gentility. Dante's, a small Italian restaurant at 21 Joy Street holds happy memories and became a firm favourite. An old world garden at the rear and interesting décor lent a cosy atmosphere, especially in winter when to complete the mood there was a large fire and a violinist playing. Beacon Hill is also home to the Bull and Finch, the nearest thing to an English pub I came across in America, and where the celebrated TV series *Cheers* was filmed. Close by is Boston Common, and on summer evenings the Boston Pops Orchestra conducted by the renowned Arthur Fiedler gave open-air concerts.

Unexpectedly one weekend we were all summoned to join the Strauss family on a visit to their ski cottage near Jackson in the New Hampshire Mountains. Although famous for its dangerously erratic weather it's a beautiful area, aspects of which reminded me of Austria, although the surrounding villages with their white clapboard houses, historic inns, and blood-red barns are typical New England.

True to form there was a huge thunderstorm just after we arrived and all the power went off! That meant we had to go and fetch water which was normally pumped electrically, from a nearby well. An early start was made next morning to climb the Black Mountain and now with clear skies we could see Mount

Washington, the highest peak in the north-eastern United States at 6,288 feet.

A turning point in my social life came with a dinner party invitation from the girls in the cottage. An English chap called John was staying for a few days as a guest of Lesley, who met him when on holiday in Canada, and it was good to socialise and chew the cud with another Limey. After a very nice meal we went up to the Ha'penny Pub and then on to the The Idler which was the nearest I'd been to a pub crawl for a very long time. I was invited to join them all for a trip to the beach a few days later and we drove up the coast to Plum Island near Newburyport, which was a novelty indeed. Unfortunately it was populated by a particularly vicious type of fly which bit 'like no tomorrow' as George would say.

Don and Frank's new joint venture was an impressive modern apartment block five miles north west of Cambridge at a town called Medford, and work centred on redecorating a number of flats which had become vacant. It was a relief to be working indoors as the heat had built up to an unbelievable level and I found it really draining. After working Saturday to make up for my day off in the week it was great to take off on the Honda and explore more of the surrounding area. I found myself at the delightfully attractive village of Lexington, scene of the first battle in the War of Independence, or the American Revolution as we Brits term it. A stone monument on the village green marked the site but it came as quite a shock to see the British described on it as oppressors and tyrants. I'd never thought of us like that!

I also made good on my resolution to take up sailing again and so joined the nearby Charles River Sailing Club. After going out with the instructor for forty minutes I was let loose in a dinghy, and from then on would often go for an evening sail which was wonderfully refreshing after a hard day's work.

The girls took pity on my feeble culinary efforts about which they would tease me no end, and I was often invited to join them for a barbecue. It was wonderful on a warm summer night to cook our evening meal out in the garden in front of their cottage, on a small stove called a hibachi. Amy's boyfriend, a very amusing chap called Gill Cass was usually there too, and often had some witty observation on local life. On one occasion he had us all in fits of laughter with his description of a cycling convention, which stopped overnight in Cambridge on its way to a protest meeting in Washington. Apparently they never got any further as next morning they found all their bikes had been stolen!

Gill and Amy were complete opposites. He being so laid back with a very dry sense of humour sometimes took great delight in winding her up. Invariably she would bite and then a broad smile would cross his face and realising she'd been had she would explode! But they seemed to rub along and their various doings were always a source of interest to us. I wonder what became of them.

Chapter Nine
The Wedding on the Beach
and Unexpected News from Home

One Friday evening at the end of July, I arrived back from work to get a message from Frank that he and Irene were getting married. Apparently they had resolved any differences or doubts over their future, and the wedding was to take place on the local beach at 7.00 am next day.

Panic ensued as I cleaned myself up and dug out some respectable clothes. Most helpfully Ruth offered to lend me her Volvo, so that I could dash up to Kittery straight away. The wedding present would have to wait until later.

A slight sea mist swirling around set the scene next morning, and at the appointed hour a small congregation of about thirty friends and relatives gathered on Kittery beach for the ceremony. Presumably due to the short notice Irene's parents were not present (and neither was Frank's mother) to give away their only daughter and I wondered how they would receive the news of the marriage back in Spain. Hopefully they would approve. It was remarkable to think that I had met Frank on a ship only five and a half months previously, and here I was attending his wedding on a beach in New England!

The best man was John Hartley and the bridesmaid was his wife Sue. It was all very informal, with the minister in a plain grey suit and several men wearing jerseys and slacks. What we would term 'smart casual' today I suppose. One or two even smoked throughout the service! Irene wore a simple white wedding dress with an Alice band holding her hair in place. Frank cut his usual dash with a smart navy blue reefer jacket with white trousers and his favourite Panama hat. I wasn't sure about the trainers though.

In less than an hour it was all over, and everyone returned to the farm for the wedding breakfast, which had been arranged on the front lawn by the sailors. This was more liquid than edible but bride and groom looked suitably pleased and relaxed, and many glasses were raised to the happy couple. A small number of us joined them for lunch at a lovely restaurant up the coast at York Harbour, as they were not going away until the following week.

Frank and Irene at their wedding reception

A memorable day ended with me rowing the Strauss girls back across the creek to their parents' house where I was entertained to supper.

Out of the blue, a few days later a letter arrived from home written by a chum of mine called Gordon Howie. He was about the last person I expected to hear from, but he explained that he was shortly leaving his current employers for a new job with a bigger construction company. As there was a gap of a few months between the two jobs, and having heard details of my travels from my parents, he had decided to come over to America and look me up. This was most welcome news but I felt it only fair to explain that the work permit and job situations were not easy. He would have to find accommodation and employment if he intended stopping any length of time, because the USA was anything but cheap. This didn't deter him and he replied that he would join me as soon as all the arrangements had been made.

So I had this to look forward to, and additionally invitations

R.F., Jim and George at Medford

to various functions suddenly came thick and fast. What a change!

One was to the home of an Irish-American called Jim, whom I was working with at Medford, for a roast beef and Yorkshire pudding lunch cooked by his wife Sarah, which was a great treat. In addition one week Mary seemed to be having a drinks or dinner party almost every night, but chaos ensued on the memorable occasion of Don's birthday party which she had agreed to host. Running behind schedule, the kitchen in a mess, she was wrestling with a heavy candlestick trying to force in a new candle when it slipped, and went crashing through the large mucky fish tank which held pride of place on the sideboard. I've never seen anything like it – talk about the parting of the seas. Cecil B. de Mille couldn't have done it better! The floor was awash with millions of tiny fish flapping around and Mary was running in circles screaming causing Alan to emerge from his room. Taking one look at the scene he waved his arms skywards and let fly a barrage of four letter words. Whereupon Ruth rounded on him and told him in no uncertain terms what she thought of his lifestyle and general attitude. Meanwhile, Don who was on the phone having an important business discussion was forced to hang up in sheer embarrassment, before eventually he and I were sent out for takeaway Kentucky Fried Chicken. So much for the birthday dinner!

Things took an interesting turn a few days later with a supper invitation from Lesley at the cottage, and she and I gradually became more of an item. Sailing continued on the Charles River and I watched an enjoyable US Tennis Championship final: Ken Rosewall beat Cliff Drysdale, and Emerson/Laver beat Okker/Riessen in a thrilling men's doubles match. It was turning into a marvellous summer.

Gordon arrived one Friday towards the end of August bringing with him the latest edition of *Autosport* magazine which was like manna from heaven. There followed a big celebratory barbecue provided by the girls on their front lawn and Jim and Sarah joined us, together with a couple of Lesley's friends, which made for a great evening. It was terrific to see a mate from home again and catch up with all the latest news.

The Freedom Trail is one of Boston's main attractions and was Gordon's introduction to America, as Lesley took us sightseeing. It's a two and a half mile route visiting sixteen of the city's notable sites, which must feature in every American schoolchild's history book, and is marked with a set of red painted foot prints on the pavement. Notices explain events leading to the colonists' efforts to gain their independence and it starts at the Old State House, now dwarfed by taller buildings, and takes you to the Granary Burial Ground, resting place of revolutionary heroes, and the site of the Boston Massacre. This was where British troops opened fire on rioting protesters, which gained us permanent notoriety and set the seal on the colonists' resolve to free themselves of Colonial rule. Paul Revere was the messenger who rode out to Concord to warn that the British were on the march from Boston, so that the patriots were prepared for the clashes on April 19th 1775 that

Freedom Trail, Boston

Gordon outside the Paul Revere House

began the War of Independence. His grey clapboard house which is the city's oldest, built in 1680, is as famous for its age as for its former owner, and is situated in the city's North End, now known as Little Italy, where the Trail ends. Highlighting the day for us was an invitation to go aboard a US Navy Coastguard cutter, and after a tour of the ship we had afternoon tea in the wardroom. A gift of a couple of sailors' hats made fine souvenirs, proving that there was no ill feeling towards us Limeys, and I kept mine for many years.

At Don's suggestion we started a four day week, working ten hours a day, which wasn't as arduous as I expected, and it was good to finish on a Thursday evening and have a long weekend. More than once he had asked 'Why don't you stay and make a million Rog.?' He was thinking of something along the lines of his arrangement with Frank but with me taking a more active role. It was an interesting suggestion to which I gave considerable thought but it would mean abandoning my ambition to get around the world, and of course going through all the US immigration formalities. How feasible this would be as I had minimal capital was anyone's guess. I did suggest that perhaps I could return having completed my journey, which he agreed was a possibility and we continued to discuss the subject intermittently.

Gordon quickly found himself some digs nearby, and even a cash in hand job doing renovation work on the house of a local lady, which kept him in funds. Subsequently he also became involved in the discussions and joined me in working for Don.

Labour Day, the first Monday in September and equivalent to our August Bank Holiday, was approaching, and Don invited Lesley, myself, and Gordon to spend the weekend at his holiday home at Wellfleet on Cape Cod. On the way down we stopped at Plymouth to view the *Mayflower*, a replica of the Pilgrim Fathers' ship of 1620, and arrived at an attractive bungalow overlooking large sand dunes scented by pine trees and salt air. Our holiday began with a conducted tour in Jeeps

Breakfast discussion at Wellfleet: R.F., Don and Gordon

over the dunes, after which we fooled around taking photos of each other, pretending to be lost in a desert. Exploration of the area took us up to Provincetown, right on the tip of the long curling peninsular that is Cape Cod. Basking in glorious sunshine, its brightly painted wooden houses and galleries set in busy narrow streets displayed a quirky charm, making it an obvious 'Mecca' for holiday-makers. It's also renowned for its seafood, clam chowder and lobster being particular favourites, but as I'm a non fish eater this aspect was lost on me. The Cape also features a series of small inland lakes which are ideal for water sports, the temperature being some twenty degrees warmer than the sea. A very pleasant change from my previous visit and it was lovely to sit relaxing in the sun after a swim.

In return for cleaning the carburettors on her Volvo, Ruth lent us the car one weekend so that we could make a trip up to Bryar Motorsport Park, a few hours north of Boston in New Hampshire, to watch some racing. We arrived quite late and pitched our tent amongst several others, before getting the 'gen' on proceedings over a drink with the fellow next door. It was just a small club meeting but very relaxed and friendly, with a large number of British sports cars such as Healeys, Triumphs, and MGs. Practice took all of Saturday and we had a great time wandering around the rudimentary paddock taking photos, talking to competitors, and generally soaking up the atmosphere. Stock car racing, which we found hugely amusing, took place in the evening on a small inner circuit sprinkled with oil, and we finally sacked out around midnight exhausted with laughter.

Leaving early next day to avoid the race traffic we drove along the beautiful wooded southern shore of Lake Winnipesaukee, in which we swam and cleaned ourselves up in the rays of a gorgeous sunset. We were in time to watch a water ski demonstration and firework display at a place called Alton Bay – all for the princely sum of 10 cents. Unable to find anywhere to camp, we drove down a side road, pitched the tent in someone's driveway, and rather surprisingly remained undisturbed all night.

For some time I had listened to tales of various people's experiences travelling around America, and had harboured vague thoughts of seeing more of the country myself. I mentioned the idea to Gordon who was immediately keen, and we began to discuss the project in more detail. Fortunately Don had no objection to my taking a few weeks off, and gradually an itinerary took shape, formed by suggestions from Lesley, her sister Janice, Carole, Gill, and several other acquaintances. We would hitch-hike across the country to California, then up the West coast visiting San Francisco, and back across on a more northerly route up around Chicago. The general opinion was that it was best to get to the Midwest fairly quickly as the interesting sights really began around Colorado.

WBCN was a Boston radio station that had a program called *Rides and Riders*. Somebody planning a long drive could advertise for people to share the driving and expenses, and equally travellers looking for a lift could state their destination on air. This was how we heard of two students called Gerry and Bruce who were planning to drive back to university at Fort Collins in Colorado, which would put us well on our way. A meeting was arranged one evening to discuss things, resulting in Friday September 17th being settled as our start date.

The next week was spent getting our kit together and finalising all the details. We borrowed a tent from a friend of Lesley, bought a primus stove and maps, and went over the route with Janice who had done a similar trip. Departure day was a rush as I worked in the morning to finish an apartment for Don, but after packing everything together and having a bath we opened some wine for a last meal. Lesley, Jan, and Carole came to see us off, and feeling rather nervous we met Gerry and Bruce outside McDonald's on Boston Common, before finally getting away at 10.30 pm that night.

Chapter Ten
Into the West

Gerry's car was a large 1964 Oldsmobile coupé and the fifth crew member was his cat Peyote, named after the drug. Reassuringly for us there was no evidence that our fellow travellers were users. The plan was to complete the journey of two thousand miles in the shortest time, and taking it in turns we drove all the following day for an almost solid thirty hours, passing to the south of Chicago. For convenience we used the motorways as much as possible and with the car running well the only unplanned stops were after Peyote was sick, and when a tyre threw a tread.

We had crossed through the States of Massachusetts, New York, Pennsylvania, Ohio, Indiana, and Illinois, before reaching Iowa. Bruce drove the last stretch to his parents' home in the small settlement of Storm Lake, where we arrived at 3.00 am on Sunday morning and promptly collapsed into bed. Refreshed by eight hours sleep and a large steak for breakfast, we loaded Bruce's Jeep Travelall, (a forerunner of the Range Rover), and I set off with him on the final leg of the journey, with Gordon accompanying Gerry.

Known as the Great Plains, this central part of the country was absolutely flat with dead straight roads running through acres of tall yellow corn as far as the eye could see. Countless Westerns depict wagon trains crossing the landscape on the great migration to California, and in places their wheel tracks could still be seen over one hundred years later. We passed through small towns comprising one main street and a few shops and bars, before reaching Nebraska and skirting south of Omaha, the capital. It was a glorious day and we drove west into the setting

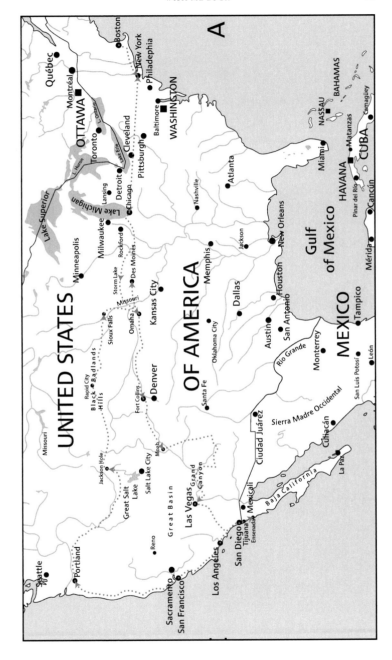

sun, stopping to pick up a couple of hikers just after dark. They must have been disappointed as shortly afterwards we ran out of petrol and Bruce had to hitch a lift himself to get some.

While we refuelled a police car drew up and pointed out that we had no rear lights, but, unable to get them fixed, we decided to press on. Some distance further, with me driving, the police pulled us up again. Just my luck! However he was very amicable and we had a long chat sitting in his car while I described my travels and showed him a British passport. Not having seen one before he was most intrigued, and after a friendly handshake we said goodbye, and I continued until we reached Fort Collins. I still have the ticket he issued. We all sacked out in some students' house adjacent to the university in the early hours of the morning.

Rod Stewart's latest hit *Maggie May* was belting out from the stereo when we awoke, and it turned out that eleven people had been sharing the place that night. Gerry took us on a tour of Colorado State University which was a very modern building with its own cinema and recreational facilities. Fort Collins was founded in 1864 as a military post named after Colonel William Collins, and nestles against the Rocky Mountains at a height of 5,000 feet.

A light dusting of early snow had already fallen, and we later drove up into the foothills to a large lake which overlooked the town and surrounding prairie. Although looking completely natural it was actually man-made, being known as Horsetooth Reservoir, and provided the town's water supply. I will always remember the absolutely breathtaking stillness up there. You could have heard a pin drop.

The next stop on our route was the city of Boulder, some fifty five miles to the south, and after we said farewell to Gerry and Bruce some other students kindly gave us a lift there that afternoon. We were due to stay with a couple called Sheila and Dan who were friends of Lesley, and after a snack and a look around we found their house and introduced ourselves. I only remember them now as being a pleasant young couple who were thankfully expecting us.

They also drove us up into the hills above the city that evening and the view at night was even more spectacular. Boulder, a city of about 65,000, lay spread before us and Dan explained that it took its name from nearby Boulder Creek. Just to the west are huge slabs of sedimentary stone known as the Flatirons, which lie at an angle of about forty five degrees against the foothills, and which are a symbol of the city. It was freezing cold so we were glad not to be camping.

After we had caught up on our sleep next morning, very English weather forced us indoors, and we spent most of the day visiting the museum which described the lives of the early settlers and their battles with the Indians. *The Anderson Tapes,* Sean Connery's latest film, was showing at a downtown cinema that evening and I reckoned it the best I'd seen for ages.

A beautifully sunny but cold morning greeted us, and Sheila drove us to the outskirts of the city and dropped us on Route 70, where we soon hitched a lift in the back of an old pick-up truck for twenty odd (freezing) miles. However the spectacular scenery made up for it. The wide prairie stretched away to meet the snow covered Rocky Mountains, the peaks of which were hidden by a layer of cloud.

Our destination was the famous ski resort of Aspen, and we had made a sign to hold up when standing at the roadside thumbing. I posed for a photo at one point and just as he was taking it a large police car drew up behind Gordon. The officer advised us in no uncertain terms that it was against the law to hitch-hike on a freeway, and after confiscating the sign, threatened to arrest us if he caught us again. I felt that it was only the large Union flags on our packs that saved us, and after walking away we waited until he was out of sight before returning to try our luck again. Being miles from anywhere there was really no other option, and luckily we did not have long to wait before a VW camper van stopped for us.

Hitching through the Rockies to Aspen

Rocky Mountain scene

Gordon writing his diary, Maroon Lake, near Aspen

Driving it was a character called Roy, and it soon became obvious that he and his mates were high as kites on marijuana, or some such substance. They invited us to partake and when we declined kept saying 'you guys are sooo straight'. However they had us in fits of laughter with a string of unlikely tales as we rolled along, the downside being Roy's unnerving habit of turning to face us in the back for seconds at a time when talking; while we prayed that he would turn around before we hit something. They began to fret though when a police car tailed us for several miles, as their bloodshot eyes and rather slurred speech would have given the game away. Everyone relaxed when he turned off and we stopped for a break. But any apprehension we felt was exceeded by the magnificence of our surroundings, and as we climbed up to 12,000 feet at sunset to cross Independence Pass we were presented with yet another wonderful photo opportunity.

Aspen was originally a mining town established in the 1880s when silver was discovered in the surrounding mountains and its early history had evidently been pretty exciting. Some of the original brick buildings still had bullet marks in the walls, and only in recent years had it become a famous ski resort, popular with film stars and celebrities.

Of course everything was very expensive, but Roy knew of a red painted Victorian house complete with 1890's décor where we could rent a mattress in the attic for 3 dollars a night. Called the Little Red Ski Haus and reckoned to be the best value in town, it was populated by travellers like us, and young ski bums who had christened Aspen 'Rip off city USA'. He even stood us dinner that evening at a quaint place with a cabaret act, which was incredibly generous of him. This was a commendable American trait that we were to experience on numerous occasions.

Exploration next morning revealed Aspen to be a curious amalgam of Western frontier town and chic Alpine-style ski resort, complete with some very expensive shops. All the latest fashions in ski wear and equipment were available and I suppose the attitude of some of our fellow lodgers was understandable. After a visit to an original saloon which had a bullet hole through the former owner's name, Roy and his mates departed and Gordon and I hitched a few miles out of town to a lake we had been told about.

Maroon Lake is so called because of the reflection in the water of the red coloured rock of the mountains which tower above it. We were the only visitors to this spectacularly scenic place, and the only sign of habitation was the odd beaver's lodge. The late afternoon sunlight danced on the surface of the lake as Gordon sat on a rock writing his diary, while I wandered along the lapping water's edge to take photos and enjoy the solitude of this stunning setting.

A hilarious conversation was under way amongst our fellow inmates when we returned to the Little Red Ski Haus, which provided the evening's entertainment. We retired for the night still laughing and I was sorry to be moving on next day.

Surprisingly our first lift was with an English girl, working in Aspen, and she took us back up to rejoin Route 70, the main highway west. A long wait just outside the town of Glenwood Springs involved another chat with the law, but he was more curious than threatening. Even so we were glad to get going when an old couple invited us to jump into the back of their pick-up truck. We were getting quite used to travelling in pick-up trucks.

Near the town of Grand Junction, so named because of its position at the confluence of the Colorado and Gunnison Rivers, they stopped to allow us a close look at a small herd of buffalo – our first sight of these legendary creatures. They seemed relatively tame but it was sobering to think that they were nearly wiped out by unrestricted hunting. Indeed it's said that it was a deliberate policy of encroaching white settlers to deny the Native Americans the source of much of their staple requirements.

A few hours further on we crossed into Utah and were dropped off outside a gas station; a small oasis in what appeared to be the middle of a desert. Wondering whether we had done the right thing, we surveyed the desolate surroundings. The landscape had completely changed, and there was literally nothing for miles around us except scrub and rock with some barren looking hills in the far distance. But fortune was with us in the shape of a young fellow named Chuck, who offered us a lift to the small town of Moab some miles further on. Not only that, but he also took us on a conducted tour of the nearby Arches National Park en route, just as sunset occurred.

The Park comprises over two thousand natural sandstone arches, spires, balanced rocks, and eroded monoliths, formed some three hundred million years ago when a sea flowed into the region. The variety of weird shapes glowing a vivid deep red in the evening sunlight made a haunting spectacle. Unfortunately since 1970 over forty of these arches have collapsed due to erosion.

The question of where we would stop for the night was also answered by Chuck when he told us that he was friendly with the town's sheriff. On arrival we made straight for the police station and were promptly offered a cell each! So for the first time in my

25. Hitching through Utah

26. The Arches National Park

27. Leaving Moab Police Station

life I spent a night behind bars – although I'm glad to say there were no other inmates and our doors remained unlocked.

Leaving our cells proved a lot easier than leaving Moab, as we had our longest wait yet of two and a half hours on the edge of town next morning. But it paid off handsomely. 'Where ya headed boys?' called the cheerful driver of a large saloon car. He was Bob Hagberg, a tarmac contractor on his way to inspect an airport runway. We explained that we were heading south to Mesa Verde National Park, a World Heritage site on account of its ancient cliff dwellings, which lay back in the western corner of Colorado. The Spanish word 'mesa' means a flat-topped steep-sided mountain; so literally 'green table'. After buying us a meal during which we described our journey he immediately decided to take the rest of the day off and accompany us around the Park.

This was a terrific offer because the site is a huge area in which you could spend a week seeing something new every day. It is twenty miles alone on a snaking road from the entrance to the Park museum, which sits 8,000 feet up with spectacular views for many miles of the surrounding canyons, mesas, and wide stretches of desert. Earthquakes in distant geological times had raised the mesas from beneath the seas, encouraging an eco-climate that suited the original human settlers. It was our first proper sight of what we think of as 'Cowboy Country', and typical of what we had seen in so many Westerns over the years.

Built into the cliffs on different levels are the remains of ancient dwellings that go back 2,000 years to Stone Age peoples, and by climbing up and down ladders you can explore the ruins. The most extensive and majestic of these is called the Cliff Palace, and shows how the early inhabitants learned to build, work, and live together in harmony, secure from wild animals and human adversaries. Circa 1270 AD it had two hundred living rooms and sheltered about four hundred people.

We spent most of the day going round with Bob, inspecting the various sites and he even insisted on buying us supper before

28. Mesa Verde

29. Cliff dwellings, Mesa Verde

leaving us by the park entrance at dusk, and wishing us good luck. What a wonderfully generous man.

Our first night under canvass was comfortable and after repacking the tent we set off next morning to the town of Cortez, where we hitched a lift with an inventor. As you do. We were certainly meeting an interesting cross section of the American public, and they seemed to enjoy meeting us and listening to our English accents. The next objective being the Grand Canyon our route ran south into New Mexico through a 'town' called Shiprock, where we were dropped off in the middle of a Navajo Indian reservation.

It was quite a shock to see the squalid conditions in which these people lived, barely eking a living from the arid land, and their houses were austere little shacks. Nearly all the men wore cowboy clothes with large Stetson hats, and drove old pick-up trucks with cattle or a horse in the back. All traces of their former life had gone. We chatted with a few teenagers, who looked fairly plump and healthy, and they assured us that they were doing 'just fine', which I found rather hard to accept.

An Indian farmer and his family took us some way further before abruptly dropping us at the roadside and disappearing into the desert. So we were in the middle of nowhere again. We waited in the boiling sun for some time before a tanker driver took pity on us and pulled up with a squeal of brakes. The size and emptiness of the landscape was awe-inspiring, and we drove for several hours along the narrow ribbon of tarmac leading south which vanished in a heat haze in the distance. The only sign of life was the occasional Indian farm shack, before we eventually reached the cattle town of Gallup.

Life became even more interesting as we stood at the roadside there, when the first of two large yellow school buses halted some way beyond us. We looked at each other and simultaneously asked 'Is he stopping for us?' To answer our question a head popped out of the door followed by a beckoning arm. 'Couldn't drive past the British flag,' said Pete the driver as we ran up. And wonder of wonders they were going directly to the Grand Canyon so we lost no time in jumping aboard.

The buses were brand new and being delivered to schools in California, but the drivers, Pete and Dave, were quite happy to stop for any traveller that they came across on the way. And boy were they an odd but very amusing assortment!

The common term used at the time to describe anyone who was anti-establishment, unconventional, or who had dropped out of society was 'Freak'. This generally covered any man with long hair looking as though he might use drugs, and the description certainly applied to our fellow passengers. Two guys lay asleep along the seats and as the afternoon wore on everyone got more drunk, with one bloke getting distinctly out of hand. They were particularly intrigued that two Englishmen were travelling around their country sightseeing, and everyone agreed this was 'Far out' – an expression that followed every other sentence. Joints were being passed up and down and frequent 'comfort' stops had to be made, until Pete decreed there would be no more until we had passed the mandatory inspection entering the State of Arizona. Quite surprisingly we did.

On this part of the journey we were following the old Route 66 which symbolises the 'American Dream', made legendary in numerous films and songs. Tales of long open roads, neon-lit diners, and quirky characters abound and it all seemed in tune with our bus and its occupants. At one point we picked up a stranded motorist who looked very uncomfortable in our company. In the course of a conversation he solemnly assured me that the Indian problem had now been solved. I was tempted to ask if this was 1971 or 1871.

Towards evening the other bus ran out of gas so we continued to Flagstaff where the unruly one was ejected, and Pete arranged for a garage to go back with fuel while we had a meal. We reached the Grand Canyon after dark and spent the night parked on

That bus!

The Bright Angel Trail, Grand Canyon

the South rim, and I have an abiding memory of sitting in that school bus in fits of laughter at the hilarious conversation of the freaks, one of whom was playing a flute. Far out man!

While three of them slept outside, the rest of us stayed in the bus, and by the time I arose the sun was well up over the Canyon. It was a truly breathtaking sight looking out across a distance of about twenty miles to the North rim, as the colours of the different rock strata continuously changed hue. The Canyon had first been explored by European Americans in the 1860s, in an unlikely expedition led by a one-armed ex-soldier. They had paddled the entire length of the Colorado River to finish some months later in Nevada.

Facilities consisted of a wooden nineteenth century hotel comprising a museum, with demonstrations of rug weaving by Indian women, and a restaurant and bar. After breakfast everyone spent the day sightseeing and we learned that escorted mule trips to the bottom of the Canyon were available; but Gordon and I decided we would like to make the journey next day on foot along a path known as the Bright Angel trail.

Later Pete, Dave, Gordon and I visited the bar which was filled with a diverse assortment of mule handlers, travellers, and hotel guests. Bursts of laughter punctuated the noisy chatter and a group of people at a nearby table struck up a conversation with us. Among them were two Norwegian girls called Karen and Inga who lived in Los Angeles. They were planning to take the mule trip down next day, but by the end of the evening had decided to change their plans and join us.

So after a delayed start next morning we bade farewell to Pete, Dave, and the gang and set off with the girls on the narrow eight mile track to the bottom. In places it was very steep and we were pretty exhausted on arrival, but the temperature one vertical mile down from the top was beautifully warm. After cooking up some soup and with no thought of snakes, scorpions, or other creepy crawlies we sacked out in our sleeping bags by the

Colorado River under a brilliant starry sky. It remains one of my life's great moments.

We paid for it next day though. I had never been so completely exhausted as I was towards the end of the climb back up, which took us six hours. By the time we reached the top we were absolutely whacked, but luckily the sky was overcast and in fact it rained heavily towards the end which helped considerably. A wonderful sense of achievement was felt by us all, for what had been an exhausting but truly unique experience.

With the Rockies now behind us we crossed into Nevada with its unfettered gambling laws, and the casino city of Las Vegas in the Great Basin Desert lay ahead. The girls had planned an overnight stop there on their way back to LA, so after a shower and a change of clothes we set off in their car arriving at 9.00 pm that evening. It was hard to get a sense of scale in that vast empty landscape, and I couldn't imagine how the early pioneers ever began to survey the area on horseback or by foot, let alone work out how or where to cross the daunting Sierra Nevada and Rocky Mountain ranges. But what a contrast on arrival! Driving along The Strip at night gives you the full-on effect of the place, with huge neon signs on every building in town – including the many funeral parlours. This struck me as being in dreadfully bad taste and it was hard to imagine ending your days there.

One of the landmarks is Caesar's Palace, a garish hotel which, as the name implied, was furnished in mock Roman style, with large columns, fountains, and Cypress trees at the front. The menu featured such culinary delights as Caesar's Caper, Nero's Orgy (an ice cream pot-pourri), the Asp's Bite, etc. Feeling better after a meal we wandered around the various tables and slot machines, and all had a go at Blackjack. I was a dollar up after two hours play before calling it a night and finding a motel.

The girls departed for Los Angeles in the middle of the most terrible dust storm which blew up next morning, getting in our mouths, noses, and ears, and blotting out most of the surroundings. Karen kindly offered to put us up at her flat when we arrived in a couple of days, so we would have a very welcome base during our stay there. After writing some cards we spent the afternoon wandering around the casinos, and were astounded by the number of people moronically feeding the one-armed bandits for hours at a time.

Andy Williams was opening in a new show at Caesar's Palace that evening and we managed to get tickets. It was a brilliant night with Andy singing some classic Carole King and Carpenters numbers, and the icing on the cake was a souvenir LP dated September 30th 1971, which I still have. It helped improve my impression of Las Vegas a little and I'm glad to have experienced the place, but have never felt the need to return.

Starting out early we had a long wait at the entrance to the freeway, before finally getting a ride for a hundred and twenty miles in a hot rod enthusiast's 1955 Ford pickup (yes another one). Our next lift took us the rest of the way to Los Angeles where George, a friendly young bloke with a VW camper van, bought us a hot dog and directed us to Karen's address which we reached by early evening.

She had a really nice flat in a modern apartment block, but I wasn't too impressed with Los Angeles which was a big sprawling city with an awful layer of smog hanging permanently above it. But next day we drove down the coast a small way to a very pleasant place called Laguna Beach, where at Crescent Bay I had my first swim in the pleasantly warm Pacific Ocean. Having swum in the Atlantic it seemed an appropriate way to celebrate our crossing of the huge expanse which is the continent of North America. In contrast to Los Angeles Laguna Beach had developed into an artist's colony since the early twentieth century due to its clarity of light, rather like St. Ives in Cornwall.

For transport we hired a large red Chevrolet Chevelle, the performance of which Gordon delighted in testing to the full! After a marvellous supper with Inga and some other friends we took a stroll up the famous Sunset Strip in Hollywood. Its trademark billboard advertising was much in evidence but it turned out to be a rather sleazy area of nightclubs, boutiques, and strip joints.

A visit to Disneyland which had originally opened in 1955 was next on our agenda, and proved to be a wonderful experience. Perfect weather complemented a fascinating scene, featuring a fairytale Sleeping Beauty castle, African jungle, high level Monorail, and a re-creation of a turn- of-the-century Main Street, complete with gas lamps, period shops, vehicles, and flower stalls. Other attractions were a corner of old New Orleans, complete with jazz band, a submarine experience, open top bus ride, and Captain Hook's pirate ship. Overlooking all this was a replica Matterhorn mountain which could be scaled with ropes.

We tried as many of these attractions as possible, but perhaps my favourite was the submarine experience. You descended into the grey painted sub which actually ran on rails without submerging, but the underwater views through the portholes were very realistic and gave the impression of sinking to the ocean floor. The sea bed comprised very convincing clumps of coral and rocks, sea grasses, fish, and general marine growth.

A Mississippi paddle boat called the Mark Twain, with tall ornate funnels and a hooting steam whistle, took visitors on a river trip past authentic looking Indian villages complete with tepees and canoes. Squaws were seen preparing meals, and braves fashioned their weapons while children played at the water's edge.

The African jungle trip took us past incredibly lifelike crocodiles, and replica hippopotamus heads popped out of the water to investigate us at frequent intervals.

In the evening sunlight a uniformed brass band led by Mickey Mouse parading down Main Street was a fitting finale to an exceptional day.

While in Los Angeles I visited the immigration office and was delighted to be given a further six months extension to my US visa.

Having got that out of the way we took off in the Chev early one morning for a trip down to Mexico. As we passed San Diego the spectacular Coronado Bridge, which stands on tall pillars, could be seen curving in a majestic arc across the harbour to the Naval Air Station at North Island.

The contrast with the United States after crossing the border at Tijuana was like night and day. The people were terribly poor and lived in shanty towns, with houses made of cardboard packing cases and odd pieces of wood and corrugated iron. Occasionally they would be right next door to an ornate palatial mansion, clearly emphasizing the disparity in wealth.

We pressed on down a good coastal highway to Ensenada, another ramshackle town looking like something from a Western movie film set. The shops were geared for tourists, and all sold the same leather and suede goods. On the return journey an old road took us through hills and general desert scenery punctuated by cactus trees, piles of old cars, and the odd shack. Stopping on a long empty beach in the late afternoon sun to eat our sandwiches we were incredibly warm, although surprisingly the sea was freezing cold. There was a long queue at the border to return, but apart from having to open the boot we had no problems and finally arrived home at 9.30 pm to shepherd's pie for supper.

It was obvious by now that Gordon and Karen had hit it off, but it was still rather a shock when he announced that he would not be continuing our trip. Whilst driving along the freeway we had seen a large sign advertising a holiday package deal to Hawaii, and the idea of going on there with Karen appealed to him. It was a setback for me as I was now left to complete the return journey alone. After initially feeling slightly annoyed, I got used to the idea, but decided to revise my plans somewhat. From San Francisco I would continue to follow the coast north as far as Portland, Oregon, because I wanted to see the giant Redwood trees, and would then head inland to cross the country on a more northerly route.

The rest of our stay in Los Angeles was spent sightseeing, which included a visit to Marineland of the Pacific to see performing dolphins and killer whales. All were highly trained and one of the dolphin's tricks was to tow a dog on a small boat through the water. After each trick and enthusiastic applause from the audience they were fed their quota of fish.

George, our initial contact, also invited us one evening to the Orange County Drag Strip to watch a very American form of motor sport. Two specially designed cars race each other down a straight quarter mile strip of road which, with their huge nitro fuelled V8 engines takes only a few seconds. They reach speeds of about two hundred mph before deploying their brake parachutes, and it's particularly spectacular at night as their open exhausts light up the sky. The noise is tremendous!

Gordon decided to come up as far as San Francisco and we left LA in incredible heat on the morning of Sunday October 10th. It had been an interesting stay and I was very grateful for Karen's hospitality. We kept to the coast road as far as Santa Barbara but had made slow progress by evening. Just as it seemed that we were there for the night a van pulled up, complete with a lunatic driver, and we set off at a great rate of knots. So I saw in my twenty-sixth birthday in the early hours somewhere near Monterey in the back of a rattling van. Apart from being stopped by the police (again!) for having no rear lights, we made good progress to reach Berkeley at 4.00 am and crashed out at the pad of two of the van's occupants.

Berkeley is some distance from San Francisco which meant a bus ride into the city, but what a contrast with Los Angeles. The place had so much more charm and character, and riding up tremendously steep streets on the famous cable cars was great fun. When they reached the end of the line they went on to a turntable where they were pushed around manually, ready for the return journey. A British trade fair was taking place, so Union flags were much in evidence on the various shops, making us feel quite at home.

Next was a boat trip around the bay and it was unfortunate

that the Golden Gate Bridge was blotted out by a chilling fog, although we did get a good view of the smaller Bay Bridge when the sun reappeared. Nevertheless I was fascinated to get up close to Alcatraz Island with its infamous prison, by then deserted, but looking even more sinister and grim as it emerged through the swirling mist. There is still controversy as to whether three convicts did escape to the mainland on home built rafts, or perish in the freezing waters of the bay. After walking around the interesting wharf area with its fish sellers, small cafés, and restaurants, Gordon set off straight back to Los Angeles.

I was sorry to see him go and in addition to my feeling rather gloomy, my feet started to hurt, which I found worrying. (It transpired this was due to some trainers which I had rescued from a rubbish bin). The previous owner had obviously had the same problem! In a little restaurant near the University I had a lonely celebration of my twenty-six years with a cheese and sausage pizza and a glass of Heineken.

Berkeley was well placed for an early start next morning, and I managed to get across to Highway 1, the coast road heading north, where I waited in the hot sun for a time and got quite badly sunburnt. You could have knocked me down with a feather when suddenly around the corner came a little Austin A40 – about the last vehicle I would have expected to see in that part of the world! The driver, wearing a black beret, was an artist of Irish descent who explained that he had owned the car from new. We set off with a blowing exhaust and followed the scenic coast as far as Cape Mendocino, where I thanked my Irish friend and started walking.

Once again the driver of a pickup truck took pity on me and pulled to a halt. Bud and his wife were a pleasant couple travelling to Portland, Oregon, and we made good time before stopping just north of Eureka. The coastline up there in the late afternoon sun was wildly beautiful, with its steep cliffs receding into a distant haze, and the roar of the incoming Pacific rollers. We were

approaching the land of the giant Redwood trees when we stopped
for the night at a camp ground, where I pitched the tent.

The Redwood National Park, covering almost 40,000 acres
of ancient forest, lay just south of the state border with Oregon.
These trees are the world's tallest living things and can grow as
high as a thirty storey building. It is not enough to know that
you walk beneath giants that sprouted twenty centuries ago: you
are in a forest that existed before the human species evolved upon
the earth. Some have arched trunks wide enough to drive a car
through, and we stopped several times to admire their impressive
majesty. It was fairly late and cold when we found a camp site
just south of Portland and lit a fire, but it didn't seem to help
much and I spent a rather miserable second night under canvass.

I thanked Bud and his wife for their company as they
dropped me at the start of the freeway east, and the first car
to stop was a Datsun 240Z sports car which I had hoped to
experience for some while. It certainly went as well as it looked
and they were becoming more common and making inroads
into sales of the usual British Jaguars, MGs, and Triumphs.
My destination was a place called Jackson Hole which was
situated just outside the Yellowstone National Park in the state
of Wyoming. I had seen pictures of the magnificent interior
and had decided it was worth a visit.

The route took me along the northern Oregon border with
Washington State, before turning south east towards Idaho. It
was featureless country and as I waited for the next lift a police
car drew up. 'In the back' said the cop who carried a large long-
barrelled revolver and who obviously didn't approve of hitch-
hikers. 'Out' he said after some searching questions as to my
intentions and a close examination of my passport, 'and watch
you don't get cut out' – meaning murdered. The opposite of a
'Freak' was a 'Redneck', the expression defining someone who
was ultra right-wing and who probably carried a gun. I was
definitely back in 'Redneck' country and received some funny

looks with the occasional fist shake or raised finger from passing drivers, which added to my sense of unease.

When I described all this in my English accent to the two long haired lads who gave me my next ride, they rocked with laughter! But it was good to be on the move, and they seemed to enjoy the novelty of my company as we travelled all day across the dull barren landscape of Idaho. I couldn't imagine living in such a place although it was apparently ideal for growing potatoes. It was after 1.00 am when they dropped me off, and so cold that I decided to spend the night in a gas station. But we had covered nearly six hundred miles so I was pleased with my progress. After spending a couple of hours thawing out a young fellow from the garage offered me a bed for the night at his home, which I gratefully accepted. He later provided a good breakfast and dropped me on the freeway at Burley, which lies about half way across Idaho. This was another example of the generosity of most Americans.

A series of lucky rides took me to within a hundred miles of Jackson, which lay just over the state border in Wyoming, but I then had a wait of two hours by the roadside. I was really frozen by the time a French-Canadian family stopped and took me the rest of the way.

Jackson was definitely geared for tourists with plenty of shops selling such diverse items as fishing flies, ice, hides, and antlers and like Aspen, featured many rustic wooden buildings with board sidewalks. Likewise it had originated in the 1800s, was surrounded by mountains, and had recently become a ski resort. With a definite aura of the Old West it even had a wooden opera house. After checking into a motel for six dollars a night I had a walk around, and got talking to a fellow heading to Yellowstone next day who offered me a lift. We watched an interesting game of American football and after a drink in a very ornate Western-style bar, I hit the sack early.

A dreary scene greeted me next morning however as it had

San Francisco: cable car with Alcatraz Island in distance

The Opera House, Jackson Hole, Wyoming

snowed overnight. Just what I didn't need! This had caused the closure of the Park, which was a big disappointment, so deciding to keep going, I managed to get a ride with a mountain guide back to the junction of the main road. Casper, the next large town which lay several hundred miles east was my objective, and I was very fortunate to be picked up by Ken and Sandy, a young couple in a VW camper van. They were planning to visit the Black Hills of South Dakota which suited me, as it was one of the sights on my list. After a short while we came into thick snow and stopped to fit snow chains to all four wheels, but by the afternoon it had cleared. We continued under a leaden sky across more drab flat country which consisted of low knobbly hills and scrubland with sporadic outcrops of fir trees, before stopping for the night just outside the South Dakota State line.

The Black Hills are an oasis of pine clad mountains and plunging canyons on the Great Plains, named originally by the Cheyenne, due to their dark appearance from a distance. They were sacred ground to the Native Americans, over which their flat-topped cliffs were used to stampede buffalo by the Lakota, before the advent of the horse made this method of killing the animals less wasteful. When white miners encroached to prospect for gold in breach of another treaty, a fierce war ensued. The area is also home to Mount Rushmore with its famous granite sculptures of Presidents Washington, Roosevelt, Jefferson, and Lincoln.

Our first stop was the Custer State Park where there was a large population of prairie dogs. Resembling big hamsters that stand up on their hind legs surveying their surroundings, they quickly disappear down their burrows at any sign of danger. These though, were quite tame and we fed them until cautioned by a ranger. An abundance of other animal life in the Park meant that we were able to get close to a herd of grazing buffalo, and to catch a rare sight of a white mountain goat. An inspection of a small building which was the State's first jail followed, but I doubted that much of it was

Top left: Ken and Sandy
fitting snow chains

Top right: The faces on Mount Rushmore

Left: Graves of Wild Bill Hickock and
Calamity Jane, Deadwood

Below: In the Badlands National Park

original. Further into the hills are ghostly rock formations which may be why this land was so revered by the Indians.

Owing to a heavy rainstorm I thankfully slept in the van, but the weather obligingly cleared next morning and we went straight up to see the carved Presidential faces on the mountain. They were very impressive being sixty-five feet from chin to forehead, with eyes that are eleven feet across. These huge sculptures were the work of Gutzon Borglum, the son of Danish Mormon immigrants, and created between 1927 and 1941. They are one of the United States' definitive monuments, and a kind of cameo of the country's short history. Washington represents the struggle for independence and the birth of the Republic. Jefferson expresses the country's political philosophy of self-government: Lincoln typifies the permanence of the Nation and the struggle for equality: and Roosevelt depicts twentieth century America, a period which saw the United States emerge as a dominant influence in world affairs.

The Black Hills lead into 'Wild West' territory and our next stop was the fascinating old frontier town of Deadwood. Its main claim to fame being that it was the place where Wild Bill Hickock was killed when shot in the back during a card game. Apart from the numerous parked cars, it had hardly changed since the 1880s, and after going up to Boot Hill Cemetery to see the stone graves of Wild Bill and his girl friend Calamity Jane, we visited the town museum, filled with absorbing photographs and relics. Dropping into a couple of Western bars completed the picture for us of those wild times.

It was then only a short trip to Rapid City where again I found a rustic motel room, and we all had showers before cooking our supper. Eating while watching TV was a luxurious change from normal, and I was pleased to be able to repay some of the couple's hospitality.

The Badlands National Park is another must-see spectacle in this area, and is as dramatic and unbalanced a landscape as any on the planet. Comprising desolate tiered cliffs sculpted by ancient water flows, grassy buttes, and jagged peaks, it is surrounded by vast prairies where bison were reintroduced only eight years earlier. After fixing a problem with the van and calling at a Sioux museum, which related events from their perspective, we reached this eerie place which was devoid of any other human life. The road runs for forty five miles right through the middle and we stopped numerous times to take photos, and also to fire off a few rounds at nothing in particular with Ken's .22 pistol. At one stop he climbed several hundred feet up a cliff and stood with his arms outstretched, silhouetted but dwarfed against the sky line in the crystal clear afternoon light. The marvellous colours of the different rock strata were accentuated, especially at sunset, when we left to rejoin the main road east.

Having stopped after dark for supper, Ken and Sandy dropped me off at a little place called Murdo, where they turned off south for Nebraska. They planned to visit a ranch and kindly invited me to continue with them, but I really felt that I should return to Cambridge and my job. However as they intended visiting New England in due course they promised to look me up, and happily we were to meet again some weeks later.

Saying goodbye to them was an anticlimax, and after spending a miserable night in a gas station I had a long cold wait next morning. Feeling generally frustrated with things, especially the unfriendly locals, I was much relieved when a young fellow stopped and took me all the way south-east, following the wide Missouri River to Omaha, a journey of nearly four hundred miles. People think nothing of driving these sorts of distances, which really brings home to a foreigner the sheer size of the country.

I quickly got a another good ride with a friendly business man intrigued by my accent and story, to Des Moines half way across the State of Iowa. He even bought me supper at a Holiday Inn, before putting me on Route 80 East for Chicago; another instance of wonderful generosity.

My good luck held when after a wait of only half an hour Phil, a painter from Jackson Hole stopped for me. He was driving non-stop all the way to New Jersey, and we only made a brief diversion into Chicago for food. After passing through The Loop, the city's central business district with its distinctive high level railway, we kept going throughout that night. Taking turns to drive and sleep, we stayed on Route 80 East all next day, except for a small detour when I went wrong. Apart from that it was an uneventful journey and I was delighted with our progress. Phil dropped me about forty miles from New York at 12.30 am, and after hitching a short ride to an all night diner I was resigned to waiting out the night there. But luck was still with me when two blokes I was talking to decided to run me into New York City! They delivered me to the start of Route 95, the freeway heading north to Boston at 5.30 am on a misty morning, and after an hour's wait a green Ford Mustang drew up.

Through one of those quirks of fate this lift killed two birds with one stone as the car was driven by Mike, an Irish chap from Cambridge. It transpired that he shared an apartment with another guy and they were looking for a third to help with expenses etc. I knew that Mary was moving back home permanently after her summer wanderings, and I would have to find alternative accommodation, so we went straight to Mike's for a viewing. I was confronted by the unusual spectacle of a guy in striped black and white swimming trunks sitting with his feet up, eating breakfast cereal in front of the TV. Of Yugoslavian origin his name was Jurus, and whilst rather surprised I was made to feel most welcome. Although a bit shambolic the apartment was spacious and conveniently central on Massachusetts Avenue, so I immediately agreed to move in a couple of weeks.

Mike dropped me in Harvard Square which seemed almost surreal after being away so long, and I walked up to 239 where I received a great welcome from Lesley, Amy, and Mary. It was really good to be back again and we had a celebration meal that night to mark my safe return and the completion of a memorable odyssey.

Chapter Eleven
A Golden Autumn

In many ways the next few weeks were some of the most idyllic of my whole journey. Perhaps this was due to the satisfaction of completing my trip around America, combined with returning to Cambridge and seeing everybody again. It was a special time in my life which I look back on with great fondness.

Saturday October 23rd, the first after my return, was a gorgeous autumn day. Lesley and I took a drive north to Lincoln in New Hampshire that afternoon and the countryside up that way was just fabulous. New England was at its finest; the bright red, yellow, and orange colours of the leaves giving an incredibly vibrant display. A perfect day was rounded off later when I took the girls into Boston for a meal, followed by a few pints of Whitbread in the Bull and Finch.

Gordon appeared the next evening, having flown back from Los Angeles, and after a noisy reunion we all went to the cinema to see *The French Connection*, one of my all time favourite films. Gene Hackman was brilliant as the wayward New York cop, with his long-suffering partner played by Roy Scheider.

North east of Boston lies Cape Cod's smaller sister the lesser known Cape Ann, with a rugged coastline and snug harbours reminiscent of Cornwall. Monday was a free day and Gordon, Carole, Lesley and I took a trip up to Rockport, a pretty fishing village lined with red, yellow, and green clapboard houses. It had quite an 'arty' community and I bought my father a garden hammock as a Christmas present.

It was great to see George again when I reported for work next day, together with Don who had been making changes. He had decided to move his office into the basement of the building on Huron Avenue, and the first week ended on a backbreaking note with Gordon and I digging through rocks and clay to make the new entrance.

But our social calendar gathered pace. Great entertainment was provided one evening when Mary gave another (more successful) party for the Hon. Jimmy's birthday, which was a riot with her and Val doing their song and dance routine. Accompanied by Don on his guitar, this consisted of songs from popular shows and musicals. Everyone was there and when the cake broke in half we all collapsed with laughter. Priceless!

A few days later Frank and Irene had a Halloween party. It is an attractive custom at this time of year to put a hollowed out pumpkin in the window with a candle and a face carved into it. This was followed by a Mexican Dinner given by the girls for the Byrons, and next on the agenda was a pyjama party at the communal house that Amy's boyfriend Gil shared with five others. It was all great fun.

Another lovely late autumn day saw us visit Old Sturbridge Village, a true-to-life New England village of about 1790. Traditional crafts were carried out by guides dressed in period costume who explained the various processes. These included a blacksmith's shop, a woollen mill, a printer, candle maker, and even a working farm, all exactly as they would have been.

I was sorry to see Gordon leave to start his new job in mid November, and after phoning my parents who sounded fine, I planned a visit home for Christmas. The idea of forming some sort of new company seemed to have petered out over the preceding months, but it still came as rather a shock when Don told me a few days later that he would only be able to keep me on for another six weeks. This caused me to change my Christmas plans so that Gordon took my family presents back with him, and I began to think about my next move.

Nevertheless in the meantime, life continued most agreeably with visits to the surrounding area and a busy social life. Concord, lying some fifteen miles north west, is another attractive village where the initial skirmish took place between the British Redcoats and the American Colonists in the War of Independence. The surrounding countryside was still very beautiful when I took a spin out there one Saturday afternoon and stood on the bridge which saw the first shots fired.

A pleasant surprise was a phone call from Ken and Sandy to say they were just outside Boston, and we met up the following evening when they came round to the girls' for a reunion supper. It was good to see them again and swap stories of our subsequent travels, and after Jurus borrowed a slide projector I gave a presentation of all my photos, accompanied by a few ribald comments! We took them around the Freedom Trail and also included a visit to the USS *Constitution* displayed in Boston harbour. This is a three mast wooden frigate launched in 1797, and was named by George Washington after the constitution of the USA. It is the world's oldest commissioned naval vessel afloat, but I was slightly disappointed that only 15% of it is original.

Lesley and Carole's friends ranged far and wide, and good times continued with a delightful visit one weekend to a couple who lived up in rural Vermont, near a gorgeous village called Weston. Sally and Jamie, with their dog Ted, lived a seemingly idyllic rural life on a farm surrounded by fields and low rolling hills. An attractive sight on quieter roads in Vermont are the old covered wooden bridges which have a pitched roof, and date back to early days. The village store was also truly old fashioned, having a central stove with a pipe going out through the roof, but it stocked everything from a headlamp bulb for a 1927 Overland to a wicker log basket. Nearby was a priory and after a walk and a general look around we called in to see an evening service given by the monks – the first time I had entered a religious establishment for a considerable while . . . Light snow flurries accompanied us as we left for Cambridge that Sunday evening, heralding the approach of winter.

Lesley (*left*) and Carole

At Old Sturbridge village

Thanksgiving parade, Plymouth Rock

Together with Christmas and New Year, Thanksgiving ranks as the third major Holiday in the USA, and takes place on the fourth Thursday in November. The origins of the festival date back to 1621 when the Pilgrims gave thanks for their first harvest in the New World. Lesley's parents Rose and Joe arrived for the celebrations and were typically mid west American – but very pleasant. They generously took us all out to dinner at Anthony's Pier 4, one of the top restaurants on the Boston waterfront. Nautical items hung on the walls, and a riverboat anchored beside the restaurant served as an unusual cocktail lounge. Turkey is the traditional fare on the actual day which was unfortunately wet and dreary, but the lunch at Janice's home was a jolly affair and helped to compensate for the weather.

The holiday continued with another visit to Plymouth Rock where there was a Thanksgiving parade and a chance to have a good look around the *Mayflower*. Soldiers in period costume, consisting of a three cornered hat and wig, a long tailed coat with wide contrasting lapels, breeches and buckled shoes, marched along the main street watched by a large crowd. They were accompanied by pipes and drums and a musket was ceremoniously discharged into the air at intervals, hopefully only firing blanks!

A few days later a letter arrived from my parents to say that they would like to see me for Christmas if possible, so I began making travel enquiries. I also heard from Gordon to say that he got back OK and was well into his new job. It was now a year since I had left home and it seemed like only yesterday since we had all set off in Jeff's Land Rover; but what an eventful year it had been. I could never have foreseen how well things would turn out on the awful day of our demoralizing arrival in Kingston, or when I was feeling so dejected in that seedy New York hostel; which had been the low point of the journey thus far.

Through one of Don's tenants I managed to book a charter flight home for 185 dollars (with the Pioneer Women's Club of New York!) and departure date was set for Monday December 20th.

When the tickets arrived I phoned my father to expect me. He sounded fine and arranged to meet me at Gatwick, so I began to get quite excited at the prospect.

With my long-term plan to see Australia in mind, it had occurred to me a while previously that I might as well visit New Zealand on the way – a decision I have never regretted. Accordingly I also made a provisional booking to sail on a P&O liner from San Francisco to Auckland in the New Year, for 540 dollars.

Meanwhile work continued on the new office and we put in some long days, although I managed to fit in a squash match with Gill, my first for over a year, which was great fun. First-rate entertainment was provided next day as well, when we watched a Harvard v Navy tournament.

And so I worked out my final week for Don, finishing at lunch time on Friday December 17th.

He had been a most agreeable and generous employer, proving invaluable in putting my finances on a sound footing, and allowing me to continue my journey onwards. For this I will always be grateful and it gave me great pleasure that evening to take him, Ruth, and Lesley to a famous Boston restaurant down near the old market hall. Durgin Park was a characteristic 'spit and sawdust' market dining room which had been going since 1827 and had proved popular over the years with statesmen, politicians, Boston blue bloods from Beacon Hill, Market men, writers and 'just plain folks from everywhere', as their brochure put it. One was advised not to argue with the waitresses who were 'a tough broad-shouldered floor show'! Electric bulbs dangled from long cords to light the place, with each table having a red checked cloth, a huge water pitcher, and a pile of napkins. There was a clamorous atmosphere but the traditional New England fare overshadowed the din, with such eclectic dishes as Durgin Park Chowder, Yankee Pot Roast, freshly baked Johnny Cake and Apple Pan Dowdy to name but a few! It was a brilliant experience and a fitting end to my time with Don.

The next couple of days were spent doing some shopping, collecting everything together, and packing it all up. I found a slightly cheaper fare at 509 dollars on the P&O liner SS *Orsova* sailing on January 29th, also from San Francisco, and after some consideration, paid a deposit. The thought of moving on felt strange after being in Cambridge for six months but at the same time was tinged with excitement. I had already been to wish Frank and Irene Season's Greetings and would be seeing them again on my return in the New Year, when the four of us planned to take a trip up to Canada to explore Quebec and Montreal. That Sunday evening the girls held a drinks party, after which I went for a farewell jar with Jurus to an Irish pub on Massachusetts Ave.

Monday morning December 20th – panic as Lesley's car wouldn't start! So a bus into Boston and then another to New York which suffered various delays including a broken windscreen wiper. A taxi finally got me to Kennedy Airport at 4.30 pm – only for the flight to be postponed until 7.30 pm, then 9.00, 10.00, and after a fight nearly broke out between the passengers and airport staff, the Laker Airways 707 at last took off at 11.30pm. Six hours late and The Pioneer Women's Club were definitely not impressed. Neither were my poor waiting parents who had to spend the night in their car.

The flight itself wasn't too bad: it was very satisfying to watch the sun come up over the horizon as we sped eastward, and after a reasonable breakfast we made a good landing back in dear old Blighty. I cleared customs OK, and there were Mum and Dad who looked surprisingly cheerful considering their ordeal. It was fabulous to be back, and after some friends phoned that evening everybody gathered at their house for a boisterous reunion. When all the handshaking and back slapping was over, a rush was made for our local, The Talbot in Belbroughton, and I ended up in my usual corner by the fire. It had been an incredible thirteen months which was well worth all the effort, and it seemed almost more incredible to have made it home again.

Chapter Twelve
On the Move Again

After an excellent Christmas and New Year's Eve during which I caught up with all the news from friends and family, I started getting ready for departure on Friday January 7th 1972. While at home I phoned Geoff who brought me up to date with what happened after we left Istanbul. He had spent several weeks in hospital recuperating before being discharged, and very bravely had decided to drive back alone. The journey had taken him a month; a wonderful achievement for a man in his situation. Since his return he had been back at work, and had heard our story from Bob.

Leaving home again didn't seem so daunting as before, as besides having a clear-cut objective, I was returning to familiar faces. My parents ran me down to Gatwick where we had supper, and after they left I tried to get some sleep on a bench. The flight was delayed for only half an hour this time and we took off next morning at 9.30 am. I was invited on to the flight deck and could see Boston and Cape Cod clearly as we passed overhead. How times change.

Wanting to waste no time in leaving New York I briefly tried hitching but didn't get far before dark, and settled for catching the bus. I finally arrived back in dear old Cambridge at 11.00 pm and walked up to the girls' to find Lesley was the only one home.

It was good to see her and everyone else again, and after a couple of days catching up she and I set off for Kittery where Frank and Irene gave us a great welcome. Disappointingly they could not come with us to Canada, but we did accompany them to Portland where Irene had to complete her immigration formalities.

A beautiful sunny morning greeted us next day and we set off at 10.00 am for Quebec. To the sound of Don McLean's new hit 'American Pie' we journeyed north through a winter wonderland of frozen lakes and snow covered forests, eventually arriving after dark. The city looked enchanting as we approached, with a multitude of bright festive lights lending it a magical quality, and we were pleased to find a quaint hotel in the old quarter. Opposite us and towering over everything, was the majestic Château Frontenac, with its numerous turrets illuminated like some fairytale castle. It is actually a large luxury hotel and sits within the walls of the old fortified city.

A day spent exploring got off to a slow start when the old boy in charge of the military museum couldn't remember the combination of the safe where he kept his keys. The wait was worth it though, to learn details of the various sieges that were part of Quebec's turbulent past, and to see the battle lines of the opposing British and French forces set out in miniature.

It brought to life distant school history lessons describing General Wolfe's scaling of the Heights of Abraham at night, to surprise the French forces at dawn thereby capturing the city.

Venturing further afield next day an enjoyable drive took us out to the Ile d'Orleans, in summer a picturesque island in the St Lawrence River. It was now covered in snow and I remember it for being the coldest place I've ever been to. After getting out of the car for thirty seconds to take a photo, we needed half an hour with the heater on full blast to get the temperature back up again. Several trawlers were completely frozen in, and going nowhere until the spring thaw. Later we drove some fifteen miles north of Quebec to Lac Beaupart, a ski area, looking very attractive in the early evening sunshine. We rounded off the day with another excellent meal at a cosy little restaurant, before dressing up to go to a lively disco at the Château.

Quebec had been fascinating and we were sorry to leave as we departed for Montreal, the second centre of our tour. Travelling along the northern bank of the St Lawrence we noticed the landscape was very flat, and after passing through the town of Trois Rivieres it became even more bland. The churches however maintained their Gothic style, which helped to brighten up the rather drab towns.

Despite having a small historic district, Montreal being a modern sky scraper type city, had none of the charm of old Quebec. We arrived in mid afternoon and it was bitterly cold as we checked in to a rather dingy hotel in the quieter part of town. Going out later we saw the new James Bond film *Diamonds Are Forever* which I felt didn't quite live up to its forbears.

Our second day was bright and beautiful but again terribly cold, which was emphasised by the clouds of condensation, looking just like steam, coming off the partly frozen St Lawrence. A small manmade island housed Expo '67 and although it was closed until June, we could see some of the exhibits of 'Man and his World'. The American Pavilion was prominent and looked like a giant golf ball made of glass. A bus tour in the afternoon was not too successful as the condensation on the windows kept freezing, which rendered viewing the sights virtually impossible. However the English/French commentary described the splendid Notre-Dame de Bon Secours Cathedral, and surprisingly there was also a Nelson's Column. But for us Montreal was perhaps most memorable for the delightful little restaurant round the corner from our hotel, where we had the best meal of the trip.

A howling blizzard accosted us next morning, with the temperature at twenty degrees below. It was too cold for me and we were glad to be on our way. But progress was difficult as we could hardly see five yards at times due to the snow blowing across the road. Gradually things improved as we left Canada's fiercely independent province behind, and drove down through Vermont to arrive back in Cambridge in the late afternoon.

A couple of days later it was time to make a farewell visit to Frank and Irene, where they entertained us to an enjoyable

Chateau Frontenac, Quebec

Meeting Senator Ed Musky

dinner. Frank took me for a spin out onto the headland in his old truck next day, where we sat putting the world to rights. Afterwards we called on some friends of Lesley's who were very pleasant, but I found the round of goodbyes was becoming rather a strain.

An interesting interlude took place on our last morning when we attended a rally in Portsmouth for Senator Ed Muskie who was running for President. There was all the razzmatazz of American politics, which to my conservative mind seemed over the top, but Frank introduced us and we shook hands. I explained that as an Englishman I couldn't be any help, and disappointingly for him his campaign was to prove fruitless.

It was a sad moment when the time came to leave Frank and Irene, and the farm where I had spent so many happy times. I will always be grateful to him for his company, advice, and the help he gave me. In his case I'm pleased to say that we did keep in touch and met again when he came over to England and stayed with my family on a couple of occasions.

That evening there was another Byron party, this time to celebrate Alan's birthday and as a farewell for me. It was as hilarious as usual and at the end of the evening I presented Don with a bottle of Scotch, which was well received. He and Ruth were setting off for their house on the Cape early next morning so I was not to see them again. I made a special point of saying cheerio to George – we had enjoyed some good laughs together and nobody could have wished for a better workmate.

The last weekend was rather a strain for everyone and I couldn't help wishing that my departure date, set for Tuesday January 25th, would hurry up. I tried frantically to organise a ride west to San Francisco, but having no luck, resigned myself to taking the Greyhound bus. Lesley and I had a quiet and gloomy last supper at the cottage on Monday evening and both of us struggled to put some sort of gloss on the situation. It was very hard, knowing that inevitably we were going to miss each other.

The bus was due to leave at 7.00 am and the weather was dismal, which did nothing to improve our feelings. We were up at 6.00 am and I tapped on Carole's door to say another sad farewell before leaving the cottage for the last time. Fortunately our departure was punctual and after an emotional parting from Lesley I climbed aboard. On a dark rainy morning we drew out of Boston heading for New York, our first stop. Feeling subdued I couldn't help thinking back to the previous May when I had first arrived to start working for Don. It all seemed so long ago, but the initial uncertainty of a new start was still a vivid memory.

The three day journey from coast to coast was to be virtually non-stop, and our route lay via Chicago, Salt Lake City, Utah, and Reno, Nevada. Those last few days in Cambridge had been difficult, but after a while I settled down and it felt good to be on the move again. There was no time for sightseeing, but prominent in Salt Lake City was a huge Mormon temple, and I remember crossing the famous Bonneville Salt Flats which were a surprisingly muddy brown colour. Our last evening halt was at Reno, which originated as the centre of extensive silver mining operations when large deposits were discovered in the area in the 1840s. It became very cold, and further on while crossing the Sierra Nevada mountain range we stopped to fit snow chains. Otherwise it was an uneventful trip and we arrived in San Francisco at 7.30 am next morning.

I had breakfast with a fellow traveller from the bus called Ed Taylor, before checking on the ship situation. At the P&O office they told me that although she was in I couldn't board until the next day. Ed generously offered to put me up at his place in Santa Cruz a few miles out of town and run me in next morning. I gratefully accepted and we spent the rest of the day sightseeing and riding up and down on those iconic little cable cars, before catching the bus south to Santa Cruz.

A beautiful morning greeted us and I felt great as we buzzed along the twisting coastal highway in Ed's little Fiat 850 convertible. Suddenly we arrived high above San Francisco and its magnificent Bay, the Golden Gate Bridge lying before us, with the sunshine reflecting off the water. It was a magical moment.

Ed came on board to see me off before the good ship *Orsova* edged away from the dock- side promptly at midday. A band serenaded us with 'Rule Britannia' and 'San Francisco', as the waving passengers threw dozens of multi-coloured streamers through the air. Thankfully unlike on my last visit the Golden Gate was not obscured by mist as we passed beneath it. To the cries of the ever present gulls following in our wake San Francisco receded into the distance, and I gazed at the northern coastline, finding it difficult to believe I had hitch-hiked all the way up it a few months previously.

We docked in San Pedro harbour Los Angeles at an early hour, and later our steward brought in tea with a copy of *Good Morning*, the ship's daily paper. A far cry from the old *Montserrat*! I was sharing a two berth cabin with a jovial Canadian called Mike Bellerby, who having met a Kiwi nurse in his homeland, was immigrating to New Zealand to get married.

Disinclined to go ashore I spent the day on board reading and enjoying the warm sunshine – a lovely contrast with the cold of Quebec. Working for Don had given me a level of financial security, and before leaving Cambridge I had treated myself to a new top-notch camera; a 35mm SLR Minolta. Conveniently placed next to our berth was a sea plane base and taking photos of them coming and going helped to familiarise myself with it.

Meal times were also more civilized than on the *Montserrat* and I shared a table with a Canadian guy called John Brownlee who had boarded the ship in Vancouver, and two girls who were immigrating to New Zealand. *Good Morning* gave a full description of all the entertainment available on board, which ranged from fancy dress balls, cabaret, cinema, camera club, to keep fit classes, old time dancing, etc. In fact there was just about everything for everybody.

The *Orsova* at Los Angeles

John and Dale in Hawaii

Midnight signalled our departure and I stood outside the Veranda Bar on the stern watching the twinkling lights of America, my home for the last nine months, fade slowly over the horizon. Our course was the Great Circle Route across the Pacific, calling at Hawaii and Fiji en route to Auckland.

It was difficult to know where to start summing up America. The things one heard about like the skyscrapers and huge straight freeways were all there as expected, but it was quite something to actually see them 'for real'. Nearly all private dwelling homes however were of wooden construction, with the historic New England houses in particular having an attractive character and appeal of their own.

As far as food was concerned, the steak was still king, and for a snack the hamburger and Coke reigned supreme. New to me at that time was the Pizza parlour, but of course since then they have become well established in the UK.

I thought the worst aspect was the crime rate which was partly explained by the pressure of life and the ease with which one could obtain a firearm. All types of guns were available – even at the local supermarket in some States such as South Dakota. A common slogan of the gun lobby was 'gun control means using both hands'! This summed up the prevailing attitude. At that time gun crime in England was fairly rare, which explained my feelings, although I was never threatened with one and only on the odd occasion felt unsafe.

Generally the average Mid-Western male struck me as being rather childish; often seeming to imagine himself back in the days of the old West. Many carried a gun and their attitude was probably due to the constant feud between the Rednecks and the Longhairs or Freaks. The closest comparison in England I suppose would be the Mods and Rockers situation. Also in my experience most blacks seemed morose and very offhand. In general, I think this attitude was due to black people feeling themselves regarded as second class citizens. Only three years had passed since the assassination of Martin Luther King, best known for his 'I have a dream' speech, and black and white segregation was still a very recent memory.

Kindness and generosity would remain for me the great virtue of the people, and in this respect many were exceptional. Being English I was something of a novelty which often helped, but the meals we were bought when hitching, being put up by Ed Taylor, and the terrific treatment I received in Cambridge were fine examples.

Even back then 'ecology' and 'pollution' were watchwords, and there were big campaigns to raise awareness of both these issues. Tied in with these was the return to the simple life by many young people, who eschewed the glitzy extravagance of the previous generation. I soon became aware of their wide-spread smoking of 'grass', and abhorrence of the Vietnam War. In contrast there was a general feeling of the need to believe in America, which was expressed in the abundance everywhere of the national Stars and Stripes flag. This was displayed on buildings public and private, car windows, lamp posts, officials' uniforms, motorcycle crash helmets, and sewn on to any article of clothing.

The terrific showmanship involved in politics was evident when we attended Senator Muskie's election rally, and gave me the impression that it was almost regarded as some sort of sporting competition.

Names that became familiar from Cambridge and district were the tube stations into Boston: Harvard, Central, Kendall, Charles, and Park Street; a journey I made many times. Star Market where we did our shopping, Storrow and Memorial Drives, Brattle Street and of course Mary's house on Mount Auburn Street; plus The Bull and Finch English pub, the Freedom Trail, and the route out of Boston up to Frank's, over the Mystic Bridge.

These, together with my hitch-hiking trip and the friends

I made are the salient memories of my stay in America; an altogether wonderful experience.

The SS *Orsova* was built at Barrow-in-Furness and made her maiden voyage in 1954. Although smart and comfortable enough with adequate facilities, she was starting to show her age by 1972. Somewhere between Los Angeles and Hawaii occurred an event that was logged in her records, and which greatly added to the interest of our voyage. On Friday February 4th we received a distress call from the American ocean going tug *Tecumseh*, to say they had a medical emergency. One of their officers had thrombosis and as we were the nearest ship with medical facilities we turned back on our course to rendezvous with them at 9.00 pm that evening. We hove-to, the crew speedily lowered one of our lifeboats to make the pickup, and afterwards received a round of applause from the watching passengers. The whole operation took place at night which undoubtedly added to the drama, and fortunately there was a happy outcome to our 150 mile mercy dash, as our surgeon saved the man's life. Another cause for celebration was the fact that we passengers had an extra two days' free cruising!

About this time it was discovered that there was an Australian stowaway on board who was reputedly being fed on bread and water by a passenger. More drama followed just before we reached Honolulu, capital of the Hawaiian Islands, when an elderly man died of a heart attack and was buried at sea. It was turning into an eventful voyage.

'Aloha' means welcome and on entering Honolulu harbour the first noticeable landmark is the Aloha Tower on the quayside. The city itself was typically American and things were very expensive, but three of us decided to hire a car and drive around the island of Oahu. This is one of eight major islands in the Hawaiian group, the biggest of which is, not surprisingly, Hawaii. President Dwight Eisenhower proclaimed them America's 50th State in 1959.

I had come to know John Brownlee, the Canadian on my table, who was a couple of years younger than me, with a mop of thick red hair and matching beard. He introduced me to fellow Canadian Dale Christensen who was my age, fair haired and of Scandinavian origin. The weather initially looked threatening but brightened up later and we quickly drove out of town and stopped at a beautiful quiet bay to swim and sunbathe. It had a lovely expanse of white sand and the sea was that marvellous turquoise colour of the Caribbean. To me the island was a cross between Jamaica and Tenerife, with the wonderful lush vegetation and palm trees of the former, and the hills and volcanic coastline of the latter. Further inland the scenery looked quite forbidding under low cloud, but gave way to large plantations of pineapple and sugar cane which was the main produce. We called at Pearl Harbour but disappointingly were too late to take a boat tour, although we could see the monument to the battleship *Arizona* where so many lives were lost in the Japanese attack of 1941. Later that evening we ascended the Aloha Tower to admire and photograph a radiant sunset before rejoining *Orsova*.

Shipboard life resumed as we set course for our next port of call, Suva, capital of the Fiji Islands in the south Pacific. On our second night Captain Woolley gave a cocktail party and the dress code was strict. Two long haired surfers in T-shirts and shorts were ejected by the Master at Arms for not wearing ties and being improperly dressed. Unwilling to miss free drinks they reappeared with borrowed ties, but to much amusement were refused again. Just then a large elderly matron bedecked in all her finery entered the saloon through the swing doors just as the ship rolled the other way and shot her straight out again!

On Tuesday February 8th we reached the Equator and a hilarious 'Crossing the Line' ceremony took place that afternoon. We all gathered around the swimming pool where several of the crew had dressed up as King Neptune and his Court. A number of passengers were liberally covered in egg yolk and other mess before being tossed into the pool. Even the First Officer couldn't escape and went in with full uniform! It was great entertainment as long as you weren't a victim too. Between Wednesday 9th and Friday 11th we crossed the International Date Line and accordingly there was no Thursday February 10th.

Saturday February 12th saw us arrive in Suva and we docked at 8.00 am. After breakfast I took an open-top bus tour which lasted for three hours and cost 1 dollar – amazing value. We were taken out of the town and along the coast for a while, before circling to return. Once again the scenery was incredibly beautiful with an abundance of wild flowers and palm trees. Many people lived in traditional houses called 'Bures' with thatched roofs and woven matted walls, and along the route we came upon small native kids dancing in grass skirts by the roadside, with the adults thumping bamboo poles to provide a beat. All laid on for the tourist no doubt – but entertaining nonetheless.

The backbone of the economy was the sugar industry, supported by coconut products and bananas, but tourism was fast catching up. Fiji became fully independent within the Commonwealth in 1970 with the Queen as Head of State. We called at Government House, a large Colonial style mansion set in a lush tropical garden of brightly coloured flowers, the only ones of which I recognised being giant poinsettias. Guarding the entrance were smart riflemen in red tunics and long white skirts to below knee level with a serrated edge.

I also spent some time hunting around the duty-free Indian owned shops for a 200 mm telephoto camera lens. After some haggling I bought one at considerably less than I would have paid in the States so was well pleased.

John and Dale had decided to stay over in Fiji and catch the next ship coming down in a month's time. They invited me to join them but I felt I should continue to New Zealand – a decision I later regretted as they had a fabulous time travelling around. We arranged to meet up again there, and so with a Fijian police

45. Fijian police band, Suva

band parading along the dockside I waved goodbye to them as we slipped our lines and pulled away.

I began to prepare for my arrival in Auckland, and it was here that I learned to iron a shirt when a kind woman watching my feeble efforts took pity on me. Meanwhile on the last day of the voyage the ship maintained a South South Westerly course at an average speed of nineteen knots towards the North island of New Zealand, where we were due to make landfall off Burgess Island.

Chapter Thirteen
New Zealand

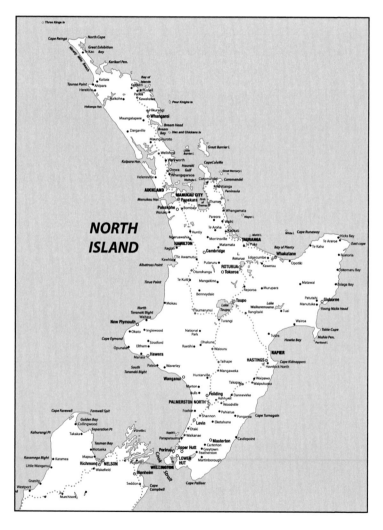

We embarked our pilot at 5.45 am on Tuesday February 15th, and I was up early to join the queue for Immigration, who came aboard at 6.30 am. After all my previous problems it was an absolute delight not to have any visa worries or a grilling about my plans. Several of us who had bought goods in Suva had slight Customs concerns but our fears proved groundless. I joined up with a group which included Mike Bellerby and his fiancée Joan, also Wayne, a returning New Zealander, whose family had come to meet him. After supper with them at the Great Northern Hotel I dossed down in his room for the night.

From the moment I walked down Queen Street, the city's main commercial thoroughfare, I felt completely at home. Familiar names like Prudential Insurance and Boots the chemist were much in evidence, and in contrast with American cities there were at that time hardly any high-rise buildings. Large permanent awnings stretched over the full pavement width to shelter or shade shoppers, and with a mixture of modern post-war and traditional Edwardian style shops and offices it was like returning to the Britain of the 1950s. A high number of private houses were of wooden construction, especially in country areas, some even having corrugated iron roofs. People were very relaxed and friendly, and as it was late summer businessmen's 'uniform' was a short sleeve shirt and tie with no jacket, smart shorts and shoes with knee length socks. Ladies looked cool and comfortable in patterned dresses. The shops all stayed open late on Friday evenings but then closed for the whole weekend.

Traffic drove on the left but new cars were very expensive as they attracted high import duty, which accounted for the large number of older vehicles to be seen. Most were British from the early Fifties, with even popular pre-war models from Vauxhall and Morris being common and looking well cared for. Wayne had personally imported a new car from Canada which saved the tax, but there was a frustrating delay with formalities, and Mike and Joan kindly put us both up on camp beds in their new flat.

Things moved quickly as on my second day I saw a vacancy advertised for a store man at NZ Motor Company, the main British Leyland agents. I went straight for an interview which seemed to go well, and was very pleased next day to be offered the job, starting the following Monday. Not bad going!

My next task was to find some permanent accommodation, so the next few days were spent checking adverts, doing odd jobs, and exploring the city and district. And very attractive it all was. Auckland sits on the earth's most recently formed volcanic field and the majority of its surrounding hills are extinct craters. One of its landmarks is the self descriptive One Tree Hill, site of the world's largest prehistoric earthwork fortification, from the top of which one had a marvellous view over the city and the Hauraki Gulf, in the distance. Among the places I visited was the War Museum set in a lovely park looking out across the water towards Rangitoto Island, a perfectly formed volcanic cone whose slopes are covered in lush greenery.

By Saturday I had found and moved into a self-catering boarding house in the Newmarket area, which meant that I could walk to work. That evening, with a couple of fellow tenants I sampled another Auckland hostelry belonging to the father of a chap from the ship. Pubs, which closed at 10.00 pm, tended to be rather raucous halls where most people stood around small high-level tables, and beer was dispensed in jugs.

Work began again the next week and involved picking spare parts from their respective bins for despatch to outlying dealers. Not madly thrilling, and being on your feet all day quite tiring, but at 50 dollars (about 30 pounds) per week the pay was reasonable and they were a good crowd. The hours were 8.00 am until 5.00 pm and it was nicely informal – the main excitement in our department being the weekly visit to collect parts in her van by a comely young Maori girl. As soon as she walked through the door the cry would go out 'Hello Daaaaaarling' from Jack the senior storeman, which always brought proceedings to a halt!

I shared a room at my digs with a chap called Ted and that weekend a friend of his took us up the attractive coast which had some nice little beaches. I considered buying a motor scooter to get around but that week we got Ted's old Austin A40 going and it was great to be mobile again. We drove into town a couple of times and also to the top of another extinct volcano called Mount Eden, for a fine view over Auckland at sunset.

The Hauraki Gulf was ideal for sailing, which was very popular, and I called at the modern yacht club to see if there were any weekend crewing vacancies. Several boats which had come across the Pacific from America were moored up, including one only eighteen feet long sailed by a Dutchman; a wonderful achievement in such a small craft.

Deciding that I would be better off in fully catered accommodation I found a boarding house in a nice area at Mountain Road, Epsom, which was run by a funny old girl called Mrs Goss. There were seven other young blokes living there and she pottered about amongst us like an old hen. Breakfast and an evening meal were provided but on closer inspection I soon realised that cleaning wasn't her strong point, as everything was covered in a thick layer of dust. It wasn't unusual either to see cockroaches, known as 'wetters' in NZ, although Mrs G was conveniently in denial when the subject was raised. I shared what was potentially a pleasant room with another Pom called Miles, so after a couple of days we had a blitz on it and managed to get it looking better. We certainly had a good laugh about it all as they were a decent bunch, which compensated for the shortcomings. Several of the lads owned cars, Miles' pride and joy being a 1956 Morris Minor, so getting about wasn't quite such a problem. Communal trips followed to the Mount Eden swimming baths, the Transport Museum, which featured a Lancaster bomber and a London bus, and also Auckland Zoo set in another attractive park.

Life and work continued very agreeably, and as one of the

Pastoral scene, North Island, New Zealand

Setting up camp, Lake Taupo

Lady Knox geyser, Rotorua

(*Left to right*) R.F., David and Graham

packers left I took over his job which involved parcelling up parts for despatch. I thought it a big improvement on picking the items as it was easier on the feet. A pleasant surprise came one evening when I was asked by the Richmond Club secretary to crew on a member's boat. Saturday thus became the highlight of my week when I got a regular slot on *Tamatea*, a forty-eight foot ketch owned by a teacher called Ross. The Hauraki Gulf with Rangitoto Island as a backdrop is an outstanding sailing area incorporating an Olympic course, and the yachts out in the bay with their billowing spinnakers made a wonderful sight. It was great to be relaxing from work and on a boat again.

Because things were going well and having heard that the job situation in Australia was not good, I decided to postpone moving on there for the time being. Reinforcing this plan was an unexpected visit from John Brownlee, who besides describing his adventures in Fiji, of which I was most envious, told me that he and Dale were staying in Wellington. It was great to see him and we discussed all meeting up again. Letters continued to arrive from home and in particular from Lesley with all the Byron/Cambridge news. There had been a huge amount of snow since I left which even buried her car, and the place was unrecognisable in the photos she sent. Brrrrr!

Easter arrived and on Good Friday I set off with David Wall and Graham Johnson, two lads from my lodgings, in Graham's old Austin Devon for a few days sightseeing. Heading south from Auckland through a beautiful verdant landscape of winding rivers, low hills, and grazing sheep and cattle, we passed through the towns of Hamilton and Te Kuiti. Our first stop was the famous glow worm caves at Waitomo, near Taumaranui. The most spectacular of all the caves (which had to be viewed from a boat) had a ceiling illuminated by thousands of their little green lights – an amazing sight.

As we crested the ridge of a range of hills, our arrival in New Zealand's thermal area was announced by the sight of Mount

Ngauruhoe, an active volcano emitting a large white plume of smoke. Everything is affected and it was interesting to see steam rising from roadside streams as we drove along. The tongue-twisting Maori names certainly took some getting used to as well. Nearby in the centre of the North Island lies Lake Taupo, and before pitching Dave's tent for the night on its shore, we went swimming at a nearby geothermal spa. There are times when life is exceptionally good, and lying in that pool with the water at bath temperature, staring up at the stars was one of them. Terrific!

After a fairly comfortable night our first stop was at Waiotapu (meaning in Maori sacred waters) which lay en route to our primary destination of Rotorua. Here we saw our first geysers and thermal pools, one of which was 300 feet deep. Named after the daughter of a one-time governor of New Zealand, the Lady Knox geyser gives a display at ten fifteen each morning. It is induced to erupt when soap flakes are poured into it, and the pressure builds up when sacking is stuffed over the mouth, causing a jet of boiling steam to shoot into the air. Another attraction was the Weather Pools that noticeably change colour and level before weather changes, probably due to barometric pressure. These sights have been attracting spectators since the mid nineteenth century, and walking amongst them was a unique experience, the only downside being the noxious smell of sulphur filling the air.

To the north-east the Maori town of Rotorua is surrounded by more bubbling water and mud pools which we spent some time examining, and the inhabitants still decorate their houses with elaborate carvings of strange figures with grotesque faces. The original village is situated on top of a hill, and comprises a stockade, or 'par', with a carved ornamental arch, a storehouse on raised legs, and a communal meeting house amidst the surrounding wooden dwellings. The interior of the meeting house was beautifully decorated with the most elaborate painted designs to the walls and rafters. With their blood-curdling yells,

50. Entrance to Maori par, Rotorua

Village food store

Approaching Picton, Queen Charlotte Sound, South Island

tattooed faces and bodies, the fierce Maori warriors must have presented a frightening sight to the early white settlers.

After driving around Lake Rotorua we took a panoramic route past several smaller lakes, and I continued to be impressed by the scenery, consisting as it did of wonderful hiking country, lush green fields and hills with many small farms, and little 'one-horse' towns. Arriving after dark at the coastal town of Whakatane on the Bay of Plenty, we found a camp site near the beach and awoke next day to a perfect morning with not a cloud in the sky.

After breakfast and a stroll up the beach we set off along the coast road through the town of Tauranga towards the Coromandel Peninsula. This wild area lies almost due east of Auckland and is separated from it by the Firth of Thames. Pressing on up the eastern side of the Peninsula the road turned to a dirt track, despite showing on the map as a main highway. This slowed us up and we could only make about 20 mph, which eventually forced us to cut short our journey. On both sides lay a lush forest of pohutukawa trees and giant 'Jurassic' ferns, and at about 6.30 pm we reached a hot water beach, so named because at high tide its hot pools were covered by the sea. However as it was very cold by this time we took their word for it.

It was decided to carry on across the Peninsula to the town of Thames and find a motel, as nobody fancied pitching the tent. The 'road' was a winding track up a mountain and then down the other side and had to be navigated in pitch darkness. All attempts at finding somewhere for the night failed, so we chose to keep going for Auckland, and despite getting desperately low on oil we arrived back at midnight. It was good to be back and Mrs Goss seemed genuinely pleased to see us. So ended our Easter adventure, which had given me an opportunity to experience more of this lovely country.

Crewing for Ross continued and one Saturday we were tacking across the harbour, out to the start line, just as the hundred mile offshore powerboat race got under way behind us. Luckily they all missed us but the wash from about fifty boats was tremendous and one of our crew went overboard and had to be retrieved. Everybody was drenched but it was a great spectacle.

I also visited the Pukekohe motor racing circuit which lay about thirty miles south, to watch the last event of the season. It was an interesting little track around a horse racing course and unlike at home I was able to stand about five feet from the edge of the road taking photos without any interference from the marshals. Getting out at the weekend always made a pleasant diversion from everyday routine, although things were about to change.

On arrival home from work one Friday evening, a letter was waiting from John saying that he and Dale had moved down to Christchurch in the South Island, and were going to rent a flat. Would I join them? It appeared that whilst walking along a beach during their sojourn in Fiji they had met a Mrs Plummer who came from there. They had an invitation to visit her and on reaching NZ had made their way to the city. Having thought it over I decided it was a tempting idea and so gave a week's notice at work. Neither they nor Mrs Goss were too pleased, but I thought it a good opportunity as it would enable me to see more of the country.

The plan was to meet John at an address in Wellington, and through a contact I had arranged to fly down in a light plane from Ardmore on the evening I finished. However my case proved too big and heavy, and after a lot of discussion the only option was to take the bus a couple of days later. So with a lift back to Mountain Road I was back in bed by 9.30 pm.

It was an early start on Sunday morning to catch the Mount Cook bus to Wellington, New Zealand's capital city which lies at the tip of the North Island. But after a comfortable day's travel south via Hamilton, Cambridge, Taupo, Taihape, and Levin, through a lush green landscape, we reached the city just after

8.00 pm. From here it was a short taxi ride to the home of the delightful Clark family in the Wadestown district.

John had not yet appeared but I could not have had a warmer welcome. Wilf Clark was a quiet man in his late sixties, while his wife Doreen was a charming, bustling, and chatty lady who gave the impression that the arrival of a complete stranger in their midst was an everyday occurrence. The contact with the family came about through their knowing Mrs Plummer. Their son Philip was an amusing chap of about twenty two who hammered out Blues numbers on an ancient piano, while their daughter Angela was a shy schoolgirl in her mid teens.

John arrived an hour later and it seemed the Christchurch idea had been scrapped as Dale had apparently got a job in Wellington, so would be moving there. Having discussed things, he and I decided to bring forward a plan to hitch-hike around the South Island, and so started making preparations over the next couple of days. The city lived up to its nickname of 'Windy' Wellington' but was livelier than I expected, with some interesting shops. A small cable car similar to those in San Francisco took us up above it, to some attractive gardens with great views towards the South Island.

The most gorgeous sunny morning greeted us as we caught the ferry from Wellington across the Cook Straight. The voyage was calm and the scenery was superb for the last hour as we travelled up a fiord called Queen Charlotte Sound, with the lovely little port of Picton at its head. Boats bobbed at anchor in a small harbour and with the surrounding mountains, it made for the most captivating scene.

Our plan was to travel in a roughly clockwise direction making our way down the Island's east coast to initially meet up with Dale in Christchurch. After a slow start and in contrast to my American hiking experience, we were given a lift for eighty miles in a police car! We passed over some rather barren hills and then along the coast to the old whaling town of Kaikoura where we checked into the Youth Hostel. Whaling here had

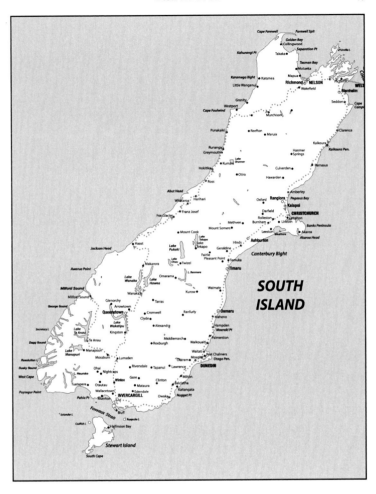

long ago ceased but it has reinvented itself as a centre for whale watching. Apart from this though, the town doesn't have much to recommend it.

We certainly didn't think so next morning as we were met with filthy weather and continuous rain. Leaving the hostel at midday we walked for three miles, getting soaked in the process, and began to think we'd be spending the night in the open. At last after four hours, a lift took us down the attractive coastal road, a feature of which was the single lane bridges which were unnervingly sometimes shared with a rail line. Having crossed part of the verdant Canterbury Plain we arrived in Christchurch at 6.00 pm and met Dale at the flat. After swapping yarns we all went to see Frankie Howard in *Up Pompeii*! I wasn't sure how two Canadians would react to this typical British humour but surprisingly they both found it very amusing.

On a beautifully clear but cold morning John and I set off on borrowed bikes to explore the area. Known to Kiwis as 'Chee-Chee', Christchurch lies about mid way down the east coast, and is the South Island's premier city. Its River Avon ran through a gorgeous park which was immaculately kept, and we enjoyed a relaxed lunch there in a perfect setting, with the colourful tints of the trees reflecting on the river in the early autumn sunlight. It was all very English and a walk round later confirmed that the city was even more reminiscent of 1950s Britain than Auckland. There was an interesting range of Victorian buildings with attractive shops and some lovely churches. Sadly many of these were ruined in the devastating earthquake of 2011. By an amazing coincidence that evening while having a drink we ran into John and Dale's cabin mates from the ship. I also collected a letter from home and was pleased to hear that everyone was well and that my sister was going to work in Bermuda. It was always reassuring to get a letter as the strikes and power cuts that characterised Britain in the 1970s gathered pace.

After clearing out the flat next morning we set off on the bikes again and rode about three miles along the delightful beach at New Brighton, which lies just north of the city. It was another perfect day and we arrived back at Mrs Plummer's quite late, before going out to a party where a good time was had by all.

Our trip continued in more fine weather when she put us on to the main road south at midday, and after walking a couple of miles we had a ride in an immaculate 1938 Chevrolet which ran like a watch.

We were dropped at the town of Ashburton which lies in the middle of the dead flat Canterbury Plain. It was lovely country and reminded John of Canada, with big pastures full of grazing sheep and distant mountains lying in a haze.

Another lift took us to Timaru at the southern edge of the Plain after which the landscape became more undulating. As our man was continuing on to Dunedin we decided to stick with him and reached the Youth Hostel at seven that evening. With a good day's travel we were now over three quarters of the way down the east coast.

When we had completed our chores at the hostel the day was spent exploring the city, whose buildings reflected its Scottish ancestry. It was reminiscent of Edinburgh or Glasgow – a smaller version one could say, and we both felt that it had more character than Auckland. Indeed the university with its prominent clock tower, built with dark basalt stone in Gothic style, is said to have been inspired by the University of Glasgow. Proceedings were enlivened by a student's rag procession which consisted of numerous colourfully decorated floats – many adorned with very fruity slogans! Another notable landmark was the exotic Victorian railway station which boasted a mosaic floor, and elaborately tiled walls. Also of interest to us was the old fashioned museum exhibiting a vast array of photographs of the first settlers to the area, complete with a collection of wagons and farming equipment from those early days.

Invercargill lying right at the southern tip of the South Island and with a similar aura to Dunedin was our next destination, and we easily managed it in two lifts, the latter generously providing us with lunch. As with so much of New Zealand, we passed along the way through very attractive country consisting of rolling green hills that provided lush pasture for huge flocks of sheep.

John had the address of some people living twenty miles north at the village of Wyndham, and leaving the hostel fairly late next morning we decided to look them up. They turned out to be two brothers by the name of John and Henry Heath who were local store keepers. They were charming people and John and his wife gave us supper, and Henry put us up for the night. Although only a tiny village Wyndham, in true NZ fashion, boasted its own racecourse.

After a good breakfast Henry took us on a mini tour of the district which is all sheep farming country, and when we had signed his visitors' book he then arranged a free bus ride back to town for us. What wonderful hospitality.

Just to the south of Invercargill is the very southernmost tip of the mainland at a place called Bluff, and here stood a signpost giving the distances to the world's most prominent cities. John took my photo beneath it and London was shown as 11,820 distant; certainly the furthest south I shall ever go.

Our goal next day was Queenstown, which lies to the north in a stunning setting on the edge of Lake Wakatipu, and two lifts in quick succession took us well clear of Invercargill. But our plan changed when our third lift said he was going on to Milford Sound, also on our list, and the centre of the South Island's fiord land. That was equally acceptable, and took us into the Otago region which provided more beautiful scenery interspersed with the occasional early pioneer's derelict stone house. As we neared the Sound the skies blackened, and rain fell in torrents to confirm the area's reputation for having the greatest rainfall in New Zealand.

Mist swirling around the mountains created an eerie Tolkienesque effect and water poured down the cliff faces in numerous falls. To reach the Sound the road goes through a mountain via the three quarter mile long Homer Tunnel. The amount of water cascading down was incredible, so we didn't stop long that afternoon, but went back a few miles up the valley to an Alpine hut where we were advised to stop the night. Fording a rapidly rising stream, we shared a bunkhouse with a party of seven mountaineers and attempted to dry out. A kerosene lamp swung

The signpost at Bluff

Milford Sound

View over Queenstown

from the ceiling and a noisy card game was in progress, while the
rest of the 'congregation' tried to read. Outside the rain continued
to thunder down.

Setting off again in brighter morning weather we walked
through the Homer tunnel without a torch – which was slightly
nerve racking. At 5,500 feet Mitre Peak dominates the Sound but
was wreathed in swirling mist, and as we queued for the boat trip
up the fiord, the deluging rain returned. Nevertheless I managed
to get a few good photos, and as the boat manoeuvred close to the
sheer mountain sides with their waterfalls, it was a spectacular, if
forbidding sight. Failing to get a lift back however we got drowned
and arrived at the hut in a sorry state.

It snowed during the night and the mountains towering above us
looked magnificent next morning as the bright sun shone off their
white peaks. Seizing the opportunity we returned to see Milford
Sound in sparkling clear weather and what a transformation from
the previous day. The surrounding mountain and woodland views
looked marvellous in contrast, and we counted ourselves lucky to
have seen its more benign face. Rudyard Kipling apparently called
it the 'Eighth Wonder of the World' – and with good reason.
Interesting diversions later were visits to our hut by Kea birds, a
species of green parrot which we fed and although seemingly quite
tame they have been known to attack sheep.

It was another beautiful but very cold day as we walked back
up the valley for about twelve miles, which was hard going with
our large backpacks. But the dramatic scenery was compensation,
as the dirt road wound through the Cross Cut mountain range.
Hearing that Te Anau, lying to the south at the head of a large lake
of the same name, was worth a visit, we eventually got a lift there
and bunked down in a caravan as the proper hostel was full. It was
lovely to turn the heater right up and relax over a good supper.
After our exertions a couple of rest days were called for, which
were spent writing letters and postcards, reading, and getting
some washing done at last. Supplies were replenished in Te Anau,

which reminded me of a small mid-west American town, with its one main street flanked by a few shops. The picturesque approach along the eastern edge of the lake had been worthwhile though, and a bottle of Cold Duck that evening with a Kiwi girl from another caravan, helped celebrate our progress to date.

Promptly next morning we set off for our original destination of Queenstown, a hundred or so miles north, and completed the journey in easy stages by late afternoon. On the approach the countryside became more undulating and the road ran the last stretch along the shore of Lake Wakatipu. On the far side towered the spectacular range of mountains named The Remarkables. And they truly were! Partly hidden by a layer of cloud which looked as if its lower edge had been cut off level with a giant knife, their snow capped peaks penetrated through to catch the setting sun. We both felt that Queenstown, a remnant of the old gold mining days in Otago, with its narrow streets and characterful buildings was the most impressive place so far. It has apparently grown out of all proportion since then and is now known as Queens City. A pity, but I suppose nowhere stands still indefinitely.

Clear skies and brilliant sunshine next day beckoned us to take the cable car 1,400 feet up to the Skyline Restaurant on the summit of Bobs Peak. From here we took in the magnificent panorama of the town, lake, and mountains – a quite wonderful scene and I felt one of the best of my entire journey. Queenstown shrank to a miniature by the huge blue lake stretching away into the distance, whilst the clouds hung level with the snow-covered tops of the Remarkables. The hydrofoil and other boats looked like water beetles as their wake made patterns on the surface, and we looked down on the occasional tourist plane buzzing along below us. The old pleasure steamer *Earnslaw* with its fascinating history dating back to 1912 lay at its wharf. Built in Dunedin, it was taken in pieces to the lake by rail, reassembled, and began its working life serving remote sheep stations. An enjoyable drink with a couple of jolly Aussie girls that evening rounded off a memorable experience.

As we were expecting mail, and the weather turned overcast with rain showers we wandered around the town and park, thankful for the previous day. But twenty four hours later it relented and Sunday May 21st produced the most perfect weather imaginable. A slight early mist soon burnt away to give a clear bright crisp morning, which is the hallmark of perfect autumn weather.

It is said that of all the towns and villages that dot the central Otago landscape none retains more atmosphere of bygone days than Arrowtown. Lying thirteen miles north of Queenstown it was once the centre of the area's gold mining industry, and an essential attraction for us. The old miners' cabins still existed on the narrow tree-lined main street, and although they were now holiday homes the place retained the aura of those far off times: Arrowtown with its gorgeous autumn colours looked its best. Gold dust could still be panned from the river behind the town and we watched a party of school children try their luck. It was hard to imagine that a hundred years previously that part of Otago had been invaded by people anxious to make their fortunes, but it was easy to feel that their ghosts still remained.

However, perhaps the real highlight for us that day was the sensational scenery outside the town around Lake Hayes, on our return journey. A combination of snow-capped mountains, Merino sheep grazing green pastures, the trees in their late autumn colours, dazzling sunshine, and another gem of a lake, made me feel that the area must rate as the most beautiful in New Zealand. It was very easy to run out of superlatives . . .

While walking back to Queenstown we got into conversation with a Scottish chap and his girl who invited us into their bungalow for tea. After we had watched the sun go down behind Coronet Peak, they kindly ran us home, to end another perfect South Island day.

From Queenstown our plan was to head across to the west coast, and after finally giving up on our long awaited mail we decided to press on. Initially the route went inland to a town

called Cromwell, but we were told that the road was closed for
repairs until 5.00 pm as a section over the River Kawarau kept
subsiding. After a long wait we made it and put up at a motor
camp on the edge of town. The contrast in scenery between the
two places was extraordinary, as the landscape quickly changed
into an area of featureless brown hills.

The barman at the local was Wilf Clark's brother in law,
and after looking him up next morning, we set off again. But
progress was almost non-existent, and after walking four miles
up the road and standing out in the dark cursing our luck until
7.00 pm that evening, we put up at another motor camp.

Walking quickly to get warm next morning we progressed a
few miles before being offered a ride to Wanaka, a small town at
the southern tip of another lovely lake of the same name. Parts of
this great lake, which covers an area of eighty five square miles, are
1000 feet deep, and fishing is a popular pastime. The scenery was
even more typical of the American prairie, with the odd cluster of
homesteads dotted around to form a name on the map. Wanaka
was a pleasant spot and after dropping our packs at the hostel,
we strolled along the lake shore and looked at the town. Heavy
rain that evening didn't augur well for the next day's objective,
which was to cross the Haast Pass. This mountain pass through
the Southern Alps is named after Julius von Haast, a nineteenth
century explorer and geologist, and rises at its saddle to a height of
1,844 feet above sea level. We were advised that the road through
the pass to the west coast was a very difficult hitch.

But we made it! In perfect but cold weather, our first lift took
us about half way, and then as there was virtually no traffic we
lay by the side of the road reading our books. Entertainment
was provided by the small local mail plane landing on a bumpy
grass strip on the other side of the fence. When I met John thirty
years later to re-trace our route, we remembered the place as we
passed it in our camper van. Just as we thought we were there
for the night, a large Mercedes lorry stopped, and we gratefully

Young gold prospectors, Arrowtown

John and VW, Lake Wanaka

Our lorry negotiating the Haast Pass

The Van Gang! John, Dave, Kirk, Barbara

R.F., Doreen Clark, John, Mrs Brownlee, Angela

clambered aboard. It was an unusual journey around the base
of sundry mountains on an unsealed narrow road, and we
only just got through one section before they were due to blast
the rock away to ease a corner. In fact the road only received
a tarmac surface as recently as 1995. Meanwhile the landscape
became noticeably more green with an abundance of the giant
ferns so prevalent in the North Island. A labourer's hut on a
construction site near the coastal town of Haast provided that
night's accommodation, and I remember thinking 'if my mother
could only see me now . . .'

After a surprisingly reasonable night we rose early and walked
about eight miles along a beautiful but deserted road through
lush foliage and more giant ferns. And then along came Barbara
Wilkie – a Kiwi girl who was touring in an old Austin van with
her dog Shag! Already on board were two Americans, Dave and
Kirk, whom we had passed and re-passed at the roadside several
times, and it was good to finally make their acquaintance. So that
made five jolly travellers bowling up the west coast to see another
of the South Island's principal wonders. We called ourselves The
Van Gang and the next few days were some of the best ever; the
sort of time one looks back on fondly years later.

On our left was the sea and away to our right stretched the
Southern Alps with the majestic Mount Cook, New Zealand's
highest peak, standing at 12,375 feet. Our goals were the Fox and
Franz Joseph Glaciers, almost side by side and named after a NZ
prime minister and an Austrian emperor.

The first of these was Fox Glacier which has formed a large
valley as it melts, and is still retreating rapidly at about two feet
per day. It's possible to follow a track up onto the glacier to view
this magnificent spectacle at first hand, which we lost no time
in doing. John was dwarfed by a cliff face of solid ice as I took
his photo and it was another memorable experience to add to
a growing list. Not so lucky further on at Franz Joseph, due to
the weather again closing in, we sought shelter in an old village

school house. But having lit a good fire, a broth was cooked up by candle light, accompanied by much merry banter to add to the atmosphere!

Rain, pouring rain, accosted us next morning, confirming the west coast's reputation for an average of three to four hundred inches a year. Returning for another look at Franz Joseph proved futile so we journeyed on with much jollity, until reaching the small town of Hokitika where a motor camp was found which even boasted TV. Barbara slept in her van as usual but we blokes had a warm little room for 70 cents each. Wine with our supper made for a really hilarious meal with all the old American humour from Dave and Kirk, interspersed with expressions like 'Faaarrr Out Man' and 'Heavy Duty', (meaning especially good) – which neatly summed up the evening.

In the old days Hokitika was the exit port for west coast gold shipments, but the main industry at the time of our visit was the carving of New Zealand jade, or Greenstone, into ornaments and jewellery. This material was originally much prized by the Maoris, and our first call was to a small factory to see how the process was carried out, before continuing north up the rugged coast in fine weather towards Greymouth.

A lazy afternoon was spent on the beach watching the big rollers pounding in, and later on the sun setting over a stretch of weird pancake-shaped rocks. These are the result of thirty million year old limestone formations, etched by sea, wind and rain. Finding a camp site we cooked a memorable supper over a driftwood fire on the beach under a starry sky with a full moon. What more could one ask for?

Our marvellous trip continued with much merriment, only interrupted by a broken throttle, which we repaired with wire. The varied scenery consisted of rocky gorges and hills covered with pine tree plantations, many of which showed evidence of earthquake damage. During a lunch stop in a café at a small place called Murchison I experienced my second earth tremor – a frightening shudder lasting about five seconds. However the locals were quite unperturbed as it was apparently a regular occurrence.

All too soon our final night arrived when we reached Nelson, the last stop before the ferry at Picton, and put up at another motor camp. We lads again shared a hut and whiled away a peaceful evening reading and listening to Barbara's selection of records. Simon and Garfunkel's classic 'Bridge Over Troubled Water' played as I wrote my diary, and always reminds me of the scene.

Departure next morning was a big rush as the others wanted to catch the 2.00 pm ferry, but John and I had to return to Christchurch to collect the rest of our kit. It was another clear day and the lakes and fiords were at their fabulous best as we followed the coast road – actually just a winding dirt track – which eventually descended into Picton. The sad anticlimax came when we had to say farewell to the gang just before they boarded. Those last few days had really made our trip, and although we swapped address none of us expected to meet again.

Adding to the anticlimax was the slow progress made from Picton, and we only reached Blenheim, about twelve miles further, by that evening. After walking for three hours next morning we finally got a lift all the way to Christchurch with a couple of freaks in a VW van, although I nearly froze in the back. On our arrival that evening the ever hospitable Mrs Plummer gave us a warm welcome. She really was a kind soul.

By now June had arrived and the next couple of days were spent around town thinking about our onward move. There was apparently no chance of catching the *Orsova*'s next sailing from Auckland to Sydney on July 7th, but we remained optimistic. As the locals would say, 'She'll be right, mate', an excellent philosophy I think. Mail arrived for us both the second day which was timely and we made ready for an early start the next morning. Having said a grateful goodbye to Mrs Plummer we got on the road, as we hoped to reach Picton that day. Eventually arriving that evening to find the daily ferry had left at 10.00 am, we put up at a rather expensive motor camp for the night. Sunday June 4th was spent waiting in Picton all day as the ferry didn't leave until 6.00 pm, but I was so glad the weather was again brilliant for our last day in the South Island.

The Clarks gave us a great welcome on our return to Mairangi Road, and, having started his new job, Dale was also still there. It was Queen's Birthday weekend (something not celebrated in the UK) so Monday was a relaxing holiday.

In the hope of making the *Orsova*'s next sailing we put our names on the reserve passenger list at the P&O office in Wellington, and cast around for odd jobs to fill the time until then. When that proved fruitless we ventured further afield to the Lower Hutt area and were offered work at the main Chrysler assembly plant, where they produced Hillman, Singer, and Valiant cars. So we were back at work that same week: it seemed no real problem getting a job then. I worked in the upholstery department putting seats together, and John was fitting the ancillary parts to engines.

We worked hard all week, which was fine as the money was good, but the routine and regimentation were arduous. There was no larking about like at NZ Motor Co. We would get up at 6.00 am and walk about two miles to the station to catch the 7.00 am train to the factory at Petone. A horrible noisy siren sounded at 7.35 am announcing the start of work until the thirty minute lunch break, half of which was spent standing in a queue for food. On Mondays and Tuesdays we worked overtime until 7.30 pm, and until 4.30 pm the rest of the week. On overtime evenings we got back at 8.30 pm which made for a long day, and made me realise that most of the strikes in the car industry at home were probably caused by the boring routine. It resembled being switched on and off like a machine and there was a high turnover of workers, most of whom were Maoris and Islanders. But it did have its lighter moments such as departure time at the end of the day. Everyone had to line up twenty yards from the time clock and wait for the siren. We were not allowed to move forward until it went off, and then followed a stampede! There was always a mad rush to get aboard the train home and claim a seat, so you desperately hoped the carriage door would stop opposite you.

Dale, down from Palmerston North that first weekend, had a company Vauxhall, and took us a spin along the coast. It was a luxury to be out in a car again and we spent some time watching the surfers on a beach near the airport. Letters continued to arrive from Lesley with Cambridge news, and I was sorry but not overly surprised to hear that Frank and Irene were having problems – mostly centred on Frank's drinking it seemed.

We crammed in all the hours we could at work but it was an effort to make the walk to the station each morning. Only the thought that it was not for much longer kept us going! Finally on the last day in June we finished, although being moved for my last three days on to the track to fit suspension parts was an improvement over the seat department. They seemed rather annoyed that we were leaving so soon, but it was great to say cheerio to getting up at 6.00 am every morning and the two mile walk to the station.

A few days spent catching up on odd jobs and writing home followed, during which John's mother arrived to check up on her son. Through a connection of Wilf's I bought a top quality down filled sleeping bag which proved invaluable over the coming months. There was still no news about places on the *Orsova* but we decided to go up to Auckland anyway. On Wednesday July 5th I put my case on the bus and we all said goodbye, prior to catching a train a few miles north to Paekakariki (wonderful name!). The Clarks had been marvellous to us and I'm pleased to say that I stayed in contact with them, and subsequently visited their daughter Angela and her family thirty years later.

They had given us contact details for a friend of theirs called Jacob Scott who lived at Havelock North, just south of Napier at Hawke Bay on the east coast. This was to be our first stop and once again the police obligingly provided transport for a good part of the journey! Then a very decent fellow took us straight to Havelock and after giving us tea at his home, plus a short sightseeing tour, delivered us to the Scott's! We had passed through the most delightful fruit growing country on the way, which left a very favourable impression, as did the lovely little town of Havelock North. To me it was reminiscent of a small English village community.

The Scott family continued the spirit of hospitality we had experienced, and Jacob kindly ran us to the nearby town of Napier, to help us on our journey. Napier is unique in that in 1931 it was completely destroyed in an earthquake and so was rebuilt in period Art Deco style. A friendly Maori gave us a lift straight up to Taupo, and after buying him a drink we went for a soak in the thermal pools at the De Brett Hotel. Brilliant! More generosity followed when John Carr, a kind young teacher took us to his parents' home for the night, and we spent a pleasant evening in his local bar until the police turfed us out after drinking up time. John put us on the main road north next morning and we reached Auckland with no problems.

Old Ma Goss seemed very pleased to see us when we called at Mountain Road for mail, and having given us lunch, invited us to stop the night. The afternoon was spent rushing round to the tax office, bank, and P&O office, and to our delight we managed to get tickets on the *Orsova* sailing for Sydney in four days time. A jolly evening with all the same old faces was spent back at 107, to round off a most successful day.

Having confirmed our departure date we decided to visit the strikingly beautiful Bay of Islands on the North East coast over that last weekend. In town we bumped into two Canadians from the *Orsova* and all went down to the dockside to view the Chilean Navy's lovely square rigged sail training ship *Esmeralda*.

Although the weather wasn't too good, it was still warm as

we headed north, and after walking the last seven miles reached the town of Whangarei fairly late to check in at the hostel. The countryside on the way was wonderfully green with some lovely beaches where foaming breakers rolled majestically shoreward. These particularly impressed John, as did the difference in temperature since Wellington. It was really tropical and great to be in shirtsleeves in mid winter.

After a slow start next morning we finally reached Paihia in the Bay of Islands just in time to take the 2.00 pm cruise round the Bay. It was on one of these beaches at the foot of a small wooded inlet that Captain Cook made his first landfall. The other passengers were a lively lot being the Australian cast of the show *Charlie Girl* which was playing in Auckland. The weather was dull all day which was a pity as the islands were very attractive, often with tall palm like 'cabbage' trees which are as much a symbol of New Zealand as the Kiwi, or the silver fern leaf. Many islands were the retreats of millionaires and the area is renowned for the deep sea fishing catches of marlin and shark made famous by the likes of Ernest Hemingway.

After heavy rain all evening the weather cleared and we made a good start on the return journey until reaching Whangarei. However, after a delay of a couple of hours we had a lift all the way to Auckland where we bunked down with a bunch of Canadians in a flat in the Parnell district. Our last night was spent reading and listening to Cat Stevens tapes.

The ship was due to sail late next evening, and that last afternoon was spent sorting out my finances which resulted in a most welcome tax rebate of 81 dollars. We went aboard for tea and the old barge was just the same, except for the departure of Captain Woolley. It felt very much like returning home.

Then it was back up to Mountain Road to get our gear together and say cheerio to Mrs Goss who had been very helpful. Some of the lads came down to see us off and we all watched a Maori concert before they went ashore. Promptly at 11.00 pm the tugs pulled us out into the harbour and a band played the Maori song of farewell before the inevitable rush to the Veranda Bar!

As usual I felt very nostalgic and after a while took my drink outside to watch the lights of Auckland fade astern, as I reflected on how well things had gone and the good times I'd had.

All things considered I felt that I'd enjoyed New Zealand more than any other country I'd visited, although I wouldn't have missed any of them. But, perhaps as a result of spending nine months in the USA, the country seemed so British that right from that first day I felt completely at home.

In 1972 it was probably the most British place outside Britain with so many similar customs, and yet it was much more rural and immediately apparent that the mainstay of the economy was farming. It was all so relaxed, and the pace of life after America was noticeably slower. The average Kiwi was an easy going bloke with an admirable 'She'll be right mate' attitude; and who could blame him, living as he did in some of the most stunning scenery in the world. The old stereotype of the Rugby loving, beer drinking, horse racing fan (there were some eighty tracks at that time) was fundamentally true. It seemed to me that the traditional colonial ties probably existed more strongly in NZ than in any other Commonwealth territory, as they still largely depended on the 'Mother' country. But things were beginning to change, and in particular trade with Japan was increasing strongly.

New Zealand memories in no particular order were: Mrs Goss and my Mountain Road digs with its cockroaches and quirky assortment of blokes; Waikato bitter, my favourite NZ beer served in a jug of course, with standing room only at little tables in most 'hotels'; the marvellously hospitable Clark family in Wellington, and the journey out to Todd Motors at Petone each morning. Old cars were plentiful and a 1930s Model A Ford was not a novelty. There were lots of other pre-war American cars and thirties Morris 8s in particular, together with numerous

British vehicles from the early fifties, such as the Vauxhall Velox and Austin Somerset. However the number of modern cars on the roads was gradually increasing. Also the tongue twisting Maori place names such as Taihape, Manawatu, Taranaki, and Ruapehu – the name of the tallest mountain in the North Island.

In fact I liked the way that the Maoris were regarded as equals and generally respected, which was not so in some other countries with a native or coloured population.

The fact that the seasons were out of step with the British months of the year did seem odd though, and summer in February took some getting used to.

The Returned Servicemen's Association (their equivalent of the British Legion) was a very strong and active organisation, and because they held no allegiance to the Queen, membership for Communists was barred!

Wages were slightly lower than in Britain and although dairy products were cheaper, clothes, and particularly shoes and household appliances were very expensive.

I was always fascinated by the tropical plant life: particularly the giant ferns that grew to a height of twenty feet or so and whose ancestry goes back one hundred million years; also the pampas grass, and the creepers that we found in the South Island, which were easily strong enough to hang on to. Naturally sheep were part of the landscape just about everywhere.

But I felt that my favourite memories were of sailing in the Hauraki Gulf around the landmark of Rangitoto Island, and travelling with the Van Gang; particularly that fabulous evening cooking our supper on the beach under a full moon with the surf crashing in the background. Finally there was our walk along Lake Hayes from Arrowtown, with a brilliant sun shining on some of the most perfect scenery in the world. I couldn't hope for happier memories anywhere. I have never for a moment regretted spending more time than originally planned in 'The Land of the Long White Cloud'.

Chapter Fourteen
G'day!

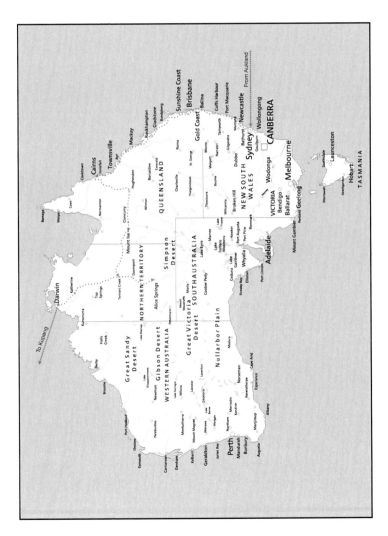

There was quite a swell during our first day at sea and John felt rather queasy that morning. Shipboard life was mostly the same, including the steward's welcome cup of tea and newspaper first thing. It was luxurious to sleep in a bed with proper sheets again after months of sleeping bags, and we all wished the voyage could last longer. There was a familiar feeling of security with everything laid on and nobody seemed too anxious to get to Sydney and begin again.

Our second day saw better weather as we ploughed on westwards across the Tasman Sea, and after a routine medical check everyone relaxed. I spent the time playing chess before competing in a fancy hat contest that evening. An interesting conversation took place with a young Aussie when I asked 'why there was often an anti Pom attitude in his homeland?' He explained that it was not really so, but they disliked us making comparisons with how things were done in the UK. I was advised to stay fairly non-committal until accepted by the locals, which was advice that served me well.

At 7.30 am on Friday July 14th we had our first view of Australia, my original goal, when we sighted Sydney Heads on the horizon. It was quite a thrill for me and even at that distance I could make out the Harbour Bridge. The sun was well up in a cloudless sky as we passed the famous Opera House and berthed at the foot of the bridge.

Thankfully there were no Customs or Immigration problems but we didn't get ashore until that afternoon. John and I, together with Jerry, another Pom, and two Canadians, Jean and Ken, who had all been on the same table for meals stuck together, and after dumping our kit at the main railway station, walked up town to collect our mail.

Our next stop was a large hotel Jerry knew of, overlooking the renowned Bondi Beach. It was called the Astra, and after being quoted 15 dollars a week with breakfast, which seemed excellent value, we checked in. First impressions of Sydney were positive and it reminded me a little of San Francisco, although Bondi Beach itself was smaller than I had imagined. Supper consisted of Hamburger Specials eaten on the beach. It seemed incredible that after so many adventures I had finally arrived in the country I set out for nineteen months earlier.

Saturday was spent exploring our surroundings and walking across the Harbour Bridge which, being a terrific height above the water, gave us magnificent views over the city. Sydney on the east coast of the continent is the capital of the province of New South Wales, and was founded in 1788 by British settlers as a penal colony. Its name derives from the then British Home Secretary, Lord Sydney. The great natural harbour with its myriad coves and small inlets stretched away either side of us, and the celebrated opera house with its distinctive white peaked roofs stood out to our right. Leisure craft of every type weaved their way to and fro on a sparkling sea. Skyscrapers and cranes in abundance emphasised that this was an altogether bigger and more cosmopolitan city than Auckland or Wellington; and a wander up to the Kings Cross area later on, with its bustling strip joints, bars, restaurants, and general night life, accentuated the American flavour of the place.

Lunch and supper with a film show afterwards were wangled back on the *Orsova*, and we continued to go aboard until she sailed a day late the following Tuesday. The poor old ship met a sad end, as in November that year three hundred passengers and crew were taken ill with dysentery. There were further complaints on a Christmas cruise and she never recovered from the subsequent bad publicity. In 1974 she was sent to be scrapped in Taiwan.

After a week settling down I had rather mixed feelings about the city, but for no particular reason. I suppose I found it difficult to get used to the pace of life which was a far cry from Auckland and dear old NZ. But the Aussies seemed a friendly lot, indeed more so than I expected, and my diary noted that I had yet to be called a Pommie bastard! Also I was very lucky to walk into a job on that first Thursday, especially as the employment situation was reckoned to be difficult.

I had been strolling through the city when I passed a small engine reconditioning shop, and on impulse looked in to see if they had a vacancy. It was called The New Process Cylinder Boring Co. and they said I could start the next day at 75 dollars a week, which was good money. The owner was a man called Ross and the firm had been started back in the 1920s by his father, using a new technique for boring engine cylinders. We worked from 8.15 am until 5.00 pm and it was a twenty five minute bus ride from the hotel. Also at weekends I had a casual job at a hand car wash at nearby Bondi Junction, in order to save up as much as possible for the onward journey.

The weather continued to be very hot and Sydney was suffering from a severe drought. In addition a petrol shortage loomed and we were told that due to strikes there would soon only be enough for essential services. Before long Jerry and Ken left to go north, leaving me, John and Jean, at the Astra. After considering alternative accommodation we decided to stay put, especially when offered our rooms at 10 dollars per week each as permanent guests. Besides, the breakfast room on the fifth floor with its view over the beach and bay provided a nice start to the day. A nearby café called Edwin's usually supplied our supper for a dollar. News filtered in from my parents, Lesley, the Clarks, and finally a letter from Frank brought the distressing news that he and Irene had separated. This left me feeling very depressed and I couldn't help thinking that he was largely to blame. Shortly afterwards another letter told me that they were celebrating their first wedding anniversary! It was hard to keep up.

John had decided to accompany me on the overland journey to England, which was good news, and we reckoned to leave from Darwin about mid September. We paid a deposit on our flights to Kupang in Indonesian Timor, and had a nasty shock

Arrival in Sydney

Lunch stop between Brisbane and Rockhampton

shortly afterwards when told that the travel company had gone bust. Thankfully the agent later agreed to take responsibility and pay for our tickets, for which we were very grateful as they were 100 dollarseach.

In between work at New Process and odd hours at the car wash I managed to do some sightseeing, and one Sunday took the boat across the harbour to spend the day at the zoo, which, unusually, had a shark pool. There was normally something happening at Bondi beach which was always populated by surfers, and at times the lifeguards practised rescue techniques in their wooden rowing boats. Jerry returned from his travels and quite often we all had a beach barbecue, which was not only fun but also served my main objective of saving money.

It was during this time that John discovered the Church of Scientology, a name that meant nothing to me but which has over the years gained some notoriety. They were offering a course on which he decided to enrol and complete by staying on for a few months. I was disappointed and would miss his company but felt that he was doing what was right for him. Ultimately he remained in Australia for several years and finally returned to Canada when all his savings had been swallowed up by the Church. Sadly I believe this has been the disastrous experience of many people worldwide.

Just as I was wondering how I was going to break it to Ross that I wanted to leave, he solved my problem by giving me a week's notice. The expected local authority contract for reconditioning bus engines had failed to materialise, which meant that he was overstaffed. As last man in I was first out, but I was delighted at the way my plans were falling into place. My last week passed without incident and after signing out on Friday night I stood in the shower scrubbing off the grime for an hour, followed by a session in the Bikini Bar to celebrate!

September had now arrived and I couldn't wait to get going again. My plan was to travel up the east coast before turning inland to Alice Springs, which lies approximately in the centre of the continent. From there I would take the highway north to Darwin on the coast and catch my flight to Kupang. Time passed quickly with preparations such as mending and washing clothes, shipping my surplus gear home, buying a backpack, and writing letters to all and sundry. On top of this there were malaria tablets and visas to be obtained for Indonesia and Nepal, a course of vaccinations to be undergone, a tax rebate to file, etc. etc. As advised, I converted nearly all my money into US dollars, and after some haggling at the bank I also got 100 dollars in one dollar bills for convenience. Together with my passport this was carried in a money belt which never left my sight, even when I was taking a shower, and especially later on the journey.

At last everything was ready and on the off chance I phoned the Hertz office to see if they wanted anything taken north. My luck was in as there was a car to be delivered to Brisbane, so I arranged to collect it next morning. Jean decided to accompany me that far to see something of the country beyond Sydney, so I wouldn't be setting off on my own. On my last night Jerry, John, Jean and I went for a farewell meal to Rushcutter's Bay, and I was very touched when they presented me with a card and a Bondi Beach T-shirt as a souvenir of my stay in the city.

Friday September 8th was departure day and I hurried into town first thing to collect the car – a Holden Torana – before returning to pick up Jean and my pack. Having said farewell to John, Jerry, and the hotel staff we headed over the Harbour Bridge and out of Sydney. Goodbye Bondi! It felt really great to be driving again and the Pacific Highway was an interesting road that followed the coast and passed through places with strange names like Mooney Mooney Creek and Tumblegum. We stopped for a young hitch-hiker who was hard work as he hardly said a word, and also made for rather a squash when we pulled off the road to try and sleep about 9.30 pm. Several times I started the engine and got the heater going as it was surprisingly cold later.

However, another fine day dawned with an initial atmospheric low-lying mist, and we drove on accompanied by our friend who didn't seem to know where he was going. Stopping at Coff's Harbour, we tried without success to locate two Canadians from the ship, so continued past fields of sugar cane through Surfers' Paradise (known locally as Sufferers' Paradise!), a large resort resembling Miami. The scenery became rather sparse, the trees having twisted thin trunks with no foliage as a result of bush fires, and away to our left lay the Dividing Range of mountains as we crossed into Queensland. I started to feel a bit low at the thought of continuing on my own as we reached Brisbane and dropped our pal off, but cheered up somewhat after a meal and a stroll round. It was a sizeable modern city and we later enjoyed the film *Nicholas and Alexandra* at a drive-in cinema.

Having passed a more comfortable night near the drive-in, we found a place in town for breakfast and Jean fixed up her bus ride back to Sydney. My luck was in again and I picked up another Holden to deliver to Rockhampton further up the Queensland coast. I drove Jean back to the bus depot and we said goodbye. She had been good company and I wished her well. I wondered if we would ever meet again but thought it unlikely, although I gave her my UK address. But we never have, and as I've said before, that's the sad thing about travelling.

Setting course for Rockhampton about four hundred and twenty five miles further on, I made good time before picking up another hitch-hiker. At one point the English football results came over the radio, and it was a most surreal experience to be driving through the Australian bush miles from anywhere as the announcer's voice intoned 'Arsenal 1, Tottenham Hotspur 3' etc.

The houses that we did see were nearly all built on stilts about five feet off the ground which kept them cooler, and dry if there were floods. My companion invited me back to his place near the town of Gladstone, which turned out to be a weird and decrepit little farm house some miles off the road. The other occupants

'Arsenal 1, Tottenham Hotspur 3', Australian outback road

Refuelling the Alfa

were two freaks and we all ended up playing Gin Rummy and smoking joints by candlelight. An unexpected ending to the day!

After a cold night on the floor, I was away early when the freaks left for work, driving on quiet dirt roads to reach Rockhampton by 8.30 am. It was a pleasant town with wide streets and after sneaking into a hotel for a wash, I delivered the car. They were very decent people and arranged a lift for me with one of their ferry drivers to Mackay, two hundred and forty miles further on. There was literally nothing but sparse bush between the two towns and I was very glad that I didn't have to try and hitch it.

We arrived by early afternoon but there were no more deliveries, so after checking the other rental companies I had a meal and got on the road. Adding to the weight of my pack was my emergency food supply, a large bag of muesli, and I realised I wouldn't be able to walk far in that heat. Four middle-aged Pommies who were touring in a camper van took me a short way further to the small town of Prosperine where I waited until dark but had to put up at a guest house for the night.

I was up early and after a short wait got two lifts, the second of which was with a freak in a Mini Cooper 'S', travelling at a great rate of knots. The road was littered with the bodies of young kangaroos that had been run over at night, and these were the only ones I had seen thus far. Dawn and dusk were the usual times to see 'roos as they sleep during the day. Happily their numbers were not reduced by us and we reached Townsville at midday.

I thought the place more drab than Mackay or Rockhampton, but hung around all afternoon as the freak was leaving for Cairns at 7.00 pm and offered me a ride the rest of the way. So after supper we set off again with the cassette player belting out acid rock 'music' that nearly deafened me and made it impossible to talk. Perhaps that was the idea? The road was incredibly bumpy and at one point turned to mud, but we finally made it and I was dropped off at the Youth Hostel at 1.30 am after waking the manager.

A welcome rest day followed, especially for my ears, and in brilliant weather I spent most of the day reading in a park overlooking the sea. Cairns is the most northerly town of any size on Australia's east coast, and although larger than I had imagined, I thought it more attractive than any of the previous places. It was extremely neat and tidy with wide streets bordered by lovely tropical palm trees and bushes, and I casually wandered around taking photos.

Some fifteen miles from the mainland on the Great Barrier Reef lay Green Island which was somewhere I particularly wanted to see. Appropriately named with a white sandy beach it stood out against the splendid turquoise coloured sea, looking every inch the tropical island. It's only about thirty five acres in area and is surrounded by gorgeous coral formations. Hiring a snorkel and flippers I felt like Jacques Cousteau swimming amongst all the brightly coloured fish, and as the sun was really hot now, I was also developing a good tan. 'What a great life!' was my diary entry.

On the return ferry I met Dave, a bearded Pom who had settled in Oz but was on holiday from Brisbane. He was considering motoring across to Alice Springs and quick as a flash I offered to share the driving and expenses! Fuelling my enthusiasm was the fact that he owned a nice little Alfa Romeo, but it should also mean I would arrive in Darwin in time for my flight on September 22nd. He moved into the hostel and after overnight consideration (and a few beers) decided to go ahead.

Before that though was a trip to Kuranda, a small village about twenty miles inland and nestling 1,000 feet higher in lush green hills. The spectacular journey on a narrow gauge railway took about ninety minutes, climbing through sugar cane plantations before we entered a series of tunnels. Exiting these, the line crossed a bridge on stilts spanning a wide gorge with dramatic waterfalls, before reaching Kuranda station which was attractively decorated with wonderful displays of native plants and bushes.

We set off for Alice at 8.00 am next morning and initially our route took us back towards Kuranda, where we had breakfast at a lookout point with a panoramic view over Cairns. Although we could have gone south on the main road back to Townsville before turning inland, we decided to cut two corners off the triangle and thrashed along a track to join the main highway at Hughenden. At one point we screeched to a halt at the sight of a huge lizard about four feet long sunning itself, but as soon as we got close it ran off into the bush before I could take its photo.

The main highway was not much better, long stretches being just dirt road with some terrible bumps which had the Alfa bottoming badly. Vegetation was sparse and the scenery very monotonous – just a flat expanse of scrub country with occasional cattle. Now and again a small filling station, usually with a bar attached, appeared in the middle of nowhere and I wondered what people did with themselves living so far from any centre. The impression of sheer size was even more evident than in the USA, especially when we passed a sign at the head of a track saying 'Wallambulla Station 320 miles'. It was hard to imagine anyone driving three hundred and twenty miles along a dirt road seemingly leading nowhere, to reach their home.

The heat built up as we travelled further inland, passing through the featureless little towns of Richmond and Cloncurry, into the setting sun and leaving behind a huge cloud of dust. After dark we ran over the carcass of a small cow which caused a terrible stink inside the car and took some getting rid of. Dave had friends living at the mining town of Mount Isa which we reached at 9.00 pm for our night stop, and we sat up until 2.00 am watching TV. As next day was a Sunday we stayed on and went swimming in Lake Moondarra. This provided the town's water supply, and although rather dirty was at least refreshing. In addition we cleaned about half a ton of dust out of the car and managed to get rid of most of the smell of cow.

Mount Isa, known locally as The Isa, is a mining town

established in 1923 because of the area's huge mineral deposits. Lead, silver, and copper are mined extensively and it's now the commercial centre for Queensland's vast north western region. I knew I wouldn't have lasted five minutes living in such a dusty uninspiring place as there were hardly any recreational facilities, and I gathered most people were there just for the money.

We had now covered seven hundred and eighty miles from Cairns and I was happy to continue to our next objective, a place called Tenant Creek four hundred miles further on near the junction with the main Adelaide to Darwin highway. It was barren country with literally nothing but a small cafe-cum-filling station every two hundred odd miles, and again I found myself wondering what people did with themselves. A drunken fight broke out at one place we stopped at which provided the answer to my question!

It was easy to see why camels had been introduced to Australia in the early days as the best means of crossing this arid land, but in 1972, before the advent of the Ghan railway from Darwin to Adelaide, most goods were hauled by road train. These were huge trucks pulling three or four large trailers and usually travelling in a cloud of dust. They were difficult to overtake and we nearly overturned trying to miss one that came round a bend on the wrong side of the road, frightening the life out of us both. I also bruised my elbow badly on the door but it could have been so much worse.

Turning south from Tenant Creek we headed towards Alice Springs some three hundred miles further on. This was the wrong direction for me, but I wanted to see Alice and thought it more likely I'd get a lift to Darwin from there. Between the two places we stopped to look at a collection of huge rounded boulders at the roadside, known as the Devil's Marbles.

By the time we rolled into town at 8.30 pm that evening we had covered just over seven hundred miles, which was a good day's motoring, considering the heat and state of the roads.

Australian road train

The Devil's Marbles, near Alice Springs

Stopping for the night near a National Park I slept by the car under the clear star-filled sky of the Australian Outback. And despite horrible thoughts of poisonous Taipan snakes and Red Back spiders crawling all over me I had a surprisingly good night.

Alice Springs lies almost exactly in the centre of Australia and mid-way between Adelaide and Darwin in the Northern Territory. Because of its position, and a water hole (named after the wife of an early surveyor) it was established as a telegraph station connecting the two, as well as Great Britain. The Park contained the springs plus a replica of the original station and buildings as they were in about 1890, together with old photographs. Its other claim to fame is the annual Henley-on-Todd Regatta held by the Todd River Yacht Club in a dry river bed! The highlight is a race between teams carrying boats that range from home-made 'yachts' to bath tubs, and I obtained membership by buying the T-shirt.

After looking around we drove out some thirty miles west to see a large rock crevasse called Standley Chasm. This is a deep narrow canyon caused by surging flood waters over thousands of years. It was in the Park that I got close up to my first live kangaroo, as until then the only ones I had seen had been run over at night.

Alice was a typical Outback town surrounded by low rocky hills, and relied mainly on tourism. It also had a fair sized Aboriginal population and we had noticed over the previous three days that they had become much more numerous. With their somewhat menacing features and jet black skin they looked quite frightening to our eyes, but I felt sorry for them as they seemed to have a pretty raw deal in life. Sadly many of them had succumbed to alcohol.

Calling at the Avis rental office next day I couldn't believe my luck as they needed a car delivered to Darwin. Perfect! Dave was heading back to Brisbane to finish his holiday so I thanked him for his company and we said cheerio. He really had been a

67. Giant termite mounds

great help and we had travelled half way across the Continent together. Then after picking up a Kiwi hitch-hiker I headed north at a steady seventy miles per hour in another Holden.

The Stuart Highway was mostly a good bitumen surface and just wide enough for two cars to pass each other. If you met a road train or truck you had to pull off on to the dirt, which sent up clouds of dust with flying stones, and broken windscreens were common. But on my journey other traffic was scarce, and what looked like a town on the map was usually a seedy cafe with a couple of petrol pumps. One such place, called Elliot, consisted of a small workshop with a partition separating the kitchen where the rest of the family were eating their evening meal.

After dropping my hiker friend at Tenant Creek, I drove up a side-track for a couple of miles just before dusk and climbed a tree in the hope of seeing a kangaroo. Except for the wind there wasn't a sound and nothing but bush to be seen in any direction. Neither were there any kangaroos. Anyone seeing me perched up there would surely have wondered what I was doing, but luckily nobody came along. After an expensive supper at a roadside cafe I drove on until 10.00 pm, and was rewarded by the sight of a baby 'roo hopping across the road in front of me. So at least I saw one in the wild. I pulled over for the night to sleep in the car, waking early and freezing cold as usual.

As the heater didn't work I quickly got going and was early enough to see a lovely sunrise. North of the town of Katherine the road became very twisty as it wound through tropical vegetation and the temperature rose higher. Huge earth termite mounds, some as high as twelve feet, were dotted amongst the trees. They were apparently built by magnetic termites and had the long axis of the mound facing almost exactly north/south.

Arriving in Darwin at lunch time, I had my first set-back as the Trans Australia Airlines office was uncertain about my onward charter flight to Kupang. They told me to check back later, so I drove around looking for accommodation, eventually settling on the YMCA which was very luxurious and modern, with its own swimming pool. Back at the airline office I was advised that the flight had been postponed for twenty four hours, but had a nasty feeling it could be for longer. Nothing was to be done, so having delivered the car, I walked back to the 'Y' for a good clean up and a beer, which improved matters.

An early phone call next morning to T.A.A. confirmed another twenty four hour flight delay so most of the day was spent lounging by the pool, reading, and doing some washing. To lighten my pack I posted some surplus clothes home, and was also roped into a keep fit class which nearly killed me. In the late afternoon I again went to the office and was told the flight was on for Sunday. So it was fingers crossed for September 24th and happy landings in Kupang! I hardly saw anything of Darwin, the capital of the Northern Territory, and in fact two years later at Christmas 1974, Cyclone Tracy decimated the city. Seventy percent of all buildings were destroyed and today it must look very different.

Sunday arrived and to my great relief all went as promised, so it was goodbye Australia. The T.A.A. bus delivered me to the airport and the turbo prop Viscount took off on the dot at 10.30 am.

Ten weeks was a relatively short time to gain a full impression of a country the size of Australia, as of course I hadn't seen it all by any means. The common belief at the time, especially abroad, was that it had a big future with plenty of opportunity, which has proved to be correct. On my way up to Darwin I came to realise what a huge open and empty country it was, the impression of size being even more obvious than in the USA, and the Outback was certainly more interesting than I expected. However I felt that there was relatively little to see in the way of major attractions such as Ayers Rock, and such huge distances between what there was, that it made hitch-hiking around as I had elsewhere rather impractical.

At that time the country seemed a cross between Britain and the USA, but with a definite lean towards the American way of doing things. But I couldn't imagine it ever becoming completely 'Americanised' because the people were so different, and indeed it still hasn't become a republic. My impression was that there was a sort of love/hate attitude towards America, many of whose ideas they were trying to imitate, but wouldn't admit to. The expected harassment for being a Pom only materialised on one occasion from a workmate, but often through the press and media the criticism of Britain was very scathing. There was a degree of truth in the old adage of the average Aussie having a chip on both shoulders.

Nowhere did I hear the expected very distinct Aussie accent either. To me there was hardly any difference from normal English in most cases, and Australian newscasters could have come straight from the BBC. However, trademark expressions such as 'Good on yer', 'She's right', and 'Fair dinkum' were widely used. New to me were 'Crook' meaning ill or broken, and 'Winj' meaning to complain. Political correctness as we know it today wasn't considered and foreigners were often referred to as 'Wogs' wherever they came from!

The Northern Territory was the only state where I came across the Aboriginal population or 'Abos' as they were termed. They were most certainly regarded as second class citizens and didn't appear to count for much at all, unlike the Maoris in New Zealand.

One of the biggest disappointments was undoubtedly the lack of kangaroos, mainly because they had been wiped out in most areas. The only obvious signs of their existence were the baby ones that had been run over at night. But according to the Kiwi hitch-hiker I picked up in Alice Springs, they were more prevalent in the Southwest of the country.

The drinking laws were more relaxed than in New Zealand and the days of the six o'clock swill were long gone. Beer or lager was ordered as a 'schooner' or a 'midi', the former being about a pint and the latter a half. A traffic rule whereby you must give way to anything coming in from your right, even if from a side road, was an oddity I had only previously encountered in France.

My favourite parts of the country were Cairns and the Great Barrier Reef, and my only real regret was not getting completely off the beaten track to visit a sheep or cattle station. Australia didn't make a great impression on me but I wouldn't have missed it, and was very thankful for all the personal luck I had there. I have to say that I was never tempted to stay. If I were to settle in the Southern Hemisphere New Zealand would definitely be my first choice. But by that time my overriding ambition was to complete my journey around the world.

Chapter Fifteen
Indonesia

After a smooth flight of just over two hours across the Timor Sea we touched down at Kupang to begin the next phase of my journey. What a shock! The airport consisted of one patchy grass landing strip and a wooden shed for customs etc. with the usual assortment of lethargic officials hanging around.

The island of Timor was split roughly in half, the northern section belonging to Portugal and the rest being Indonesian. Kupang, the capital of Indonesian Timor lay at the extreme western end of the island some six miles from the 'airport'. My plan was to work my way up through the Indonesian islands to Singapore by boat, and then on to Malaysia and Thailand. Only myself and a French chap called Pierre left the plane, which was going on to Bali, and after clearing customs without problems, we bargained for a taxi into town.

There were 480 rupiahs to the Australian dollar, and the hostel where we were dropped wanted 500 rupiahs a night, which we thought excessive. Kupang was not very big and we walked down the shabby main street with its various vendors, before finding a very ropey joint up some broken steps for 100 rupiahs. It was called 'Wisma Selam' and we had a dirty little room with two old bedsteads and mattresses over which they spread a semi-clean sheet. Welcome to the third world! It was rather a shaky start but we felt better after a couple of hours and for what amounted to ten pence a night one couldn't expect too much.

Three other blokes were staying there, two Australians, Jim Scammel and Jim Gillespie (the two Jims), and Ulrich Wild, an amusing Swiss. Later on we all went for a meal and arranged to

check out the shipping position next morning. The sun was still hot even at 6.00 pm and after dark the street vendors selling fruit, peanuts, cigarettes, and snacks from little wooden shacks did business by candle light and paraffin lamps. The people seemed pretty friendly

Friendly locals! Kupang, Timor

and many of them had red teeth from chewing betel nut. In addition to the women, many of the men also wore long multicoloured sarongs. I retired to bed happy and despite getting eaten by mosquitoes, felt that things were really moving in the right direction.

The market, Kupang

Boat building, Flores

Everything in Indonesia was very haphazard, as we found out next morning when calling at 'Pelni' the local shipping agents. Supposedly a boat was due in three days time, calling at Flores, the next island in the chain, but nothing was definite so we could but hope. The town was completely un-modernised with little tourist influence, and wandering around the dusty streets and the crude market place with its rickety wooden stalls was an eye-opener. A great variety of fruit was available and we spent some time there eating fried banana. Even large cockerels were for sale – tethered to heavy stones to prevent them from roaming. It was impossible to go anywhere without shouts of 'Hello Mistair', and if we stopped to buy something an interested crowd soon gathered to watch the bartering. At the sight of a camera a large bunch of kids would appear from nowhere, and loved having their picture taken even though they would never see the result. Our evening meal cost 125 rupiahs including coffee, so it was cheap living.

Partly to kill time due to the uncertainty over the boat, I checked for flights to Bali at the office of Zambrud, a local airline running DC3s, but they were expensive and I would miss seeing the islands in between. Then we were told the ship should be in next day.

Needless to say there was no sign of it next morning and with nothing complicated like a radio, the only way they could check was to send a man onto the roof with binoculars. Another day went by with mounting uncertainty and I began to doubt the wisdom of not flying on to Bali. If I got to Flores would I be stuck there indefinitely? To help pass the time we tried one of the small fishing boats in the harbour, but they wanted 1,000 rupiahs per head to take us, which we reckoned was too much and maybe too risky. Then came news that the ship was in and several people went to speak to the captain who was non-committal regarding passengers and prices.

Eventually things were settled and an Australian lad called

Russell and I, arranged to be dropped off at Larantuka on the eastern end of Flores. From there we would make our way to Ende further across the island where we were told that we could catch another boat to Bali. So, having bought our tickets we waited at the harbour for them to finish loading their main cargo of grain and cowhides, before finally sailing at 11.30 pm. The ship was a scruffy little tramp steamer called *Warni III*, and after loading they rigged up tarpaulins over the hatch covers to protect passengers from sun and spray. Fortunately the sea was flat calm and it felt good to be on the move again.

After watching the lights of Kupang pass to starboard I settled down amongst the locals and their belongings and slept quite well. I awoke feeling rather clammy and it soon got very hot, so we were glad of the covers. The only cool place was right up in the bow, and as we stood in the breeze watching the flying fish I was reminded of my days on the old *Montserrat*. Two large sharks swam lazily out of our path before we voyaged up a narrow passage between small islands to reach Larantuka.

Immediately I felt the place to be a big improvement on Kupang, being much more tidy, quiet, and completely devoid of any tourist facilities. The people gazed at us in amazement and a crowd of kids followed us everywhere calling out 'Hello Mistair'. Just out of town it became really primitive with huge palm trees towering over the inhabitants' simple thatched huts. On the beach there was a large wooden boat about forty feet in length, under construction, and it was fascinating to see how the individual planks were shaped. One end was jammed between rocks, and with the aid of steam from a fire, gradually bent over until a heavy rock could be placed on the other end to set the shape. The planks were then fixed to the internal frames with wooden pegs, no nails or screws being used. A framework over the boat, roofed with palm leaves, protected the workmen from the powerful sun. Dug-out canoes were plentiful together with small inter island boats with triangular lateen rigged sails.

Balinese temple

An offering to a 'god'

After haggling with our prospective Chinese driver, we found that it would cost us 4,000 rupiahs to get to Ende further along the coast. This, together with the uncertainty of getting a boat from there made us decide it wasn't worth it. So back on board we approached the first officer about staying on for the rest of the voyage up to Surabaya in Java. From there we could backtrack to Bali. We spent the evening nattering in his cabin, and thought we must have made a good impression when, to our delight, he agreed to reduce the fare by 850 rupiahs!

As the ship wasn't due to leave for twenty-four hours, I wandered off along the seashore next morning, and it was very peaceful when I finally escaped the kids. Originally colonised by the Portugese – who named it Flores ('flowers') for its lush fragrant forests – the water's edge was quite rocky as it's volcanic by nature. The western end of the island is home to the fearsome looking Komodo dragons, the world's largest living species of lizard, which grow up to ten feet long, and which will attack humans.

I swam and lazed in the sun before meeting two boys fishing with homemade spear guns, who just had to have their photo taken. As soon as the camera came out, a passing water carrier rushed up to be included as well. To these people I was the richest man in the world, owning a watch *and* a camera. Later I drank coconut milk with some locals who were fascinated by my Australian red towel sun hat. Giggling girls stood in the background and when one was offered I had to refuse as politely as possible! Judging by their interest in me it seemed as though they had never seen a white man before, and I began to feel like Captain Cook or another early explorer, especially as all communication was in sign language.

Russell suddenly appeared to say the ship was sailing at 4.00 pm so we rushed back – but not before having to drink more coconut milk with an insistent family – and so just made it with a few minutes to spare. The sun was hidden by the huge volcano that towers over the village as we headed away to the north of the island, and I was very fortunate to have had the chance to visit somewhere seen by relatively few tourists, even today.

After a very uncomfortable night squashed between the locals, and suffering from ear ache, I was concerned when the ship came to a halt about 9.00 am. This was apparently caused by a faulty propeller shaft and it was a relief to get going again before too long. As the staple diet on the ship was white rice and fish, which I don't eat, I was after all glad of my large bag of muesli.

Another rough night with a rising wind ensued as we came out of the lee of Flores, and a load of water sloshing across my face woke me. Everyone became gradually more soaked, before the engine stopped and we lay drifting for four hours. I was glad of John's sleeping bag cover which kept most of the water off me but I had horrible visions of being shipwrecked. The wind finally died with daylight, but at about 9.00 am the engine stopped again for an hour. Then towards evening, as we came out of the shelter of the island of Sumbawa, the wind rose once more and the crew rigged up a tarpaulin to try and keep the water off us.

By morning the ship was rolling all over the place, which it continued to do for the rest of our third day at sea. At least it was bright and sunny but there was not much to do except play cards, chess, or read. Living conditions were very cramped and everyone looked forward to reaching Surabaya. A school of dolphins followed the ship for a while in the evening, and as I wrote my daily diary entry the sea got up again to herald another rough night. And so it proved with everyone getting wet and praying there would be no more breakdowns. Thank heavens there weren't.

But by the time we entered Surabaya harbour next day we were enveloped in a really muggy heat, and extremely glad when the ferry landed us ashore at last. It was a bustling and very noisy place, being the main port and city at the eastern end of the island of Java. Transport was either by 'betjak' or smoky little three-wheeled Vespa taxis. The betjak was a pedal tricycle in which the passenger sat in front of the driver, usually with a sun shade to protect him. Russell and I took a Vespa to the bus depot and booked our tickets on an overnight bus that would take us via a ferry to the island of Bali. This accomplished, we treated ourselves to a hearty meal – a marvellous indulgence after the rice and muesli I had been living on for the past few days.

The bus was waiting when we returned much later and away we went into the night with a real nutcase of a driver at the controls. A brief early morning ferry ride then took us across the short strait to the island, before the nerve-racking journey continued for the last seventy miles to Denpasar, the capital.

Everything we had heard about Bali was true! Quaint little thatched-roofed temples dotted our route, nestled amongst most lush green vegetation. We had travelled past immaculate terraced paddy fields, with oxen pulling ploughs controlled by men up to their knees in mud wearing coolie hats; just as we had imagined. Every kind of fruit appeared to be available and although the people were poor I had the impression that a tremendous amount of care and attention went into everything they did. Denpasar certainly did not have the scruffy and unkempt look of Kupang.

We had heard that Kuta Beach a few miles further on the southern tip of the island was the place to make for, and we soon found a clean little 'losmon', or guesthouse there. Losmon 'Indra' was ideally situated just off the beach among palm trees and exotic plants. Contrary to our expectations, food was incredibly cheap. A huge bowl of fruit salad was 25 rupiahs and it was possible to live like a king for about 10 US dollars (4 pounds) a week. The beach was a long sweep of sand fringed by coconut palms, and having had an exhilarating swim in the surf that afternoon I was thrilled with it all. Once again life seemed too good to be true.

After much haggling Russ and I hired a little Honda motorbike next morning and buzzed around on it checking out our surroundings. It was great to be mobile again and with the exception of one Western standard hotel everything was very rustic and unspoiled. Others from Kupang were also staying at our losmon so it was good to meet up again. That evening we all went to watch a musical ceremony at a small temple. Bali had its own version of the Hindu religion, whereas the rest of Indonesia was mainly Muslim. The gamelan band consisted of about thirty-five men playing a variety of percussion type instruments, which produced a most uncanny jangling sound, unlike anything we had heard before.

Our next objective was Mount Batur, a large active volcano in the centre of the island, whose crater enclosed a lake with a perimeter of about twelve miles, surrounding a smaller recently active volcano. It made for an impressive view, and after lunch at a little place right on the lake's edge we had a wonderful ride up to the north coast, before heading east along a terrible unmade track. It was a great laugh until we both came off the bike after dark on a bend with loose gravel. My right knee was gashed to the bone and it hurt like merry hell. Eventually we were directed to a doctor's house, where he bandaged us up and kindly gave us supper with his family. A trip to the hospital in Denpasar was necessary next morning where they poured all sorts of jollop on my knee before stitching up the wound. The local anaesthetic they gave me was so local I could feel everything they did, and was in absolute agony for the rest of the day.

Our mornings always began with two or three Balinese appearing at the losmon trying to sell us batik paintings, wood carvings, sarongs, or other goods. Batik is the ancient art of decorating cloth using wax and dye, and usually depicted their Hindu gods or mythical creatures. After bargaining successfully or otherwise we would drift down the road to one of the little bamboo 'restaurants' for breakfast, which usually consisted of a large fruit drink and salad. The rest of the day would be spent on the beach or riding the bike. In the evenings we would sample the cuisine of another cafe and linger over our supper before retiring fairly early. Somebody had a radio cassette recorder so we could listen to music tapes or read, which all made for wonderfully relaxing times.

One morning a funeral procession came past the losmon consisting mainly of women bearing gifts on their heads for the departed person. In Bali the procedure is most unusual in that the burial takes place and the grave is then fenced off with bamboo. After some weeks the body is exhumed and cremated in accordance with their brand of Hinduism.

My twenty-seventh birthday on October 11th 1972 will be remembered largely as the day I got properly stoned! Since trying marijuana for the first time in Jamaica, I had smoked it on a number of occasions without any real effect, and rather wondered what all the fuss was about. But when Russell produced some stuff he'd bought locally, we lit up and suddenly it all happened! It was a pleasant, very relaxing, almost soporific experience but caused us to go into fits of laughter at the most ridiculous things. In addition it seemed to promote pangs of hunger which we called 'the munchies', so that we would later potter down to one of the little snack bars to enjoy a rich fruit salad. I'm not sure that long-term use could be good for one, and once back home I never tried the stuff again – just viewing it as an amusing part of the travelling experience. But it certainly took my mind off my knee.

Of all the people I never expected to see again I thought Barbara, the van girl, from New Zealand the least likely. But as I walked back after breakfast one morning who should come cycling along the road but her. She didn't recognize me at first but we then had a long chat about those days in the South Island, and she subsequently made it to the UK and stayed with my family.

My leg was fairly swollen and hurt if I stood for long, so a couple of trips to the hospital were necessary to have the bandages changed. Because of the humidity the wound was slow to heal and I had to be careful to keep it dry, which meant no swimming.

But thankfully I was still able to use the bike and continued to explore the island. I spent one memorable day riding along the south coast through typical Balinese scenery and small thatched roofed villages, which all had their own little temple. There were reputedly ten thousand on the island and I stopped at one to watch a religious ceremony, before going on through groves of coconut palms and past peasants toiling in the paddy fields with their oxen. It was incredibly beautiful, heightened by the sun sparkling off the sea, and that evening we watched a rehearsal of the colourful Monkey Dance at a local temple, to end a magical day.

In their religion the monkey is sacred, and scattered around Bali were many monkey temples. Giving food to a monkey amounted to making an offering to the god of all monkeys, which we were careful to do. A short way down the coast, perched on the cliffs, was a particularly enchanting monkey temple which we would visit to smoke a joint while watching a blood-red sun drop slowly below the horizon. It was a memorable and entrancing part of my Bali experience.

All too soon the day came to move on, and I went into Denpasar to collect my knee prescription and buy a bus ticket back over to Java. Then after packing my kit and a late lunch, Russell, Phil, and I wished each other all the best, and I caught the 4.00 pm bus, complete with another lunatic driver, up to the ferry at Gilimanuk. So it was goodbye to Bali – a truly fascinating place, which was at that time in the process of being 'discovered'. I felt certain that it wouldn't be so cheap or unspoilt for very much longer and have never returned, preferring to remember it as it was.

The bus pulled into Surabaya at 3.00 am and dropped me off at the railway station, which opened an hour later. After a scramble to get a seat we set off at 5.00 am, travelling westwards across the main island of Java. The flat countryside consisted mostly of paddy fields and having stopped at a few minor stations we reached the larger town of Yogyakarta, or 'Jogja' as it was known. It resembled Surabaya but was much less noisy due to the high number of betjaks and bicycles in use. Here I planned to stop for a couple of nights before catching the onward train up to Jakarta. An Australian fellow traveller knew 'the' place to stay. It was a sleazy dive called The Aziatic and was only a slight improvement on Wisma Selam in Kupang, but feeling bushed we sacked out for a while. Later we took a stroll around town and I'm amazed at this distance in time to read in my diary that we tried to find the local dance. What that was all about I don't know but it was probably a good job we were unsuccessful.

However, the main reason for staying was to visit the Water Castle complex at Taman Sari which I had heard about. This once served as a pleasure park of palaces, pools, and waterways for the Sultan and his courtiers. The architect of this elaborate retreat, built a couple of hundred years earlier, was Portugese, and it was said that on its completion the Sultan had him executed to keep his hidden pleasure rooms secret. Everything gradually fell into disrepair and an earthquake in 1865 left much of it in ruins. Nevertheless there was enough to see to make the visit worthwhile, but by midday it was so hot I had a couple of iced drinks and lay on my bed for most of the afternoon.

My Aussie pal had moved out so I had to take a single room in the annexe over the road, and my initial impression of quietness proved false, when people started letting bangers off for most of the night. What with that and the heat, sleep was elusive.

So I was glad to board the 11.00 am train for Jakarta next morning, although this was the start of a most uncomfortable twelve hour journey. It was very crowded, with only hard wooden slatted seats and adding to the discomfort was an oven-like heat. We travelled past more paddy fields before the terrain became increasingly mountainous and the train began to climb. Eventually the country flattened out and gave way to a vista of fields with peasants toiling away under the merciless sun. The heat on board was incredible in spite of the air conditioning and waiters serving iced drinks – at extortionate prices, needless to say. After dark there began a series of frustrating stops for no apparent reason but at last we pulled into Jakarta and I staggered off the train with the ultimate in numb bums! When I finally located the Youth Hostel it was full so I had to sleep on the floor, and dozed off to the sound of humming mosquitoes.

Jakarta was a large city of some six million inhabitants and has been the capital of Indonesia since the country's independence from Dutch administration in 1945. The centre was very modern with numerous high rise office blocks and hotels, and the familiar betjaks looked rather out of place. Motor scooters buzzed in and out of the traffic, loaded with families, radios, baskets of chickens, and sometimes even a pet dog.

The next stage of my journey involved getting up to Palembang on the neighbouring island of Sumatra, which lies across the Sunda Straight from Java. From there I planned to get a ship to Singapore. An American bloke from the hostel had the same intention so together we checked the train times to the ferry at Merak. There was a train leaving very early next morning, and after buying my ticket I called at the British Consulate and sat in the reading room, cooling off and catching up on the news.

Our alarm went at 4.15 am and after some misunderstanding with our betjak driver we finally reached the right station. The train was mainly for emigrants who it seemed were being forcibly moved to Sumatra. Many of them had been living under railway wagons and were a sad and pathetic sight. The journey took four hours and the ferry across the Straight left promptly on our arrival.

However the crossing, past many small islands, took a further six hours and was much longer than expected. The Sunda Straight was the scene of a fierce Second World War naval battle when two allied cruisers engaged a much larger Japanese force. Both were sunk, but not before inflicting heavy damage on the enemy.

We spent most of the voyage in the VIP room trying to avoid the incredible humidity, which even had the locals suffering. On arrival at Pandjing we found a room for the night as we were both too tired to go on further that day.

Next morning at 7.00 am we boarded the train for Palembang. As usual it was jam-packed and a Chinese woman opposite me had a dozen hens tied together under her seat. People sat with handkerchiefs over their mouths and noses to keep out the dust and smells, and the iced drink sellers continued to do a roaring trade. Amid all the chaos, six inspectors came round to check our tickets, one armed with a sub-machine gun.

It was another twelve hour journey and the Sumatran scenery was completely different from Java. The coconut palms had disappeared, and the vegetation in a very flat landscape looked almost European. Most surprisingly there were even peat bogs in places. We passed through the occasional village and it was noticeable that although made of bamboo, many houses had tiled roofs instead of the usual thatch. Some were raised up on stilts. Now and then the train stopped at a small station and we passengers could alight to stretch our legs. On these occasions you had to be careful not to leave your pack unattended for too long, as pilfering was an ever present worry. It was helpful to travel with someone else, as you could keep an eye on each other's kit.

We arrived in Palembang feeling pretty grotty and ran into an American couple I had spoken to in Jakarta. Gary and Betty-Jo had been trying unsuccessfully all day to get tickets on a Pelni Lines ship leaving for Singapore that night. This was disappointing news, but after a shower we felt better and went for a meal and a wander around.

A day of suspense followed. We heard of a cargo ship supposedly going to Singapore and went to the agents who confirmed this to be the case. 'Yes it's leaving tomorrow night and yes it can take two passengers for 7,500 rupiahs each with a cabin'. But they wouldn't take a deposit or our names. 'Just come round in the morning' we were told, which was typically vague. The rest of the day was spent wandering about pretending not to hear the shouts of 'Hello Mistair – where are you going'? 'Where are you from?' etc.etc.

Palembang was a crowded unattractive city mainly comprised of squalid slums. Hanging over the city and the river was an oppressive low mist and streams of raw sewage ran everywhere. This left me wondering about the disease rate, and from a hygiene viewpoint it's a wonder we didn't get food poisoning. In the middle of all this filth, needless to say, was an immaculate white mosque with a tall slender tower. No shortage of money there! We watched a man sitting cross-legged doing some sort of trick with a snake, but he seemed to take exception to our presence, so after giving him a variety of hand signals we wandered on. Later I bumped into the two Jims and Ulrich from Kupang who had just been to see a film. It was great to meet them again but somewhere in the cinema Jim Scammel had been relieved of his wallet containing 6,000 rupiahs, which underlined the need for constant vigilance.

Tuesday October 24th and our luck was in. The ship was indeed sailing that night and together with the others we were able to buy tickets, which was great news as I didn't feel like hanging around Palembang for another week. Apparently the immigration authorities had told the company that they must take all seven of us. It was a pleasant change to have officialdom assisting my progress.

After fixing all the details, I strolled around town and the market place, taking a few photos, before having a hilarious celebration lunch with the two Jims and Ulrich. Then it was down to the wharf to clear customs and board the ship which was moored in mid-stream. The Musi River was wide and brown with dozens of sampans and other wooden craft moored along its banks. You certainly wouldn't have wanted to fall in

it. Our ship, the *Bintang Sumudra 1* (*Ocean Star 1*) was a bit
of an old tub but as we had a cabin it was a big improvement
on the *Warni*. The evening meal of, you guessed it, more rice
was eaten in the cramped wardroom under the stern gaze of
President Suharto's portrait.

I went to sleep before we sailed at 11.00 pm but was awoken
shortly after 2.00 am to find the ship heading straight for the
river bank! They slammed it into reverse just in time to avoid a
collision, but then decided to drop anchor in mid-stream and
wait for daylight and the tide to turn. We were under way again
at 11.00 am next morning and moved slowly down river past
isolated small villages with thatched huts and fishing sampans.
Gary the American had a guitar and everyone had to sing a
song. My choice was 'Moon River' which seemed particularly
appropriate, although Andy Williams wouldn't have lost any
sleep over my performance – unless he was in the next room.
The pilot was dropped off in mid-afternoon and at last the mist
cleared as we entered the river mouth and the open sea. So as we
dodged past several moored tankers and changed up to cruising
speed, it was farewell to Indonesia.

Some of the things that lodged in my memory were the boys
rolling water barrels along the streets in Kupang, the bicycle
repair stations and betjak taxis, and the primitive toilets and
splash baths. A proper shower was a luxury. Generally speaking
the people were very friendly, although less so in Sumatra, and
travel, albeit tiring, wasn't too much of a hassle. Bali was the
jewel in the crown as far as I was concerned and would have been
the only place I could safely recommend. The rest of Indonesia
though, was an interesting experience and I was certainly glad I
travelled through it on my way up to Singapore. In all it had cost
me about 140 US dollars (about £60) to get from Darwin, which
I thought good value and well worth the effort.

Sunset over the monkey temple

Rail halt, Kotabumi, Sumatra

Palembang, Sumatra

Ride 'em, cowboy! R.F. and Ulrich, Tiger Balm Gardens, Singapore

Chapter Sixteen
Northward and a Big Scare
(Singapore, Malaysia, and Thailand)

Estimates for our arrival time in Singapore on the second day of the voyage kept changing. First it was 3.00 pm, then 5.00 pm, and the next guess from the engineer was 8.00 pm that evening. Somewhere along the way we crossed back into the Northern Hemisphere, and the sun shone as we steamed on through an emerald green sea past numerous small islands. I watched them slide by from on top of the bridge before joining the others in a frantic clean-up session as we neared our destination; the idea being to present ourselves in the best possible light to the authorities. Finally we dropped anchor in the quarantine area at 5.30 pm to await the immigration officers. Luckily everything was in order and we moored in our berth after dark amongst dozens of other ships. Singapore looked most spectacular as we went ashore, with its great variety of brightly illuminated buildings.

Ulrich and I, plus the two Jims, booked in at a cheap hotel, and after dumping our kit found a good restaurant. Here we unashamedly stuffed ourselves to the limit with wine and all the trimmings. I had mushroom soup followed by a mouth-watering mixed grill, then bananas in rum, and after the incessant rice of previous weeks it was just the best meal ever. We retired to bed feeling comfortably bloated!

First stop for us all next morning was the main post office where I collected mail from my parents, Lesley, and a fellow inmate from Mountain Road, Auckland. The old British influence was still evident, and in contrast to Indonesia, Singapore was immaculately clean and tidy. There was a fine of 500 dollars for littering which was obviously an effective deterrent. English

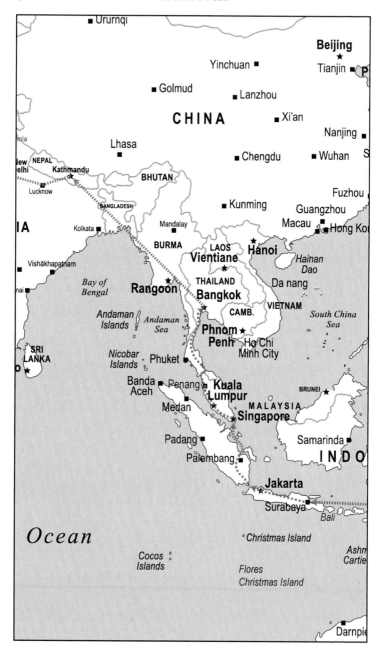

was the widely spoken official language so getting around was no problem. My knee was still sore, and I had it dressed by an elderly Chinese pharmacist who told some harrowing tales of life in Singapore under the Japanese occupation during the Second World War.

The majority of people looked very affluent and exotic cars, especially Mercedes, were numerous. Singapore's importance as a trading hub was emphasised by the solid mass of shipping stretching across the horizon and the constant stream of barges loading and unloading them. Street names were mostly English and I spent several hours in shops on Orchard Road checking duty free prices on camera lenses and portable radio/tape recorders. Eventually I rather guiltily splashed out 116 US dollars on a wide angle lens and a radio cassette recorder, but it caused great hilarity when I recorded our conversation back at the hotel. My voice sounded very different on tape although I hadn't lost my English accent as I had imagined.

We all spent a day at the botanical gardens and later a large bird park on the western end of the island. Both were gorgeous places and even away from the city, everywhere was beautifully kept. It would be a model today for this country.

Another fascinating attraction was the Tiger Balm Gardens, built by two brothers in the 1920s who became millionaires from the manufacture of Tiger Balm ointment. These consisted mostly of mythical Chinese figures and animals, and acted as a substitute for a normal zoo, which Singapore didn't possess in those days. Further entertainment was provided when I was given two complimentary cinema tickets to the film *Soldier Blue*, by a man from Warner Brothers whom I chatted to at a bus stop. As you do!

Prior to moving on again, I rushed around one morning, posting off all my cards, letters, and a Balinese painting, in addition to numerous other small jobs. The lads were staying on awhile so I regretfully took my leave of them, for they had been great company, and I felt slightly apprehensive as I caught the train to Kuala Lumpur at 8.00 a.m. on Tuesday, October 31st. Then after clearing Malaysian customs at the station with no problems we crossed the Johor Causeway to reach the mainland.

Surprisingly, the overall neatness of Singapore continued on into Malaysia, and the train was a big improvement over those of Indonesia. We travelled at quite a speed past paddy fields and through rubber plantations. The trees all had the bark missing for three feet or so from the ground, and each had a cup tied on to the trunk collecting the latex. The sight of Kuala Lumpur on our arrival was quite a shock – I wasn't expecting to see such a huge modern city with so many gleaming skyscrapers. But exploration had to wait as a heavy rainstorm began shortly afterwards and I had to take a taxi to the Youth Hostel.

Then as now, Kuala Lumpur was the capital of the Malaysian Federation, and as I discovered on my wanderings next day, was an extraordinary mix of modern glitz and ornate colonial style buildings. In particular the Sultan Abdul Samad Building, railway station, and central mosque, were all built with most ornate domes and turrets. The former is the city's main historical landmark, built in the late 19th century, and is among KL's earliest Moorish style buildings, and absolutely palatial. It seemed to have no use other than as a spectacular tourist attraction and was well worth a visit. I've seen nothing like it before or since. The weather held good so I walked a fair distance and also visited the city's most interesting war memorial and museum. The modern Parliament building was set in beautiful parkland and the whole place left me with an impression of solid efficiency; definitely a city on the way up. There were only three of us staying at the hostel so I had supper alone at a local Chinese restaurant where everyone shouted at the top of their voices.

I could easily have stayed longer but needed to keep moving, and my next objective was Penang Island lying off the northwest coast some two hundred miles further up the Malaysian peninsular. I decided to try hitching there from KL, a decision that almost caused me to abandon the journey. Setting off early next morning it didn't take long to get my first lift and we made good progress up the main road north. At that time it was what we would today term a 'B' road, and narrowed in places where it passed through quite dense forest. My second lift was in a Mercedes truck which had a wooden cab with no doors, and after throwing my pack into the back I climbed up between the Chinese driver and his mate, who spoke no English.

We followed the road for some miles before suddenly pulling off it and bumping down a jungle track. I assumed that they were probably dropping something off at a village, but before we had gone very far the driver pulled up in a small clearing. A slow smile came over his face which I can still picture today, and we sat there for about twenty seconds – although it seemed far longer. I really thought that it was all over for me. I was completely alone; no-one knew where I was, and wearing a money belt containing several hundred dollars. There was a knife in my pack but it was well out of reach, and in any case I was stuck between the two of them so couldn't jump out. After what seemed like an age they both climbed down and went to urinate in the bushes. There was no one about and I heard them talking in low voices but obviously couldn't understand what they were saying. I sat in a cold sweat until having finished they returned and we set off again, passing through a couple of villages with their wooden huts built on stilts. At neither of these did we stop, and eventually rejoined the main road where, to my huge relief, after a few miles they dropped me off.

I've been over the incident in my mind many times and am still puzzled by it all. Whether they considered robbing me, or worse, I will never know. Had they just needed a 'pit stop' they could have chosen any number of places on the main road as there was relatively little traffic on it. In all the thousands of miles travelled it was my biggest scare so far, and together with negative reports I'd heard of Thailand and India, made me consider flying straight home.

Thankfully my other lifts were uneventful, and we passed through numerous rubber plantations which gave way to green plains scattered with limestone outcrops hundreds of feet high, before reaching the city of Ipoh. This had apparently changed little since its colonial heyday as a tin mining centre, with striking landmarks such as the Anglo-Moorish railway station, similar to that in KL. It rained hard later as I boarded the ferry from the quaintly named town of Butterworth, for the twenty minute crossing to the island's capital George Town, and arrived, soaked, at the Youth Hostel about 6.00 pm.

The thought of flying home was still in my mind next morning as I took the funicular railway which rose 2,300 feet to the top of Penang Hill, in the centre of the 108-square-mile island. The cool air up there was very pleasant and helped to restore my equilibrium, though it was impossible to see any great distance because of the heat haze. But I had a good lunch there and as Churchill said 'Things always look better after lunch' – albeit his lunches tended to be more liquid. Having descended, I went on to view Fort Cornwallis, built some two hundred years previously by the British East India Company, where old cannon still stood facing out to sea.

George Town was a mix of old colonial buildings and genuine Chinatown, with busy markets, strange medicinal shops, and twenty-four hour food stalls. These were 'no-frills' places providing a mix of Malay, Indian, and Chinese cuisine usually served on a large banana leaf and eaten standing at the roadside. The familiar betjak tricycle taxis weaved in and out of the traffic and were very handy for getting about cheaply. That evening the most terrific thunder and lightning storm arrived, with torrents of heavy rain, as a reminder that it was monsoon season.

The local bus took me along the north coast next day to find some superb beaches. White sand, thatched huts, and waving

Exotic Kuala Lumpur railway station

Betjak taxis, Penang

79. The Snake Temple, Penang

80. Thai school children, Bangkok

coconut palms appealed to me as much as ever, and although overcast it was still hot. Lying on the beach I was quite burned but dipping into the beautifully warm Indian Ocean was wonderful.

I later visited the Chinese Snake Temple, so called because it was home to a species of Pit Viper that lay curled around joss stick stands and ornamental prayer tables. They were believed to be the disciples of the God 'Chor Soo Kong', and are so named from a pit organ between their eyes which see in infrared and can detect their prey's heat signature in complete darkness. Their venom is extremely powerful and usually lethal. Shaking a bit I posed for a photo with one around my neck while holding another in my hands, as the keeper explained that their fangs had been removed but could re-grow! They felt very cold to the touch and I was glad enough when he'd taken the photo and removed them.

That day, November 4th, was the start of the Indian New Year and was the cause of much celebrating in their homes by the Indian community. Throughout Malaysia the population was divided into Indians, Straits Chinese, Malays, and a smaller number of Eurasians.

I had intended to take the 7.00 am train next morning from Butterworth on to Thailand, but missed it, as I overslept. However, thanks to a cancellation I got a seat on the 11.00 am bus and we travelled past more paddy fields and rubber plantations up to the border. Just as we were waiting to cross through it, two armoured cars appeared. Communist guerrillas had apparently been active in the area, but after an hour's wait we continued and went through Thai customs without problems. In fact they went through everyone's bags except mine. Then came the crunch! Some miles further on there was a roadblock. Before I knew it two customs officers were on the roof emptying my pack, but were not looking through any other luggage. They hauled me out when they found the radio and with some difficulty I eventually persuaded them that it wasn't new. I then had a go at them for emptying my pack without calling me out first, which rather took them by surprise.

Without further ado we reached Hat Yai, the first town across the border, and as it didn't look a very interesting place, I decided to catch the overnight train up to Bangkok. The journey turned out better than expected as the train was up to Malaysian standards and I slept quite well. Drizzling rain greeted us next morning, reminding me of childhood holidays in North Wales, and we travelled all day through rather drab scenery. In fact my impression of that part of Thailand was that it was half under water. In places people were chest deep ferreting around with what I presumed to be some sort of crop, but looking unlike normal rice paddy fields.

We made numerous stops at little country stations with neatly trimmed hedges, and elaborately painted temples with steep red roofs brightened the flat landscape. The food and drink sellers did a good trade even though my carriage was fairly empty, and as we neared Bangkok at 4.00 pm my suspicions about the friendly Thai seaman who'd bought me breakfast were confirmed. With no beating about the bush he gave me his address and asked if I would sleep with him that night! I politely declined saying I had to meet friends and made a hasty exit. 'Another time perhaps'? It was a sad fact but seemed the general rule in that part of the world that if someone was unusually friendly – watch out! They wanted money, sex, or both, and this was confirmed by other travellers with similar stories.

On arrival I was confronted for the first time by signs in a language with no recognisable letters. This was Thai script, a series of squiggly lines with letters looking as if they were upside down, which made finding your way around very tricky. So I had some difficulty locating the Youth Hostel as few people spoke English, until a Buddhist monk put me on the right bus. I then had to take a barge across the Chao Phraya River, the city's main waterway. As all the taxis charged exorbitant prices I eventually

managed to get the rest of the way on another bus. Feeling like
Dr Livingstone, I crept under a mosquito net for the first time
that night, as the wretched creatures were particularly active.

The hostel sat in the grounds of the modern Chulalongkorn
University and the students' respect for their teachers was most
noticeable. When passing them the boys stopped to bow and the
girls gave a little curtsy with their hands in the prayer position.
Luckily there was an Aussie there who knew his way about town,
and having caught the right bus into the city, I bought a map
from the Tourist Office and began to get my bearings. Most of
the day was spent collecting post and sorting out my affairs. My
next destination was Nepal, and because the adjoining country
of Burma was closed to tourists, it was necessary to fly there.
An airline ticket to Kathmandu cost 107 US dollars, using my
student card reduction, so I booked the flight for five days' time.

A letter from my parents caused me some concern as they
had no news of my suitcase sent from Sydney containing all my
photos, although the parcel of clothes posted from Darwin had
arrived. Thankfully it did eventually turn up.

As it is today, Thailand was a monarchy and the people were
strict Buddhists, every boy having to spend a period as a trainee
monk. They were to be seen everywhere with their shaven heads
and bright yellow robes. Many men grew a disgustingly long
nail, usually about four inches in length on a finger of either
one, or both hands. Apparently this was a form of snobbishness
indicating that they were above doing any kind of manual work.
They looked rather effeminate to me, although they didn't go
around holding hands so much as in Indonesia, where it was very
common practice and considered quite normal.

As I was the hostel's only inmate on my second night I
decided to move to a hotel recommended as nearer the centre –
and livelier. It certainly was! The Thai Song Greet (known as the
TSG) turned out to be a seedy hotel-cum-brothel, and perhaps
fortunately was full. So I found a room in a scruffy Chinese run

joint nearby for twenty baht a night; the baht being the Thai unit of currency, which divided into 100 stang. Twenty baht equalled one US dollar so although rather noisy, it was cheap and fitted the bill. A large illuminated Pepsi Cola sign hung precariously from the front wall so I christened my new digs 'The Pepsi'. Returning later after a rainstorm I found everything soaked, as the roof leaked. Uttering profuse apologies the manager and his assistant moved the bed around and fixed me up with dry sheets, but the roof probably still leaks to this day. I dined at the TSG every night as they had a menu in English, but there were no kindred spirits about and I really missed the company of the Jims and Ulrich.

The next three days were spent on foot wandering around the city sightseeing. I walked down one of the main canals which had hundreds of wooden sampans crammed along its banks. Whole families lived permanently aboard these craft and made their living selling market produce to passers-by.

The Thai word for temple is 'wat' and there were some three hundred of them scattered among the modern city buildings, so I could only try and see a few of the most prominent. The majority of these 'wats' paid homage to the God Buddha, and the deity was depicted in gold, jade, and emerald to give just three examples. The marble temple housed a huge gold Buddha about twelve feet high – an incredible sight and no doubt a major security headache for the authorities. In addition to these was the temple of the reclining Buddha, built on the orders of the King a hundred years previously. The figure was about sixty feet long and covered in gold leaf, but I thought the temple of the jade Buddha the most impressive 'wat' of all, with the most amazingly intricate workmanship imaginable. It was difficult to describe them in words and only a visit can really do these temples justice.

The Royal Palace was another spectacular building, which certainly put Buckingham Palace to shame, but I was not allowed in to the grounds as I wasn't wearing a jacket and tie. I also tried

The gold Buddha, Bangkok

The floating market, Bangkok

83. Thai monk

to see the Royal Barges but was very disappointed to be told that they were locked away in a concrete pen.

Many of the side streets were full of small companies of which a particular trade would fill their street. For example all coffin manufacturers occupied one street, then you turned a corner and they were making neon signs. The next street would be for car part stockists, and so on. Business must have been very competitive for them all.

I was up at 6.15 one morning as I wanted to take an early ride up-river, and was in time to see the monks begging for their daily ration of rice from the devout. They carried a tin around their waist into which all donations were placed, but it was impossible to know if this was just a ritual or if they really ate all their bounty.

It was a bright morning and I went miles on one of the speedy passenger launches which were powered by a car engine, with a long propeller shaft protruding from the stern. People used these craft for their daily commute to work as they zipped along at about twenty knots, and the river was the main artery for a large variety of traffic. The price was a bargain one baht but they charged me two for the return journey! At lunch time it was encouraging to hear good reports of Nepal from three Aussies I met.

Something I particularly wanted to see was the infamous bridge on the River Kwai some eighty miles to the west, so I was up early again to catch the 8.00 am train. I was enjoying Bangkok but it was very pleasant to escape the noise, crowded buses, and exhaust fumes for the day.

The existing bridge lies slightly upstream from the original wooden structure depicted in the film, of which nothing remains, and is really quite unexceptional. Both were heavily bombed by allied planes and the two middle spans of the new bridge had obviously been replaced. It felt rather eerie walking across it, knowing that it was part of the infamous 'Death Railway', but

I was most interested to see it and examined an original train and a converted diesel lorry that were used on the line. Some nine thousand allied POWs died during its construction, and appropriately there is a well tended war cemetery in the nearby town of Kanchanaburi. There is also a Japanese monument to the dead but I was incensed to read that the prisoners died of 'illness'. There was no mention of the sheer brutality and starvation they suffered, which struck me as an insult to visitors' intelligence. After spending three hours around the bridge, cemetery, and town, I caught the return train to complete a most worthwhile visit. Frankly I admit to finding it as interesting as most of the temples, but I probably differed from the average tourist in that respect.

On my last morning I rose early as I wanted to get a good photo of a monk, which was difficult, as they were not willing subjects. Having finally achieved this, I packed my kit before departing the Pepsi and catching the bus to the airport. There were no delays so the Thai International Boeing 707 lifted smoothly off the runway on time, and Bangkok was lost beneath the clouds.

Chapter Seventeen
Nepal

Later we made a half-hour stop in Calcutta to offload the noisy Indian contingent, and had to remain aboard during the process. Two very tatty Indian soldiers stood guard at the bottom of the steps to ensure we did so. The Kathmandu Lodge had been recommended as a suitable place to stay, so having got clear of officialdom at the airport I made my way there. Although very basic it was conveniently neither full nor a brothel! It even boasted a hot shower – sometimes.

Tourism to the Kingdom of Nepal had only begun quite recently because until 1951 the country had been closed to foreigners. It was after the successful Everest expedition of 1953 that restrictions were gradually relaxed and visitors began to arrive, albeit in very limited numbers. These only really increased in the mid sixties with the advent of the 'Hippie Trail', when young people seeking enlightenment began to make the overland journey from Europe that I had originally planned. The Russian invasion of Afghanistan in 1979 effectively closed this route.

The city of Kathmandu lies in a green oval-shaped valley at the junction of the sacred Bagmati River and its tributary Bishnumati, and is surrounded by small hills, and fields of wheat, corn, rice, and jute. In the distance stretched the magnificent silver peaks of the Himalayan mountain range, with Everest or Sagarmatha, to give it its native name, visible on a clear day. On top of one hill sat a monkey temple emphasising that religion in Nepal was a complicated and intricate combination of Hinduism, Buddhism, and other beliefs. Numerous temples with their distinctive tiered pagoda roofs were prominent, and just off Durbar Square was the

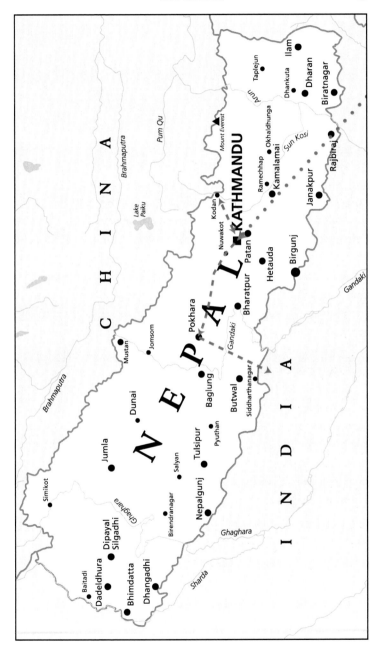

Abode of the Living Goddess with its profusely carved wooden balconies and windows. Visitors could enter the courtyard to look up into the window of the Goddess who would appear for those requesting to see her, but no photography was allowed. The Nepalese year was an unending cycle of festivals and the various daily rituals and religious practices indulged in by the people were a constant source of interest, and sometimes amusement, to the visitor.

My first impressions of the country were favourable, and although everything was very primitive and shabby, it displayed a certain charm. Many of the buildings had a half finished look, as though the workers had departed at the end of the day and never returned. The Nepalese people were delightfully friendly and in contrast with some other countries, one could walk around without being shouted at or bothered at all. I attracted no special attention and felt completely accepted, rather than some kind of novelty. The population consisted of a variety of races and tribes, with the Newars, Brahmans, and Chettriyas occupying the central region. Men were usually dressed in a long white shirt under a dark waistcoat with baggy white trousers, and wore a topi hat as a symbol of national pride, while the women wore a sari with a shawl covering their shoulders. In rural areas the practice of piercing the nose and ears, and the wearing of heavy metal jewellery was common among the women. 'Namaste' was the traditional greeting used by the Nepalese with their hands placed together and accompanied by a slight bow.

The smoking of marijuana and hashish was completely legal in those days; indeed there were Government registered stores where different varieties of drugs could be sampled at one's leisure. It was amazing. And it wasn't just the visitors who indulged either – many of the locals could be high as kites at any time of day or night. Great amusement was caused by the sight of one man proceeding down the middle of the main street whilst whirling madly round in circles – quite obviously on another planet! Not

Nepalese temple, Durbar Square, Kathmandu

85. Nepalese villagers

En route to the Chinese border

Village scene, Nepal

The market, Kathmandu

surprisingly this state of affairs wouldn't continue indefinitely, and a year later in 1973 the Drug Enforcement Administration came into being which ended open trading. Having strolled around town, I eventually wandered into a cafe where a big smoking session was in progress and was immediately included. Hashish could be smoked or eaten in cake form, and a while later, very much the worse for wear, I somehow found my way back to the Lodge and slept like a log.

To see more of the country, I took a Land Rover trip after a couple of days up to the Tibetan border. In 1950 Tibet had been invaded by The People's Liberation Army of China, and being Communist territory, was a source of some interest. The 115 mile journey over mountain roads took about five hours, which included a stop to change a flat tyre. We travelled through numerous small villages with their primitive single story thatched-roof houses, climbing all the time past hillsides steeply terraced for growing cereal crops such as millet and corn. Efforts were being made to remove rock falls in several places along the road, and at times we waited for a bulldozer to clear a way through for us. In places both men and women could be seen hunched over with enormous loads on their backs held in place by a strap across their foreheads.

The Friendship Bridge spanning fast flowing rapids was the only crossing point into Tibet, and I stood on the bridge watching the Chinese soldiers fifty yards away changing guard. They looked typically as shown on newsreels with their green uniforms, peaked caps, and exaggerated movements. I would love to have taken a photo of them but this was strictly prohibited, and there was a Nepalese soldier with me all the time, to make sure I didn't.

On the return journey a stop was made at some hot springs and we watched the locals bathing and doing their laundry. We moved on when it started raining again, which hid potentially beautiful views of the mountains on a clear day.

Kathmandu continued to be a great source of entertainment and an added dimension was my meeting a jocular Australian called Nick who was also staying at the Lodge. He was on his way to Poona in India seeking a Yoga Guru who he believed could cure his back problems. Nick was a great character and we hit it off straight away.

As we walked around, we noticed more and more weird happenings and often found it difficult to keep straight faces, although I admit we were sometimes under the influence ourselves. We stood for a long time watching the rituals concerning a small square temple just off Kanti Path, the main thoroughfare. Along one side of the temple was a row of prayer wheels which people would spin as they walked around it in a clockwise direction. These wheels were cylindrical religious scrolls mounted on vertical spindles, and on each corner hung a small bell which the person would also ring before continuing on their way. Sometimes the procedure was mimicked by a traveller with no idea of the meaning behind these practices, but the locals were quite unconcerned. The Nepalese were completely oblivious to our presence and we really felt like spectators from another world.

Small clay oil lamps lit the dark streets and alleys at night as the whole place came alive with people rushing up and down, ourselves included, as we went to dine at The Hungry Eye, The Blue Monk, or some other famous Kathmandu hostelry. We were in stitches of laughter one evening when the waiter was stoned and all the orders got muddled up! Things caught up with me a day or two later however, when I went down with a cold and stomach bug and felt pretty awful.

During this time I was trying to work out my onward travel arrangements to enable me to reach home by Christmas if possible. I had heard reports of various tour companies travelling west although it was hard to get firm information. But one possibility seemed to be a German bus going to Istanbul, from

Religious ceremony, Kathmandu

The stupa at Swayambhu

On top of the world!

Leaving Nepal – the Hamburg bus

where I could get a train on to London, and I planned to find out more.

In the meantime Nick came out with the rather scary news that he was planning to smuggle some hashish back to his homeland. One morning he took me with him to meet the dealer concerned. First we had to meet a man who led us by a roundabout route through the city's side streets to the dealer's house in a back alley, where we climbed some stairs to the first floor. Sitting cross-legged on the floor were three men who were intricately carving such things as Hindu gods, picture frames, and assorted wooden furniture. These were then cleverly hollowed out and filled with whatever contraband the purchaser required. While Nick negotiated, a customer came in for cocaine and the dealer produced a bottle (worth several thousand dollars), weighed out three grams, and sent the man on his way. Nick agreed to buy two ornate six foot high wooden gateposts which would be filled with hashish and shipped to Australia, where his father was manager of one of the country's main airports!

After all this excitement, I hired a bike for a day as it was glorious weather, and rode out to the ancient stupa of Swayambhu, perched on top of a nearby hillock. Sitting on its huge white dome was a gold spire with the Buddha's inscrutable all-seeing eyes gazing outwards, while lines of multi-coloured prayer flags strung from its tip, fluttered in the breeze. Monotonal chanting from the monks, accompanied by shrill trumpets, gongs, and clanging bells echoed over the valley to welcome the new day. The view from there seemed somehow surreal, with the vivid green of paddy fields and hedges contrasting with the mountainous backdrop in the distance.

Just before going out to eat that evening, news reached us that King Birendra's personal astrologer had forecast a giant earthquake for the next night, which 'will claim three quarters of Nepal's population'! The fact that he had been slapped in jail was neither consolation, or conducive to a good appetite. But perhaps thinking it was his last supper, Nick kept ordering more and more food while the rest of us watched in amused amazement. I suppose if the end is nigh you may as well go out with a full stomach!

It may have been news of the impending disaster that prompted my decision next day to book a ticket on the German bus going via Delhi, Lahore, Kabul, and Tehran, to Istanbul. It was due to leave four days later on the November 25th and the cost was 70 US dollars (30 pounds), which would mean that I should make it home for Christmas. Having sorted that out, I met up with Nick who had clinched his deal on the gateposts which were to be exported to his home in Oz.

After a suspenseful night everyone breakfasted as usual next morning, so no doubt the astrologer's head was on the block. Later Nick and I took a bus about an hour's ride from the city to the small village of Dhulikel, which I had passed through on my border trip and thought worth a second look. It was another perfect day with the mountains in the background, and the entire scene with the peasants working in the fields and on the terraced hillsides was unforgettable.

But the crowning glory was at Dhulikel itself. The village is situated at an altitude of 5,000 feet above sea level amidst quiet surroundings and flowering hillsides, and we sat looking over a wide valley at the line of Himalayan peaks stretching before us, from Cho Oyu in the east to Himalchuli in the west. We stayed for the sunset, watching them gradually turn from a brilliant white, through orange, to red – with one peak resembling a fire's glowing coal – and finally back to a dull white. It was a breathtaking spectacle and as we took the bus back to the city we regretted not spending more time up there.

But time had almost run out and my last full day in Kathmandu had arrived. I decided to spend it back at Dhulikel, so after going to pay the balance of my fare to Istanbul, caught the bus again. The scenery and view up there were just terrific and

I could hardly stop taking photos. Then about 4.00 pm the sun slowly began to sink and I watched the whole incredible sequence again, before walking back down the hill to get the return bus. Those last two afternoons had been just superb, and it was scenes like those which made all the hassle and discomfort worthwhile.

Together with Tony, a shaven headed American writer, who was also joining the overland trip, Nick and I went for a final supper and I interrupted mine with a trip to the barber's shop. Then disappointingly, just before going to bed I discovered that my wallet was missing. Luckily it contained nothing really vital but I lost my International Student and US Green Cards, which put a damper on things.

I was woken up at 5.00 am and after a quick wash, said cheerio to Nick and we wished each other luck. I wondered how he would make out. (It was some months later that a letter arrived from Poona saying his back was greatly improved and that the gateposts had arrived home safely)! Then Tony and I headed for the bus, which pulled out of Kathmandu at 7.00 am.

Our transport was a single-deck ex-Hamburg city bus owned by two Germans, Dietmar Muller and the bearded Karl Frank, who also shared the driving. Old Dietmar ran on a fairly short fuse and when frustrated was prone to noisy outbursts, often punctuated with the word 'Scheisse' and fist shaking. His outbursts could be due to a luckless passenger, road conditions and other traffic, or awkward officialdom, and initially caused much hilarity amongst us. The bus had brought tourists out overland from Hamburg to Nepal whence most had continued onwards, but a few passengers were returning by the same means and we numbered about twenty in all. Normal seats took up most of the space but two pairs of bunks were fitted at the rear for anyone wanting to try and sleep, and excess luggage, vehicle spares etc, were sheeted over on the roof.

Our journey began with the hairy ascent of a mountain pass, followed by an even hairier descent. At one bend the road had partly subsided and we all got out while Dietmar manoeuvred round it. The outer rear wheel was on the very edge of a big drop and it was a tight squeeze all the way over the pass, but we were rewarded at the top with a last terrific view down Kathmandu Valley.

A rest stop was taken at lunch time by a freezing cold river in which a couple of blokes were brave enough to go for a swim, before we continued to our evening halt at Pokhara. The town is well known as the starting point for trekking parties, and here we filled up with fuel and had supper. There were often barriers across the road and the correct permit for each section was required before we were allowed to continue. From Pokhara we headed south on the last section until 11.00 pm, so as to be near the Indian border for an early crossing next morning.

Departure from Nepal caused no problems, with no one having to leave the bus. All that was required was the signing of a form saying what personal items were being taken out. The country had been a wonderful experience for me, with many fond memories, and almost immediately it would all seem like a dream. The thought of returning to see more of it greatly appealed, and I was to do so ten years later for a lengthy trek around Annapurna. I was very shocked and saddened to hear in 2001 that King Birendra and the entire Royal Family had been murdered.

Chapter Eighteen
Overland

What a contrast to our exit from Nepal: we now suffered from notorious Indian bureaucracy. Having passed through a road check point, a narcotics inspection was then made, when a turbaned official came aboard asking if anyone had hashish? There were several rude replies! Fortunately matters weren't taken any further and we drove on for some miles and finally came to the immigration post at Gorakhpur. There we stayed for four hours while officials laboriously copied details of everyone's passport. It was impossible to rush them – one just had to be patient and polite, but as with most officials in those parts, a degree of authority seemed to impart a feeling of God-like superiority. Thankfully they didn't carry out a full search of the bus, which would have taken up more time, and after eventually getting clear of them we stopped at the nearest town for supper. Surprisingly, as it was a Sunday, there were problems changing money which caused some difficulties.

We drove all through that night which was quite scary as, several times when doing about fifty miles per hour, we came upon a lumbering bullock cart with no lights. Additionally, approaching Indian truck drivers were very reluctant to move off the narrow tarmac road to enable our vehicles to pass. The countryside was quite green and flat, with villages whose dwellings were constructed with a mixture of mud and stone, scattered along the way. Soon we reached Lucknow, capital of the state of Uttar Pradesh where we stopped for a wash by a roadside pottery shop. It had an impressive assortment of earthenware pots, jugs, and ornaments to browse through, but many were

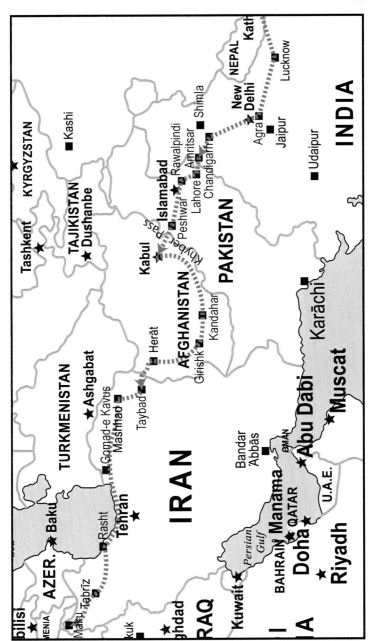

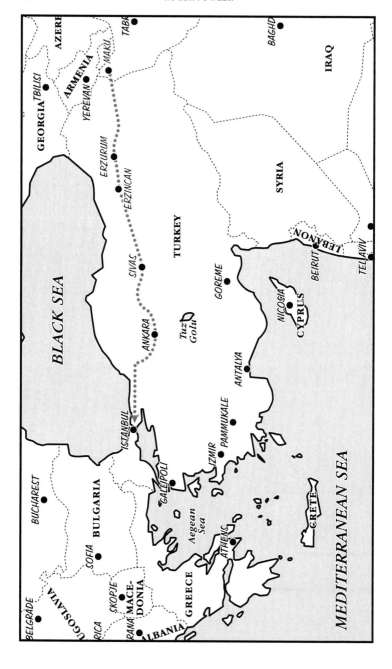

unsuitable for us as souvenirs as they were too big. The city was the site of the 1857 Indian Mutiny and there were an exceptional number of British Raj-era buildings still to be seen.

All along the route we encountered an interesting selection of animals. A huge elephant with its native driver had ambled through the border post, and we saw several camels loaded with straw and other goods. If you didn't have a lorry, a camel or bullock cart was the next best thing. On numerous occasions flocks of hideous looking vultures sat by the roadside feasting on carrion, while overhead circled huge hawks with five foot wingspans. Added to the mix were the ubiquitous cows which wandered freely in most towns and cities. They are revered and worshipped by Indian Hindus who consider them sacred, and are often seen at religious festivals garlanded with flowers.

Our lunch stop that day was at Agra, and we fought our way through chaotic traffic jams consisting of lorries, bullock carts, bicycles, and pedestrians, to look around the famed Taj Mahal. Commissioned in 1632 by the Mogul emperor Shah Jahan to house the tomb of his favourite wife Mumtaz Mahal, it's a stunning architectural masterpiece of solid marble construction, inlaid with precious stones, which in bright sunlight glistens a dazzling white. Set in formal gardens bounded on three sides by a crenellated wall, the inner hall containing the tomb is deathly silent (sorry!) and echoes the slightest sound. It was designated a World Heritage Site in 1983. I was dwarfed standing in front of it for a photo, and after a couple of hours we were off again heading for Delhi.

Being a petrol-head the first thing I noticed about New Delhi was enormous numbers of old style 1950s Morris Oxfords, which were built under licence in India and re-named the Ambassador. The YMCA was full, so five of us took one of these taxis and eventually found a guest house with one spare room. And in we went! Every hotel in the city was full, it appeared, largely due to the Asia '72 exhibition taking place at the time. Hitherto

Traffic jam, Agra, India

Army band, Red Fort, Delhi

Khyber Pass warning notice

Decorated Pakistani lorry

washing and teeth brushing had taken place at the odd village tap so at least we were able have a proper scrub up.

The layout of New Delhi with its large open squares and wide tree-lined avenues reminded me of London, which was not surprising as it was largely designed by the British architect Edwin Lutyens to be the seat of British Indian administration. Together with other buildings, he designed the Viceroy's House, requiring two thousand staff, plus India Gate. Connaught Place with its white colonnades was the heart of the central business district and it was there that I headed next morning to get some photos taken for my Afghan visa. I arrived at the same shop as Karl and Dietmar, but by the time they were done it was too late to get to the Afghan Embassy so I spent the rest of the day visiting the Red Fort, and an observatory built by one of the Maharajas, with huge astronomical instruments.

The Red Fort was also built by Emperor Shah Jahan in 1638 and so named because it was constructed of red stone and marble. It stands in the centre of Delhi and was originally the residence of the Royal Family. Inside its huge walls were well-kept gardens and I watched an Indian army band playing military music there. They were traditionally dressed in white jackets with black belts, black trousers with a red stripe down the sides, and smart white puttees covered their boots. The downside to wandering around these places was being pestered for 'baksheesh' by the kids, so at the Fort I pretended to be French and unable to understand any English, which confused them. It was rather disconcerting though to walk around with two hundred dollars worth of camera equipment and refuse a skinny kid enough for a square meal, but as someone said 'You can't feed them all'.

A short distance away is the Jantar Mantar Park Observatory, built in 1723, which consists of thirteen giant architectural astronomy instruments; the primary purpose being to compile astronomical tables and to predict the timing and movements of the sun, moon, and planets. A good view of them all can be had from the top of the sixty-foot high sundial, which is accurate to a second.

Surprisingly most people's spoken English was not too good, that of taxi drivers being especially poor, although most of the signs and street names were in English. Apart from that it was much like any other big city and the noisy three-wheeled scooter taxis reminded me of Bangkok. The Indians love their beaurocracy and for security reasons I wasn't allowed to photograph the Parliament building. I imagined they saw spies in their curry.

Mention of curry reminds me that it didn't then have the popularity with us that it has today, and we felt fortunate that evening to find a restaurant that did reasonable Western meals. But my Kathmandu cold returned and I went to bed feeling very rough. I felt even worse next morning, with a terrible sore throat, and spent a frustrating time at the Afghan embassy waiting for my visa. Having finally obtained it I was halfway back to the city centre when I realised I'd left my camera bag at the embassy. In a hot sweat I took a return taxi to find, by great good fortune, that it was still there, but kicked myself for being so stupid. Later I scrounged a meal and a hot shower at the YMCA which improved things, before we left Delhi on the Grand Trunk Road at 8.00 pm that evening. It was another all-night drive to make the Pakistan border early, as it only opened once a week on a Thursday.

India lived up to its reputation for being shambolic, when we were stuck for two hours in a crazy traffic jam of highly decorated Indian trucks. There were dozens of them with no-one giving an inch, and things got very frightening when their drivers started banging on the sides of the bus, damaging some of the body panels. We really thought we were in for trouble, until we eventually managed to get clear – only to meet further bedlam on arrival at 9.00 am on the Pakistani border at Amritsar, holy city of the Sikhs. Formalities took all day until 5.00 pm but at least no-one was made to empty out their bags. I felt sorry for the crowd of back packers arriving by train who had to stand in a queue all that time, and was certainly glad that I chose to take this bus. Having had a taste of India I knew I couldn't have endured the hassle of their railways. We stopped for supper at Lahore, where crowds of locals again surrounded the bus, banging on the sides and straining to peer through the windows. Fortunately the situation didn't escalate further, and we continued all through the most uncomfortable and incredibly cold night via Rawalpindi to the border at Peshawar. At dawn we stopped for tea with some Pakistani drivers in their fabulously decorated trucks. The cabs of these had to be seen to be believed, with ornate cushions, rugs, and a roof headlining with hanging tassels. Far superior to the most luxurious Rolls!

December had now arrived and our next objective was the crossing of the famous Khyber Pass which runs for twenty eight miles between Pakistan and Afghanistan, climbing to about 3,500 feet through the Spin Ghar Mountains. On the approach the landscape became very dry and arid, with stone forts resembling something straight from the *Arabian Nights*. At the foot of the Pass sat a large sign in English warning travellers that photography of defence installations and tribal womenfolk was prohibited. Additionally people were advised not to stray from the main road and only to travel before the hours of darkness. Attacks on vehicles crossing the pass by armed bandits were fairly common so that most made the journey in convoys.

Our exit from Pakistan was quite speedy and while Dietmar completed the formalities and paid the required toll fee we ate freshly baked bread and drank tea, brewed in a large brass samovar, with some dubious looking locals. Most of them were armed and had bandoliers of cartridges displayed prominently across their chests. The owner of the tea house had a loaded .303 rifle propped on the counter, and one money changer wanted to sell me his Berretta pistol and ammunition for 70 dollars. I declined the offer as politely as possible, without knowing if it would come in useful. In fact it was possible to buy all kinds of firearms in Pakistan or Afghanistan, as there was a thriving backstreet cottage industry manufacturing good working copies of many of the world's renowned guns.

We set off mid morning in bright sunlight, leading two Pakistani trucks, and climbed steadily past numerous fortifications and rocks engraved with the badges of famous regiments that had fought there. It was desolate country with plenty of opportunities for an ambush, and I most certainly wouldn't have wanted a breakdown anywhere along the route. But thankfully we reached the end of the Pass at a place called Torkham, without incident. There then ensued a big argument with the border authorities as an American passenger had no visa and was refused entry. Perhaps he was foolish not to have his papers in order but feelings turned against Dietmar, who wouldn't refund him any money when he had to leave the bus.

At last we were away again – only to run out of fuel after just a short distance when, with a wheeze from the air brakes, we ground to a halt. Mercifully this didn't happen on the Pass, but as this was the second time it had occurred, there was some annoyance among us passengers. I couldn't think why they let it happen, as it was a laborious and time consuming business on a diesel engine to bleed all the air out of the system before it could be started again. By good fortune we were near a village, which, like most in those parts, was fortified by high walls running around its perimeter, where some fuel was scrounged. While Dietmar and Karl attended to the bus, we spoke to the village elders in sign language as they only spoke Pashto, the official language of Afghanistan. They wore the long grey tunic and baggy pants typical of Pashtun men and we thought they were a big improvement on Pakistanis and Indians, as was the country itself, which, although rather wild and barren, was quite unblemished in comparison. The womenfolk were kept well out of sight during this time.

The Kabul River flows along the steep and rocky Kabul Gorge, which we descended on a contorted twisting road that then climbed like that of an Alpine pass up to the Kabul Plateau. Slow moving camel trains were common on the roads, but we avoided hitting any and after refuelling, reached Kabul after dark. First impressions were of a surprisingly modern city compared with what we had seen so far, and Tony and I found a reasonably priced hotel where after supper, I soaked in a hot bath.

At that time Afghanistan was ruled by King Mohammed Zahir Shar, the last monarch to reign, and in fact he was deposed the following year. So I'm glad I saw the country before it descended into its current chaos. A three day stop in the city was announced by Dietmar, as he wanted to get the bus serviced and repaired. This was most welcome, as it gave us time to rest and look around. I spent the next day arranging my Iranian visa and wandering round the shops which invariably had a radio in the background blaring out Afghan music. Many were stacked with leather-ware and the elaborate Afghan coats that were all the rage among young people. One of these would make an ideal Christmas present for my sister, and later I hit on the idea of buying my parents an ornamental rug. After looking at several, and seeking advice, I settled on what was apparently an eighty year old Turkoman prayer mat – at least I hoped it was, as it cost me 70 dollars. (It was reassuring to find out some months later from a carpet expert that it was the genuine article). Besides solving my Christmas present dilemma I reasoned that a few prayers might be needed later if things got difficult! Feeling very pleased I joined some of the others for a decent meal by candlelight, eaten to the exotic sound of sitar music.

But I awoke next morning feeling absolutely terrible. My cold which had come and gone since Kathmandu felt as though it had turned into pneumonia, so after going to pick up the rug I went straight back to bed, wondering if I would ever see England again. The room was extremely cold and after I complained to the management about the lack of promised heat, a wood stove was brought in and a pipe shoved straight through the wall! I spent most of the next day in bed also and began to feel some improvement after dosing myself with all kinds of pills.

The idea that Dietmar was involved in some sort of smuggling racket had been circulating among us for a while, and after meeting the others while sightseeing Tony told me that they were convinced this was the important stop. There was no sign anywhere of Dietmar or Karl or the bus, which was supposedly being serviced, although we were due to leave at 6 next morning. It was a worrying thought . . .

Leaving the hotel, we joined everyone else outside Siggi's Restaurant at the appointed time – and there we waited and waited. Even so there was no sign of Dietmar or the bus until they finally rolled up at midday, by which time tempers were getting rather frayed. The damaged panels had been replaced and re-sprayed so that it looked smarter, although there had apparently been an argument over the cost, which caused the delay.

But at last we were under way again and drove on all afternoon across the desert; desert exactly as the word implies with camel trains, and wandering nomads herding their sheep and goats, as they had for generations. Our route on a new concrete road that had been jointly financed with Russian and American money took us south-west skirting the country's mountainous central region. As the day wore on I began to feel worse and worse, and when we stopped for an evening meal at a mud tea house I was violently sick. We sat cross-legged around a kerosene lamp and all I could manage was to slowly sip some tea. However on reaching the city of Kandahar we found a good hotel and after a decent night's sleep I felt better. Thank heavens – as even at this late stage I had awful visions of somehow having to be flown home.

More featureless desert was the order of the day, as the bus followed the concrete ribbon which now looped north-west towards our last major stop at the ancient citadel of Herat.

An Afghan village

The local bus, Kandahar

The old fort, Herat

One for the album!

Heavy rain at midday accentuated the already bleak landscape, and the mud coloured villages looked completely incongruous surrounded by great pools of water. It made a depressing scene. Again we arrived after dark and searched in the rain for a while before somehow finding another reasonable hotel.

But it was a pleasant surprise to find that Herat was a fascinating city, dominated by a huge fortress that had been built by Alexander the Great. Dating back to 330 BC it had been used as a headquarters by numerous empires over a span of two thousand years, and had been destroyed and rebuilt many times through the centuries. Lying around at the foot of its huge walls were a number of archaic broken cannon, and the fort itself was in a dilapidated state, although since the time of my visit it has been restored by UNESCO.

Herat had originally prospered in the Silk Road trade to India and China but now, as in Kabul, the shops specialised in leather goods, Afghan coats, and this time, fur hats as well. One or two sold only the colourful round kola hats worn by the men, which denote which region they are from. But it was disappointing to also see tins of canned food for sale marked 'A gift from the people of West Germany to the people of Afghanistan'. I wondered how those good folk would have felt had they known that their donations were being sold for a profit, and I'm always reminded of this when I see collections being made for some foreign charity. So little of what's given ever seems to reach the people it's intended for.

Nevertheless it was a lively place with gaily decorated horse and buggy taxis trotting up and down the main street. Just about every type of trade was conducted, and improvisation was often a vital requirement for business. One enterprising outfit was making rubber buckets and shoes from old car tyres. But many people were very poorly clothed, often with no shoes at all, and everyone looked terribly cold. Together with a fellow Brit called Robin I visited the bustling market place and tried on the full length burqa dress worn by all Afghan womenfolk. Our photos were taken as we posed in a shop doorway but we wouldn't have fooled anyone. Rounding a corner later we came upon the bizarre spectacle of a street vendor standing with about a dozen bras over his arm! They were in different sizes and colours and while we gaped in disbelief a man shopping for his wife (hopefully) sidled up and started haggling over the price. This must rank as the Afghan equivalent of British women buying their husband's underpants in M&S.

Four of us took one of the narrow muddy lanes off the main street that evening to visit the Turkish baths, which being pretty dim and gloomy resembled something from a medieval scene. They were very popular though and probably the only place where most of the locals could go to get warm. Being the last to leave, I emerged after dark to find the streets as busy as ever as I hurried back to the hotel. To my delight there was a fire in the room, which was a real treat.

The first snow appeared next day and the Afghan plains looked more bleak than ever when we set off again at first light for the short journey to the Iranian border. Formerly known as Persia prior to 1935, the government then requested all countries with which it had diplomatic relations to use the indigenous name of 'Iran'.

Although we had seen nothing to suggest that Dietmar was engaged in any illegal activity, and certainly no proof, any concerns were brought sharply into focus when we heard chilling stories of tourists who had unknowingly been used as carriers. Smugglers would hide drugs on their vehicles and then retrieve them later when safely across the border. Apparently one method employed was to hide contraband in a vehicle's fuel tank by dropping it in on the end of some string. The penalties for drug smuggling were severe and if you were caught, it was virtually impossible to prove the drugs had been planted on you. A lengthy jail term, or – even worse – a death sentence, was the

Frying tonight! Herat

Curious onlookers, Rasht, Iran

Maku, Iran

Group photo on the Turkish/Iranian border. Tony on the right

likely outcome. Formalities took all morning as we queued to take the regulation four anti-cholera pills and then again to show our passports in the office. Contrary to our expectations however they didn't rip the bus apart, and only made a cursory inspection of our luggage, so that we left intact.

The barren plains together with the cold weather continued, and when we stopped for a break some one hundred and ten miles further on in Mashad, the temperature had plummeted to eighteen degrees below freezing. Besides being the second most populous city in the country it was reputed to be the coldest too. It was known as a place of religious pilgrimage for Shia Muslims, centred on the fifteenth century Goharshad Mosque, with its reflective turquoise dome.

The Mosque is entered through a large courtyard and is covered in the most beautifully ornate tiles. Without realising quite where I was, I wandered in while absent-mindedly gazing around me, but was hastily escorted out again by two officials who were very offended by my presence.

Rather than take the direct route through to Tehran, as originally planned, it was decided to detour up to the Caspian Sea and follow that coastline. After a few wrong turns with Dietmar losing his temper, which was a regular occurrence, we eventually found the road north-west. He had apparently been asking directions to a nearby town over the border in Turkmenistan which confused everybody. We passengers settled down in readiness for a cold night and worked out a rota system for the four bunks.

A pleasant surprise was waking to find that a breakfast stop had been called on the shore of the Caspian Sea, in very mild and sunny weather. We continued along the coast, passing through the odd town and stopping at one point to walk along the beach. The sea was quite warm and not too salty, and the area was a summer resort for wealthy Iranians who had their holiday homes along the seashore. It would be interesting to know if they still exist.

There was quite a contrast between Iran and Afghanistan, with the cities being much more clean and modern, and the people better clothed. Pictures of the Shah and his wife and son were in all the shops and public buildings, and apparently the regime was strongly enforced with a huge number of political prisoners in jail. I found myself wondering what became of the two Iranian boys I was at school with, and where they now lived? Interestingly they were always known as Persians then.

The girls on the bus caused great interest and Tony who had a towel wrapped around his shaven head for warmth, was the subject of much mirth among the locals. To my surprise the Iranians proved very friendly and would wave and cheer whenever we passed through a town or village. When we stopped for our evening meal and to repair a jammed throttle at the city of Rasht, an inquisitive crowd gathered around the bus. They looked friendly and unthreatening but a policeman soon appeared to disperse them. The small boys began taunting him so out came his baton and he really laid into them, hitting them around the ears, and backside. Another policeman joined him and it became a kind of game which lasted for half an hour or so, and they were obviously glad when we pulled away.

Another cold all-night drive was in store, and from Rasht we turned inland to follow the main road to Tabriz and on towards the Turkish border. Dawn found us crossing more desert, with wandering camels and their masters being the only moving things in that flat landscape. I was still surprised at how cold the desert could get, and came to realise that camels could not only withstand great heat but also sub-zero temperatures too. It could have been a scene straight from *Lawrence of Arabia*.

Our breakfast stop was at the town of Maku, some twenty kilometres from the Turkish border. It was a strange place lying in a deep bowl of overhanging sheer cliffs, and I struck up a conversation with the local policeman who spoke reasonable English. He was a portly fellow of about fifty who had seven children and twenty-two grandchildren. His wife had died, and hearing that I had an unmarried sister of twenty-three, made me promise to return with her! Guessing that she wouldn't be too keen on the deal I didn't ask how many camels she might be worth.

The crossing from Iran into Turkey proved straightforward, although Dietmar later confessed to greasing a few palms. Some of us posed for a photo shoot with a mixed group of jovial Iranian and Turkish border guards.

So off we set, but about three hundred yards into Turkey, Robin asked Dietmar to stop as he had left his scarf in the office. Dietmar refused and continued driving, which caused uproar before we finally managed to persuade him to wait a few minutes. Perhaps this was due to some unknown agenda but it was an example of his Jekyll and Hyde personality – one minute quite affable, the next he'd flown into a terrible carpet biting rage.

We had now entered the Eastern Anatolia region of Turkey and the stories I'd originally heard of stone-throwing mobs in the area sprang to mind. Luckily we never experienced them and began our crossing of the country on a northerly route. Nomadic figures occasionally appeared in a flat green landscape, with white capped mountains in the distance, but by sunset we were gingerly climbing a snow-covered mountain pass with a jammed front suspension. Karl thought a shock absorber had collapsed under the fearful pounding of the last few days, but it turned out to be ice in the air valve.

At nightfall we crawled into the principal city of Erzurum for our evening stop, which someone reckoned to be one of the coldest populated places in the world. I can't vouch for that, but standing at nearly 6,000 feet above sea level, it certainly felt like it, with thick ice covering everything. Afterwards there were problems getting the engine re-started as the diesel fuel had frozen, and it had to be thawed out with paraffin lamps before we could continue on into the night.

After a spell in one of the bunks I awoke to find a comfort break had been called at sunrise and the worst of the mountain climbing was behind us. The scenery reverted to being very dull, with nothing but more featureless drab plains, punctuated only occasionally by a river or the odd shanty style village overlooked by its minaret. We stopped briefly in the city of Sivas which lies just under half way across the country, and by evening had reached Ankara, the capital, where we expected to stop overnight. But more controversy followed when Dietmar announced that he would be driving straight through to Istanbul, and ultimately he had his way. So we set off on the last two hundred and eighty miles of the journey, to arrive on the shores of the Bosporus in the early hours of the following morning. I found it hard to realise that I had almost reached my goal, and began to consider staying for a few days in Istanbul to savour the fact.

Tuesday December 12th, 1972, was indeed a historic day for me and marked the realization of my overriding ambition. I stood on the bridge of the ferry as we crossed the Bosporus and at 3.30 am next morning stepped ashore on the European side. At first it seemed rather an anticlimax, but by the time we had parked the bus outside the old Yucel Tourist Hostel in Sultanhamet, the full significance of the event hit me and I found it impossible to sleep.

At first light I strolled around the vicinity which was just as I remembered it; the hostel, the Police station on the corner, the Pudding Shop, and the Blue Mosque were all just the same. Later I joined the others for a leisurely breakfast at the Pudding Shop, before checking in at the hostel. The little Turkish submariner was still the manager, and after I jogged his memory he told me that Geoff had stayed there again to recuperate after leaving hospital. I was even in the same room as before, and after dumping my gear, collected some welcome post from home and spent a very satisfying day wandering around all the old haunts, reflecting on the past two years, and feeling thoroughly nostalgic.

Perhaps I shouldn't have been surprised that so little had

changed, but at the time it felt uncanny. The streets hadn't altered at all, neither had the Covered Bazaar, or the old wooden houses nearby. There was the same manager at the hostel, the same waiter at the Pudding Shop, the same manager where we garaged the Land Rover, and I could almost have sworn that the dodgy looking money changer who approached me was the same thieving blighter that conned me back then!

I walked down to the Galata Bridge that straddles the Golden Horn, and stood there amidst the bustle, traffic noise, and smoky river ferries, thinking of everything I'd experienced, the people I'd met and places I'd seen, and had to pinch myself to realise that I'd travelled around the world.

Strolling back up the hill as the city's minarets stood silhouetted against the setting sun, Hans Christian Andersen's proverb 'To travel is to live' came to mind, which suitably fitted the moment.

Outside the hostel, Istanbul

Ambition accomplished

Chapter Nineteen
Journey's End

A celebratory meal with some of the others took place at the Pudding Shop that evening, which doubled as a farewell to Tony, who had joined the bus with me in Kathmandu but was leaving it next day.

My original intention was to travel back across Europe by train but the price turned out to be excessive and so I decided to stay on the bus – a decision I was later to question. The route would be essentially the same but more direct than our outbound Land Rover journey – through Greece, Macedonia, Yugoslavia, Austria, and across Germany to Hamburg from where I could catch the ferry to Harwich.

After another day's relaxation in Istanbul (and two welcome nights in a proper bed) we set off westwards towards the Greek border near Ipsala. The big surprise of the whole trip up to this point had been the relative ease with which we had crossed through all the borders, even though we knew that Dietmar had bribed a few officials along the way. It wouldn't work anymore however, as we found out on trying to leave Turkey. This was the first proper check and set the standard for the rest of the journey.

All the baggage had to be unloaded and inspected, including all the tools and extra stuff on the roof. They really went to town and we learnt that on the way out across Turkey, people had been observed smoking joints, and the bus was thus registered as a narcotics carrying vehicle. So why we hadn't had all this hassle on re-entering the country was something of a mystery. Everyone was told to open their bags and we stood around in the freezing cold while customs officers started their inspection. Then, after opening a few packs and getting a hostile reception, the officials got tired and trooped us all inside their office. There we were made to sign forms declaring that we weren't carrying any drugs.

At last we left Turkey and crossed into Greece where the whole rigmarole had to be gone through again. Only this time they were more interested in the bus and we watched proceedings while having a snack inside a warm restaurant. First they looked into the fuel tank, then unscrewed parts of the bodywork before calling in Dietmar for interrogation. He must have come up with the right answers because a couple of hours later they reluctantly gave permission for us to go on our way. By now it was late and an overnight stop was made at Alexandroupolis, the first town we came to. So ended the first day!

Under way again next morning we passed through Xanthi before reaching the coastal town of Kavala where Dietmar announced that the bus was to be 'serviced'. The general opinion was that he was making his 'drop' but it seemed an unlikely place. Nevertheless we all had to get out before he took the bus to the 'garage'. But one of the French blokes was asleep in the back and woke up a mile or so down the road. Apparently Dietmar nearly went through the roof when this chap appeared and immediately ordered him out!

Before leaving next morning he informed the assembled company that he knew of three people who were carrying hashish and piously advised them, and any others, to get rid of it or he would be forced to report them. I have no idea if anyone took his advice.

And so we continued on our merry way, branching north from Thessaloniki up through Macedonia and Yugoslavia, via Skopje, Sarajevo, and Zagreb, to the Austrian border just north of Maribor. It was here that the next drama unfolded, when everyone had to lug their kit from the bus to the customs room, where a huge Alsatian dog with its handler appeared. It was supposedly trained to sniff out drugs and spent the next hour being led from pack to pack, and then all around the bus. The customs boys looked genuinely surprised that nothing was found and, after a few further questions, let us leave.

It was originally intended that we would stop for a day in Salzburg, which I was looking forward to, but that idea was scrapped and we pressed on in the usual rush to arrive at the German border just before dawn. Here we had to clean out the bus, on Dietmar's orders, to make a good impression with the customs officers who were really awkward and obstinate. They were determined to find something, so the unloading routine had to be repeated all over again. Only this time they made everyone open their kit outside in a temperature of seven degrees below freezing. Everything was carefully inspected, antique carpets were measured, and duty was levied even on the goods of people who were in transit through Germany. Somehow my stuff escaped, but by the time they finished we were all frozen and fed up with the whole business, and I regretted not taking the train. There was one comic moment though when Dietmar and Lutz, a retired postman from Bremen, were shouting at each other in English before suddenly realising they both spoke German and switching to their native language!

At last, after six hours we got the all-clear and headed for Munich where there was a hurried lunch break for a couple of hours, and several German passengers left the bus. After a supper stop it was another all-night drive to Cologne, which we reached at 10.00 am next morning and where others departed. Following a quick breakfast we shot off again in another rush but during a break at the Autobahn services two policemen took an unwelcome interest in our bald tyres. Spinning some yarn Dietmar got away with it and persuaded them to take no further action, which was lucky for him and perhaps for us too. By mid afternoon we had reached Bremen, where we said goodbye to Lutz and Jorgen and at 6.00 pm arrived in Hamburg.

Nobody was sorry to see the back of Dietmar who had been

a pretty difficult character to put it mildly and leaving the bus for the last time, Robin and I made our way to the Youth Hostel. They were reluctant to let us in at first as we didn't have our student cards but after some arm twisting they relented. After this we found a nearby dockside tavern and ordered some good strong beer and a meal, while managing to keep clear of some incredibly drunken German seamen. It felt really great to celebrate our safe arrival after what had been a very eventful journey from Kathmandu; the sort of experience that's usually classed as 'character building'!

The morning was spent killing time in Hamburg and the cleanliness of the city and its environs was very impressive. Even the dockside was virtually spotless and the underground trains were immaculate compared with those of London. But everything was extremely expensive, even more so than in America, which was saying something. Then it was time to collect our kit from the hostel and board the ferry for the overnight crossing to Harwich.

The voyage went smoothly and after a night at sea, our first glimpse of England was a murky coastline, before Harwich appeared through the mist. We docked promptly at 10.00 am and it was hugely gratifying to step ashore on to English soil again.

An American girl called Colleen wore my sister's Afghan coat through customs, which we cleared without comment, and it was then a short coach ride to the station where we boarded the waiting London train. Robin went off to try and find a direct connection to Gravesend, so in the general rush I regretted that we never had a chance to say cheerio. I intended spending the night in London as I wanted to visit the US Embassy to see about renewing my visa, so upon arrival we all wished each other Good Luck, a Merry Christmas, and went our separate ways. Having come so far and shared so much, it was sad to say goodbye, but that is unfortunately the nature of travelling.

I made straight for the Regent Palace Hotel in Piccadilly where I'd stayed previously, and the receptionist's face was a picture as this scruffy back-packer, weighed down with all his gear, crossed the foyer. But with a few sideways glances he found me a room, and after dumping my kit and having a quick wash, I went straight off to the Embassy in Grosvenor Square. It seemed incredible to be walking around London again after all the places I'd been to, and mingling amongst the happy Christmas shopping crowds on Regent Street. It was also a great relief not having to keep one eye on my kit all the time, which had become very tiring. Finally I returned to the hotel and luxuriated for nearly an hour in the best hot bath I've ever had; and the icing on the cake was Frank Sinatra's voice over the radio singing 'My Way'! A few drinks and a meal later led to an equally satisfying sleep in a proper bed.

I caught the train from Euston up to Birmingham New Street next morning for the last leg home, and on arrival called on a friend of mine who worked in the wholesale market there. He was amazed as he hadn't expected me until after Christmas, but offered me a lift to my parents when he finished work.

A haircut and a few coffees passed the time while I waited, before Jim ran me the last few miles home to end, on December 23rd, 1972, what had been the adventure of a lifetime.